INVASIONS
WITHOUT
TEARS

INVASIONS WITHOUT TEARS

The Story of Canada's Top-Scoring Spitfire Wing

in Europe during the Second World War

MONTY BERGER

BRIAN JEFFREY STREET

Vintage Books

A Division of Random House of Canada

Toronto

Originally published in hardcover in 1994
by Random House of Canada Limited, Toronto.

Canadian Cataloguing in Publication Data

Berger, Monty
Invasions without tears

ISBN 0-394-22427-2

1. World War, 1939-1945 - Aerial operations, Canadian.
2. Canada. Royal Canadian Air Force. Fighter Wing, 126 - History
3. Spitfire (Fighter planes) I. Street, Brian Jeffrey, 1955-   .
II. Title.

D792.C2B4 1995   940.54'4971   C94-931111-1

To our families

CONTENTS

INTRODUCTION

I N THE SPRING of 1941, Monty Berger resigned as acting city editor of the Quebec *Chronicle-Telegraph* to join the Royal Canadian Air Force, not with lofty visions of flying Hurricanes or Spitfires into combat alongside the "Brylcreem Boys" of the RAF, but as a lowly radar technician, starting at virtually the bottom rung of the RCAF ladder. There would be no sheepskin-lined leather jacket or silk scarf and goggles; he would not know first-hand the charged atmosphere of waiting in dispersal huts for the order to scramble, or the split-second margins that often decided one's fate in the air when battle was joined. Even more surprising, not least of all to Monty Berger, was that he made this dramatic turn in his previously well-charted life as a result of advertisements placed by the RCAF on behalf of the Royal Air Force. He was twenty-three years old, unmarried, an Honours graduate in economics and political science at McGill, and had also earned an M.Sc. in journalism at Columbia University in New York—all of which suggest he might have preferred a more glamorous occupation than repairing radar sets. But like many of his countrymen, he was eager to contribute to the war effort.

So it was that Monty Berger put a promising career in journalism on hold for what turned out to be a four-year "hiatus" in Europe. In that time he saw a great deal of the war's progress, most importantly as the Senior Intelligence Officer attached to the RCAF's famed 126 Spitfire Wing. He rose to the latter capacity in circumstances that were equally serendipitous, and quickly found his niche.

To his own astonishment he also experienced a considerable amount of adventure. He was the first RCAF ground officer to reach Normandy following the Allied invasion in June 1944, landing at dawn on D-Day +1 after a harrowing trip across the English Channel. Later he helped establish his unit's mobile headquarters at various airfields in France, Belgium, Holland and, eventually, Germany itself, while the high-flying Spitfires of 126 Wing roamed the skies over Europe in support of the ground forces moving relentlessly toward Berlin. And he stayed with the wing when it became part of the British Air Forces of Occupation following the Nazi defeat in May 1945.

Based at Utersen in northern Germany during that first summer of victory, Monty Berger wrote a history of the wing's brilliant accomplishments. His story was constructed mainly from operational summaries and record books he had maintained during the wing's travels on the continent. To this rich fund of material, now the stuff on which official accounts are based, he added his own personal insights. If nothing else his manuscript was proof that his reporter's instincts had not been wasted after all.

In fact, Monty had landed in the midst of a better story than he could have imagined. The sheer number of pilots involved—several dozen in each squadron, there being as many as five squadrons attached to the wing at one time—imparted an epic quality to his story.

Moreover, his recognition of the important role played by the wing's groundcrew—more commonly known as "erks"—was unusual. Yet, as Monty explained in the introduction that accompanied an early draft:

Most people in the Air Force—any air force—don't fly. They would if they could, but they can't. These poor unfortunate birds are called "Penguins." Most are doomed to see their service careers out in Canada or in England, but a few have sampled the atmosphere of battle conditions, have got as close to real fighting as they could in their jobs. They have had ringside seats to the great battles of history, both on the ground and in the air. To a penguin that is paradise.

Notwithstanding his elevated status as the wing's Senior Intelligence Officer, Monty, too, was a "penguin," equal in that respect to an armament assistant, airframe mechanic, pigeon loftsman or any of the seventy-odd ground trades listed by the Royal Canadian Air Force at the war's end. "These penguins," he added, "lived with the 'pigeons,' their pilots, knew how they thought, how they worked.... They shared, as much as they physically could, in all their experiences, and helped to make this most modern weapon—a mobile wing—one of the greatest fighting machines in history."

Monty's depiction of the "pigeons and penguins" who made up 126 Wing captured the heroism and absurdity that was a daily part of their lives—or so it seemed upon reading a draft of the manuscript in the autumn of 1990. From this evolved a mutual desire to see the work published—almost fifty years after it was written. Several considerations reinforced this notion, including a shared belief that the story of 126 Wing was long overdue.

Thus the present account, while a collaborative effort, is based largely on Monty Berger's original text. It is not an "official history," even though it has depended mainly on primary sources in its preparation

Nor has the aim of the original version changed significantly. It was to provide a lively, though comprehensive account of 126 Wing's operations from its formation as "126 Airfield" in Redhill, Surrey, in July 1943, to its participation in the liberation of Europe almost two years later.

In one important respect, however, the present account differs from the original text. Here, Monty's own contribution to both the character and accomplishments of 126 Wing is given the attention it has long deserved, alongside that of the pilots who traditionally have won most—if not all—of the glory.

And why not? For as Monty himself has long insisted, the "penguins" were there, too.

We would like to express our appreciation to Cameron Graham, who was instrumental in bringing about the present collaboration; Donald Stewart of Paris, Ontario; and the following for their timely and invaluable assistance: Gustave Bédard, of Sillery, Québec; Eldon Deacon, Minden, Ontario; George Killen, Kamloops, British Columbia; Kenneth Pigeon, Brantford, Ontario; Betty Lynn Reinke, Toronto, Ontario; Rod Smith, Vancouver, British Columbia; Garry Whitmore, Victoria, British Columbia; and Leonard Wilson, of Stratford, Ontario.

Harrie van Grinsven of the Dutch historical association "Nistelvorst," was a continuing and bountiful source of support. The Royal Netherlands Air Force, its Historical Section and in particular Hank Kauffman, were understanding and supportive in our research.

Our thanks also to Pierre Labranche of Gloucester, Ontario for his photographic expertise.

The staffs of the Directorate of History (Department of National Defence), and the Canadian Armed Forces Photographic Unit, were particularly helpful—as usual. The cooperation of Douglas Steubing, editor of Airforce Magazine, was also very much appreciated.

Douglas Pepper, Executive Editor at Random House of Canada, nurtured the project to completion with astonishing patience, good humour and much faith, for which we are especially grateful.

Finally, we would like to thank the many former "126-ers" who gave us their recollections, advice and encouragement.

Monty Berger   Brian Jeffrey Street
Montreal   Ottawa

"Now fades the glimmering landscape on the sight,
And all the air a solemn stillness holds."

Thomas Gray
"Elegy Written in a Country Churchyard"

PROLOGUE

"An Unforgettable and Marvellous Experience"

THE PUBLIC ACCLAIM bestowed on Spitfire pilots during the Second World War began with their part in the epic Battle of Britain in 1940. More than half a century later it is not so difficult to imagine ruddy-faced young pilots scrambling to their aircraft with a fearsome determination—if one may paraphrase Pope—to quit this earthly sphere and rush headlong into the skies to meet whatever peril awaited. Never mind that "the Few," as they were known afterwards, were not always the peace-time playboys or "weekend Biggles" newsreels depicted. As former Canadian Press newspaperman Carl Reinke, who joined the RCAF's historical branch as a Flight Lieutenant, put it, the pilots were so often depicted as "glamour boys" that "some of them were in danger of believing it."

Canadians, too, were afflicted by this unique symptom of wartime hubris. Some had flown with RAF squadrons from the war's outset, and could boast of having left their mark among the contrails that swirled over the Kentish countryside in 1940 in defence of the scepter'd isle. Those who arrived later with overseas contingents of the Royal Canadian Air Force were eager to experience not only the new vocabulary of Second World War aerial combat—"Watch out for flak," "Bogies now bandits," and "Tally, ho!" were common enough—but also the adulation that came with being a Spitfire pilot. Flying over Malta in 1942, or the battlegrounds of Europe following the Normandy Invasion in 1944, they pursued their deadly craft with a boldness and tenacity that was in keeping with their reputation. Looking back, another borrowed poignancy suggests itself as we imagine the young airmen taking off, confident of their immortality: in the words of Southey, "Live as long as you may,/the first twenty years/are the longest half of your life."

The truth was the average Spitfire pilot was only slightly better off than his First World War compatriot. And compared with today's "top guns," his circumstances were downright primitive. His aircraft had no radar, no autopilot—no electronics of any sort. "He had a total of fourteen seconds' ammunition," said Paddy Barthropp, a former RAF pilot. "He needed to be less than two hundred and fifty yards from the enemy to be effective. He and his foe could manoeuvre in three dimensions at varying speeds and with an infinite number of angles relative to each other. His job was to solve the sighting equation without becoming a target himself."

Barthropp added:

> His aircraft carried ninety gallons of fuel between his chest and the engine. He often flew over thirty-five thousand feet with no cockpit heating or pressurisation. He endured up to six times the force of gravity with no "g"-suit. He had no crash helmet or protective clothing other than ineffective flying boots and gloves. He had about three seconds in which to identify his foe, and slightly longer to abandon the aircraft if hit. He had no ejector seat. He was also a navigator, radio operator, photographer, air-to-ground attacker, rocketeer and dive-bomber. Often, as in my case, he was only nineteen years old. He was considered too young and irresponsible to vote, but not too young to die.

So much for the romanticism associated with a fighter pilot's existence. Yet, in spite of this, Barthropp concluded that "every hour of every day was an unforgettable and marvellous experience shared with some of the finest characters who ever lived."

The same would be said by most, if not all of the Canadians who served with the RCAF's famed 126 Spitfire Wing. Formed at Redhill, Surrey, in July 1943, as part of the RAF's Second Tactical Air Force, its mandate was to carry out air-to-air combat and ground attack sorties in direct support of the British and Canadian armies once they landed on the continent.

From its inception, 2nd TAF (as it was known) was a mixed bag of RAF and Royal Canadian Air Force squadrons flying everything from Mosquito night-fighting bombers to Hurricanes, Typhoons, Mustangs, and, of course, Spitfires. Each belonged to an "airfield," soon to be known as a "wing," which was assigned to a higher element—in 126's case, 83 Group. The Canadian element consisted of a half-dozen or so Spitfire squadrons, and several wings, including 126, which consisted of 401, 411 and 412 squadrons. Later, two more squadrons—402 and 442—were added as the Allied front moved into France, Belgium, Holland and, eventually, Germany, the last stronghold of Hitler's Third Reich.

By then, the wing could lay claim to a host of impressive statistics indicating the extent to which it had participated in the liberation of western Europe. Most important to its Canadian pilots was that it was the top-scoring wing, having shot down a total of 361 enemy aircraft, with another twelve probably destroyed and as many as 156 damaged in the hotly contested skies over Europe.

On the ground, too, the wing had inflicted a heavy toll, including some 4,468 enemy vehicles, 493 locomotives, and 1,569 rail trucks destroyed or damaged. The number of enemy troops killed or wounded in the course of such operations could not be counted. The wing's casualties, in the crude jargon of the day, were relatively light. Only ninety-six pilots were killed in action; others died in accidents or became prisoners of war.

No simple explanation for the wing's phenomenal success offers itself despite the passage of time. True, it profited from being in all the right places at all the right moments during the war—the invasion and breakout from the bridgehead at Normandy; the frantic Allied attempt to close the so-called Falaise Gap; Operation "Market-Garden" in Holland; the winter offensive in the Ardennes;

and the crossing into Germany in 1945. But other wings with 2nd TAF participated in the same operations, without achieving nearly the mastery of the air and ground that belonged to 126.

Certainly the wing's leadership had something to do with its achievements. But so, too, did the conditions in which the daring young specialists operated. Carl Reinke observed that life with a fighter wing on the continent after D-Day was "as different from that in other commands as the continent itself was different from the U.K." He added: "The main business of the 2nd TAF was army support. That meant everything had to be subordinated to two factors: continuity of operations and mobility. And living under mobile field conditions meant doing without many conventional comforts and conveniences."

Predictably, 2nd TAF's operations inculcated a strong individualism, even a cockiness among the pilots. "You sensed a difference as soon as you walked into a fighter mess," Reinke declared. "Whether it was under canvas or in some abandoned farmhouse or an ex-German mess, the picture was the same: aircrew strutting or lolling about in outfits which could best be accounted for as utilitarian." These, Reinke noted, consisted of varying combinations of khaki and air force blue battledress, rollneck sweaters, "a bright bit of silk as a scarf," civilian windbreakers and even hockey sweaters.

If the pilots lacked good sartorial instincts, they at least knew the nature of their business. Reinke added that the airmen almost always wore a revolver over their eclectic, Joseph-and-his-many-coloured-coat outfits. Their flying boots, too, were "often a study in themselves," he observed, "their loose tops revealing as varied a bunch of items stuck down inside as one traditionally expects in a small boy's pockets—navigation maps, a couple of emergency ration packages, a knife or two, chocolate, and perhaps other incidentals." These constituted the fighter pilot's survival kit.

"It seemed a deliberate casualness, a pose at first," Reinke declared. "Then there were the styles in haircuts, mainly either a close-cropped 'crew' cut, or none at all for two or three months. Added to which was an apparent indifference to regular shaving and a suggestion of general griminess…. The completely uninhibited language around a fighter mess also was a bit startling after the comparatively genteel ways of an RCAF mess in the U.K., but it fitted into the overall atmosphere. Or probably helped create it."

Further study often revealed a logical explanation for many of the pilots' idiosyncrasies in dress, "even for the habit of wearing an open shirt collar turned down outside the jacket," as though the men were at a sporting event. The cockpit of a Spitfire under its bubble of Perspex became uncomfortably warm at altitude. Such habits evolved from the fact that pilots generally made several sorties a day, often on short notice, and were expected to maintain a constant state of readiness. "It saved wear and tear worrying about whether one had picked up all the essentials, like maps, revolvers, Pandoras [emergency ration kits], before going out to the kite each time."

Moreover, the young aces were not always the "tough killers" they imitated. "More than one fighter pilot actually disliked the work, while carrying out his duties competently and with determination," Reinke said. "Doing 'rail cuts' or bombing bridges or shooting up locomotives was a satisfaction; you were able to see the damage you'd created and how it would impede the enemy. But, not having had the army's conditioning to front-line slaughter and mutilation, many had to force themselves to fire their guns when an enemy column of men or horse-drawn carts was in their sights. Some didn't."

To illustrate, Reinke recalled an incident that occurred in April, 1945. Several pilots were standing outside a tent, waiting for the evening's movie to start. One of them was describing how that afternoon he had attacked a column of trucks. "There wasn't any sport to compare with shooting Jerries as they dived for the ditch, he insisted, with a kind of chuckle. But none of the others made a syllable of comment or picked up the theme in any way. The topic died, in a void."

Not atypical, Reinke added, "was the reaction of one squadron commander ... as he concluded reporting to the intelligence officer how he had spotted a column of about fifty German soldiers pedalling along a road on bicycles." The pilot had "knocked over" at least five of them. "As he turned to leave the IO's tent, only half-jokingly, he muttered: 'Five men on bicycles. What a ——— I am.'"

Yet, as Reinke concluded, "no team ever came off a playing field more bursting with exuberance than a squadron returning from a tussle with Jerry fighters on anything like reasonable odds—and 'reasonable' meant as long as the number of Jerries who had 'jumped' the Canadians had not been more than three or four to one. Almost inevitably, under such circumstances, one or two Germans had been shot down. And that meant a change on the wing's scoreboard, which was 'The Thing.'"

As the war progressed and the wing's tally increased, such seemingly contradictory behaviour became part of a pilot's daily existence. The ferocity of the air war impressed each man differently. Take, for example, an excerpt from a combat report filed by Flight Lieutenant J H Everard of 401 Squadron. "I gave this [Me 109] two two-second bursts from seventy-five yards quarter astern," he wrote. "On the second burst, it exploded and I was unable to steer clear of the debris. Part of the pilot's body hit my mainplane inboard of the starboard cannon and dented it. Superficial damage."

The risks were rudimentary. In combat, pilots could be either injured or killed, or shot down. Lectures on the latter possibility did not instil much confidence among the airmen—one observed that, to effect a successful escape, a downed pilot "really needs to be a combination of miner, actor, linguist, thief and all-around tough guy to get away with it"—so they concentrated on staying alive in the air, while doing as much damage to the enemy as they could. More worrisome at times were the unexpected, and incredible incidents that almost led to catastrophe. One pilot nearly crashed when his escape dinghy suddenly inflated in his cockpit, and he had to fight to regain control of his aircraft. Of course, none of the other pilots would ever let him forget the episode. The lesson was not lost, either, on the powers-that-be. Henceforth, it was ordered that all pilots carry a metal spike with them in their aircraft.

Humour, often derived from the most dire circumstances, played a vital role in the wing's ability to perform its function. Fatalism was also present. One pilot admitted he had always felt "the survival equation was sixty per cent luck, twenty-five per cent skill, and fifteen per cent guts" for those pilots engaged in attacking ground targets. In a dogfight, however, he allowed that the importance of skill and coolness under pressure rose dramatically. Everard's action, cited previously, suggests as much. But even this did not always guarantee a satisfactory outcome. Everard, for example, was later shot down and captured.

Associated with humour and fatalism was a surprising gallantry, which expressed itself in odd situations. Carl Reinke discovered this the night he sat with some airmen watching a short film depicting a fishing and hunting trip in British Columbia. Following a scene in which an Indian had hauled in a net filled with salmon and clubbed several of the fish trying to wriggle free, the airmen had shouted: "Hey, did you see what he did to that poor fish? Did you see him clobber the fish?"

Later, a scene in which large packs were loaded on the backs of several "mongrel dogs" drew similar howls of protest.

Nor were such attributes found exclusively among the pilots. Various ground personnel—mechanics, armourers, photographic specialists and other so-called "erks" who kept the Spitfires in top-notch flying condition or helped with duties essential to the smooth operation of a mobile air unit—could lay claim to being as much a part of the wing's character and success. There was risk, too, in their work, as evidenced by the dozen or so casualties among the wing's groundcrew. They were killed either during raids on the Allied airfields in Europe, or in "freak accidents" that happen only in wartime. Several were captured.

Most pilots readily agreed the erks, despite their relative anonymity, were indispensable to the wing's success. "Their abilities extended beyond servicing aircraft," acknowledged former Squadron Leader W A (Bill) Olmsted, DSO, DFC and Bar, "for their drive and inventiveness allowed them to acquire and devise living comforts which were much better than what the pilots enjoyed." The wing's Senior Intelligence Officer, Monty Berger, shared this view. "In the long course of the wing's travels on the continent," he said, "it was observed that the erk was capable of making himself much more comfortable than his senior officers." This included the enjoyment of such amenities as electricity, much coveted by the pilots but often inexplicably denied to them. The erks, on the other hand, possessed sufficient mechanical know-how to tap into existing lines and were thus assured of a ready source of lighting. In a pinch, too, they could be relied upon to show their instincts for comfort, as Leading Aircraftsman Eldon Deacon, a despatch rider with the wing, demonstrated one night. While following a car taking the wing's commanding officer to a meeting, his motorcycle inexplicably ended up in a ditch. The CO and his driver came back to pick him up, and together they resumed their journey in the car. Shortly after this, realising they were lost, they adopted the most sensible course of action, which was to stop and wait until first light. The CO and his driver slept uncomfortably in the car as a result. Deacon, on the other hand, awoke the next morning in excellent shape. Having grown up on a farm, his first thought had been to find a haystack, where he slept the night in relative luxury.

Few would deny that such common-sense ingenuity was typical of the wing's erks. Nowhere was this demonstrated better than in muddy Holland throughout the autumn and winter of 1944/45, when the wing's personnel were called upon to operate in the flooded gumbo surrounding their airfield. Here, too, the wing's intelligence staff found itself operating in less than ideal conditions. Despite the weather, sweeps into enemy territory continued. "I remember one day when we were in the mud and rain and wind of Volkel aerodrome," said Monty. "We did thirty-two briefings and thirty-two debriefings in one day. The traffic there was terrific."

Conditions on the continent were often horrific, especially in the days immediately following the Allied invasion in 1944. Donald Stewart, who was also an intelligence officer with 126 Wing, said that when the Spitfires began operating from an improvised airfield at Beny-sur-mer on the French coast, the clouds of dust raised by squadron after squadron taking off left the men on the ground choking. Later, an infestation of wasps made life almost unbearable. Flies, which had appeared in great swarming masses as a result of unburied dead soldiers, soon resulted in an outbreak of dysentery among the men. "Many pilots were too weak to fly," Stewart recalled. This was confirmed by one of the wing's medical officers, who noted as well that pilots who carried on regardless of their affliction showed a tendency to black out when performing aerobatics. Adding to everyone's misery, the truck carrying the wing's supply of toilet paper had been destroyed. "Good job our relations were writing often," Stewart commented dryly.

Through it all, the erks continued to perform their duties with a heroism that has been unfairly overlooked in the annals of modern military history. They were responsible for the motor transport that carried personnel, kit, tentage, servicing equipment, as well as messing, signals, radar and other sections. More than two hundred vehicles of various types were required in support of the wing's operations, including articulated high-load trailers, water and petrol bowsers, generator tenders, lighting trucks, ambulances, flying control and intelligence vans, workshop lorries, and despatch motorcycles. Erks made the daily ammunition, petrol and ration runs, too, which sometimes meant a return trip overnight of several hundred kilometres. No less incidental, as the supply of war booty increased, was the average erk's ability to render serviceable various items that were captured during the wing's travels, which included everything from "one-lung" Jerry motorcycles to amphibious jeeps and Mercedes limousines.

They also established canteens, provided laundry and mending services, and sold trinkets made out of spent shell casings—almost always at a profit, and more often than not at the expense of the officers. Nevertheless, pilots returning from England filled the spare ninety-gallon fuel tanks on their Spitfires with beer to be shared amongst the erks, "which guaranteed extra care on their part to execute perfect landings," recalled Olmsted. The beer was intended to ensure a groundcrew's gratitude, but in fact such generosity as much reflected a pilot's acknowledgement of their already superb skills. In his memoirs, Olmsted readily admitted that in his entire operational tour with the wing he "never flew a machine ... that malfunctioned because of sloppy maintenance."

Perhaps as a result, morale was seldom a problem among the wing's personnel. The pilots did their job, and so did the erks. Along the way, their collective antics and light-hearted pranks provided many memorable moments. Donald Stewart recalls the day someone filled a trench around the medical officer's tent with water, then went to a nearby farmyard and brought back several ducks, which were later discovered by the unsuspecting MO when he crawled into his tent to retire for the night.

The wing was known also for such extracurricular activities as baseball tournaments and outdoor boxing matches. These were pursued avidly, and sometimes in the most unlikely surroundings. Few considered unusual, for example, the idea of a game of softball played on the embattled coast of France, or in the mud of Holland.

Then there was the wing's eight-piece "Spitfire Band," which travelled the continent. George Killen, a corporal in the wing's medical section, remembers the band's command performance in Brussels. "Those Belgian girls hadn't danced in a long time and all our guys were kept busy," he said. "We opened with 'O Canada' and were most alarmed when the Belgians tried to dance to it!"

It was fair to say that such diversions were taken almost as seriously as the war itself. Flying Officer Arn Gibb, a pilot with 412 Squadron who also played lead saxophone in the band, was shot down one day during a mission, but made it back to the airfield that night to claim his regular spot on the stage. They played the usual favourites borrowed from the reigning giants of swing, and were popular among the airmen. Donald Stewart, who was one of the original members, recalls they also performed for various dignitaries and officials. Once, after putting on a show for some RCAF brass visiting from Ottawa, Stewart was asked if the band needed anything. He answered that, as a matter of fact, they could very much do with a string bass, as they had a player but no instrument. With this, a high-ranking member of the group promptly turned to his aide and barked, "Make a note of that!"

"Within a week," Stewart said, "a bass fiddle was flown over to us from Canada. What a war!"

It was, indeed. Some of the wing's other adventures included opening up captured blockhouses on the French coast (which produced vast quantities of excellent wine), and flying former Luftwaffe bombers on sightseeing tours of occupied Germany at war's end.

By then, of course, 126 Wing would have earned its motto, *Fortitudo vincit*—"courage wins." Unofficially, it seemed as though the pilots and groundcrew had simply adopted as their creed the contents of a long briefing document, entitled "Invasion without Tears," issued on the eve of the D-Day landings. Among its many memorable offerings was the curious advice, directed mainly at the erks: "It's a long walk to the war. Better ride." And (accurately, it turned out): "Footballs and cricket balls will be useful." In regards to the landing in France, the document was somewhat evasive. It read: "Soon you will be setting out on the greatest adventure of your life... If anything goes wrong, use your own initiative ... GOOD HUNTING!"

The truth was, no matter what sort of mental talisman they carried with them throughout their travels, obviously it worked—as the numbers on the scoreboard testified.

And that, as Carl Reinke suggested already, was all that mattered.

1

ORDER OF BATTLE

THE WING's operational record book put the matter bluntly: the weather, it said, was definitely "pro-Nazi."

For weeks, an icy mist and low cloud had all but grounded operations from the airfield at Nistelrode, also known as B88, or (mistakenly, it turned out) simply Heesch, which in fact was the name of another Dutch village a few kilometres away. The pilots and groundcrew of 126 Wing had moved to this site north of Eindhoven in early December 1944, with the expectation they would be able to exploit their proximity to Germany. But as time passed, they grew increasingly frustrated. The weather favoured their adversary, who was putting up stiff resistance elsewhere in Holland and to the south, in the region known as the Ardennes. The wing's Spitfire pilots were eager to do their part in an Allied counter-offensive. Nor was it far from their minds that they had yet to properly strike back after a costly New Year's Day attack on Allied airfields. Instead, they waited. Those few days in which flights actually got off the ground saw little action beyond shooting up locomotives or other ground targets. Then it began to snow. Not even the Canadians, who should have been accustomed to such adversity, found it amusing.

By mid-January 1945, "duff days"—when the weather was

unsuitable for flying—had become almost routine. To keep the airmen occupied, the wing's intelligence staff laid on endless briefings, which normally might attract a sizeable audience but in the circumstances drew standing-room-only crowds. Certainly getting "genned up" was better than shovelling the steel-plated runways after yet another snow squall. But of course they did that, too.

Finally, on January 14th, conditions improved. To its credit, the wing made the most of its opportunity. A weather recce started the day off at 0848, and following its report of generally favourable conditions the first patrol was in the air by 0917. It was a late start, but a start nonetheless after almost seven days of unwelcome inactivity. The record also shows that despite being under-strength— one squadron had returned to an armament practice camp in England—"a considerable amount of sorties were flown, and once again the Hun paid the price." The wing's diarist added: "Outstanding teamwork was evident in listening to the R/T during this morning's very successful show in which eleven enemy aircraft in all were destroyed."

It was a compelling understatement. The Spitfires of 401 Squadron had in fact pounced on a dozen or so FW 190s still in the circuit over the occupied Dutch aerodrome at Twente. Five went down. Three of the victories were credited to a single pilot, Flight Lieutenant Johnny MacKay, DFC and Bar, of Cloverdale, British Columbia. Then 442 Squadron came along and, with the element of surprise on its side, destroyed three more of the enemy's aircraft. Fifteen minutes later, after the wing's leading attackers had cleared out, the Spitfires of 411 arrived on the scene and caught the enemy trying to get more aircraft off the ground. Flight Lieutenant R J (Dick) Audet, DFC, who had made history the previous month with the incredible feat of destroying five enemy aircraft in a single operation, shot down another FW 190. His wingmates added two more.

So much for the diarist's almost nonchalant entry in the ORB. The day's action stood out as a dramatic example of the coordinated boldness and predatory zeal with which the wing carried out its operations.

In addition to the FW 190s that were destroyed, one of the pilots with 401 Squadron had added a locomotive to the wing's scoreboard. The wing's own casualties were minimal. Two pilots were lost that day, Flight Lieutenant R J Land of 401 Squadron, who was probably brought down by flak over Twente, and Flying Officer A J Urquhart of 442 Squadron, who had bailed out over enemy territory. Their whereabouts were unknown. Nevertheless, Urquhart was credited with having destroyed an FW190.

The weather promptly closed in again the next day. The recreation hall where briefings took place was soon as jammed as before. For pilots still relatively new to the wing, aircraft recognition tests were held. The wing's intelligence staff offered quizzes to relieve everyone else's boredom. They also tested a new system in which the Spitfires were dispersed at the end of the runway while the pilots waited in readiness in a specially fitted caravan. Precisely one minute and fifteen seconds from the time an order was received by Flying Control to scramble the pilots, the first Spitfire was in the air. The wing's Group Control Centre complimented such alacrity.

For the most part, though, they waited out the duff days of overcast skies, snow squalls, wind, rain and even hail. The loss of four pilots flying Blue Section with 412 Squadron, disappearing somewhere over the area of Nijmegen after a snowstorm shut down the airfield at Nistelrode, was all the more maddening. Not until January 23rd would the Spitfires enjoy another opportunity to press the attack. This time, they would penetrate Germany itself, where they were to inflict more damage to the enemy's increasing use of jet-propelled fighter aircraft, shooting down five of the new Me 262s and damaging six others.

Nevertheless, as everyone in the wing realised, there was still a lot of work to do. And more foul weather lay ahead—weeks of it, in fact.

For the eleven hundred Canadian airmen associated with 126 Wing, their Cook's Tour of the continent having stalled in the slush of Holland, time was wasting. They had grown accustomed to the momentum they had built since the wing's formation a little more than eighteen months before, not to mention the celebrity that came with having chalked up the most sustained number of victories in the air war over Europe since D-Day. Impatient to get on with the job, their diarist continued to complain about the weather.

"The most snow we have seen since leaving Canada," he grumbled during one particularly bad spell.

The next day, the wing's Spitfires shot down more of the enemy's so-called "jet-jobs," and for the time being all was forgiven.

They were far from complete success yet. But they, more than any other air force, had proven what the Second Tactical Air Force was all about. For this, one needed only to look back to the circumstances in which it had risen.

The Allied victory in North Africa in May 1943 dramatically altered the course of the Second World War. Having vanquished Rommel's famed Afrika Korps after three years of bloody fighting, the British in particular could look forward to promoting their interests elsewhere. Even as Allied troops were hurled at Sicily a short two months later in an attempt to draw Hitler into a costly campaign in the Mediterranean, military strategists in London were busily preparing for Operation "Overlord," the invasion of occupied Western Europe, scheduled for the spring of 1944.

To succeed on the coast of France would require overwhelming numbers of men, ships, landing craft, tanks—and, not least of all, aircraft. Strategic bombing, aimed at cities and various industrial targets, would continue to play a role. However, from their experience in the desert, the British had learned the importance of tactical air operations in direct support of ground troops. Two formations, the RAF's highly-experienced Western Desert Air Force and the North-West African Air Force, which had supported the British Eighth and First armies respectively, were combined at the end of the Tunisian campaign into a unified Desert Air Force. Later, it became known as the First Tactical Air Force when it was assigned to operations connected with the invasion of southern Europe.

Meanwhile, in anticipation of the landings at Normandy, it was decided to create a Second Tactical Air Force, similar to the First. Elements required to achieve this would be drawn from both Army

Co-operation Command and Fighter Command in England, initially with the latter providing the new organisation's overall framework. Additional personnel and resources would be allocated from the desert theatre.

From the outset, 2nd TAF's order of battle suggested the magnitude of its future role. Several groups would operate in support of the British Commonwealth element in the main invasion force. 2 Group, originally with RAF Bomber Command, consisted of the few light-medium day bombers still operating from the U.K. It had long been considered as "something of a cuckoo in the nest," according to Christopher Shores, an expert on 2nd TAF, "all other groups being equipped with heavy bombers and operating at night against strategic targets." The remaining elements consisted of 83 Group, which would operate in support of the 2nd British Army, and 84 Group, assigned to the 1st Canadian Army.

Further evidence of 2nd TAF's importance could be found in the man who would be assigned to command it. Air Marshal Sir Arthur Coningham, KCB, DSO, MC, DFC—the list went on—was known as an efficient and hard-working air commander. Leading troops from New Zealand during the First World War, he had earned the nickname, "Maori." Later he became a pilot; and during the interwar years he gained the reputation as an expert on long-range flying. More recently, he had commanded the Western Desert Air Force, which had conducted many of its operations in concert with Montgomery's British Eighth Army. His experience in tactical air operations was unquestioned.

Air Vice-Marshal Harry Broadhurst, commanding 83 Group, had also led the Western Desert Air Force, having taken it over from Coningham at the end of 1942. His appointment would have special significance for thousands of Canadians, for it was to 83 Group that a number of overseas fighter squadrons of the Royal Canadian Air Force were assigned in the spring of 1943. These included 403 and 421, which combined as 127 Airfield, based at Kenley, and 401, 411 and 412, which formed 126 Airfield at Redhill, also in Surrey. Together, they constituted 17 Fighter Wing, one of three such units in 83 Group. The Canadian airfields were equipped with Spitfire IXs, the latest incarnation of Sir Reginald Mitchell's superb fighter air-craft, although 401 and 412 squadrons had yet to progress past the lesser thoroughbred, the Spitfire V.

Like the Sopwith Camel in a previous conflict, the Spitfire—in its many incarnations—has firmly established itself in the public's imagination as the foremost fighter aircraft of the Second World War. Historians will point out that the North American P-51 Mustang was at least as good, if not more versatile. And, during the Battle of Britain, more RAF squadrons had been equipped with the feisty Hawker Hurricane, which many pilots preferred. It was said to be easier to fly. In combat, too, the Hurricane was not markedly inferior to the Spitfire, as evidenced by the fact that it shot down three times as many enemy aircraft in the summer of 1940. But it was not as fast. So, the Hurricanes attacked the incoming waves of Luftwaffe bombers, while the more agile Spitfires took on the fighters. Their dogfights over the English countryside soon became a rivetting spectacle, to the point where the unfolding drama was narrated by BBC newscasters. The RAF (and its Commonwealth airmen) put on a "jolly good show," too. The more keenly interested could listen to the chatter of pilots on their open-channel AM radios. The result was the airmen—and more particularly, the Spitfire—emerged, alongside the longbow and Nelson's wooden walls, as a defining symbol of British resolve in the face of adversity. Even many of the Luftwaffe's pilots believed the Spitfire single-handedly saved Britain from defeat.

The aircraft which had so effectively challenged the Luftwaffe that summer was an early variant of Sir Reginald Mitchell's original design. The Spitfire I, which entered RAF service in 1938, had a top speed of 362 mph. Both the Mark I and its immediate successor, the Spitfire II, were powered by Rolls Royce Merlin engines. Their armament varied, as different combinations were tested. But for the most part the early Spitfires went into battle with eight wing-mounted .303-inch Browning machine guns.

Further models evolved later that year, each with progressively more powerful engines. In March 1941, the Spitfire V was introduced. With a top speed of 374 mph, improved range and a rapid rate of climb, the version proved itself in sweeps over occupied Europe. There, its principal adversary had been the Me 109E.* Battle-tested in the Spanish Civil War, the "Emil," as it was known, was faster than the Hurricane, at least as fast as the Spitfire, and arguably able to outclimb and outdive both. Nevertheless, an improved version, the Me 109F—or "Friedrich"—soon entered the fray. By the summer of 1942, yet another model appeared, the Me 109G, or "Gustav." It would become the most numerous variant of the almost 33,000 109s built. Its top speed was 428 mph, and its rate of climb was an equally impressive 4,000 feet per minute. This performance was somehow at odds with many of the Gustav's design features, which seemed either magnificent or comically absurd. "There's some beautiful engineering in it," said Tony Bianchi, an English expert in the restoration of vintage Second World War fighter aircraft, "and some excellent quality workmanship as well." The overall impression, he added, was that it was "sort of a Mercedes job." Even today, the aircraft's fuel-injected Daimler-Benz engine is a marvel. In some technical aspects, too, the Me 109 was ahead of its day (neatly let-in seams where sections of the all-metal stressed skin fuselage were joined, for example, were superior to methods used on comparable versions of the Spitfire). It was also, admittedly, an excellent gun platform. Like the Allied fighters, its armament varied but not significantly: a potent array of cannon and machine guns in the engine cowling and wings ensured it would not be taken lightly.

However, the Gustav—as well as other versions of the 109—had its share of imperfections. For one thing, its landing characteristics were described as "malicious," owing mainly to the peculiar geometry of its undercarriage, which was splayed out with several degrees of "toe-in" on the wheels. This gave the aircraft an alarming tendency to dig in, if not cartwheel on landing. To avoid this, a pilot wanted to be absolutely sure he was landing straight, which meant he needed to see

---

* The use of Me 109 (and, elsewhere in the text, Me 110) has been adopted as it was common during the Second World War and is the more familiar now. However, purists use the designation Bf 109, for *Bayrische Flugzeugwerke*, the firm that designed the aircraft and was later reconstituted as Messerschmitt A.G.

what he was doing—something the Me 109 afforded in the smallest measure. Most fighter aircraft of that era were notorious for their poor visibility, but some were clearly worse than others. Squadron Leader Paul Day, a contemporary fighter pilot and senior member of the RAF's Battle of Britain Memorial Flight, once noted the extent to which armoured glass and structural columns at the front of the Spitfire's cockpit tended to obscure a pilot's forward visibility. The addition of a reflector gun sight on top of the instrument panel undoubtedly exacerbated an already poor situation. In later models, some ten feet separated the cockpit and the Spitfire's four-blade constant speed propeller, which meant at five hundred feet of altitude a pilot was blind to the next three miles under the nose of his aircraft. Moreover, the Spitfire's trademark elliptical wings, while aerodynamically useful—and certainly essential aesthetically—further obscured an area of the sky "from which all sorts of nastiness is likely to emerge," as Day pointed out. In combat, an aircraft was especially vulnerable from behind, which meant pilots needed to be able to see in that direction as well. But the Spitfire's relatively small cockpit prevented a pilot from turning completely to look. To compensate for this, a tiny rear-view mirror—Day called it a "make-up mirror," it was that small—was fixed outside the canopy. It was virtually useless.

Indeed, in many respects it seemed the only concessions the Spitfire made were to aerodynamic performance. Yet Paul Day, like his predecessors in the Second World War, ultimately praised the aircraft. "I think Mitchell got it absolutely right," said Day. "As a dogfight aeroplane of that era, it's pretty good."

By comparison, Day's first words upon climbing into the cockpit of a restored Gustav were uttered in disbelief. "Good grief!" he exclaimed. Day estimated the cockpit offered twenty-five per cent less working room than the Spitfire. "The overall impression is actually very discouraging," he said of the cramped conditions. Hauling shut the 109's greenhouse-like canopy, which swung down on hinges, he added: "Well, this certainly isn't for the squeamishly claustrophobic!" Day could not imagine having to wrestle with the contraption in an emergency.

More generously, Day admitted the Gustav's main controls were all well-to-hand, unlike the Spitfire's, which had its throttle quadrant on the left and undercarriage control on the right. This meant a pilot needed to cross his hands on take-off to retract the landing gear. And some of the instruments in the Spitfire's cockpit were difficult to see, particularly in "high-workload situations," a contemporary euphemism for aerial combat. In comparison, the 109's instrument panel was easy to read and functional. But the cockpit was still uncomfortably small. In the Spitfire, despite its lack of elbow room, a pilot could get a lot of back-stick on the control column, which was more than could be said of the Gustav.

"I certainly wouldn't want to go to war in it," Day concluded.

Luftwaffe pilots had little choice in the matter. It should be said, too, that many of them grew accustomed to the 109's idiosyncrasies and flew it both confidently and aggressively. P B "Laddie" Lucas, a fast-talking former Fleet Street reporter who achieved his greatest fame as an RAF Spitfire pilot during the siege of Malta, said: "We always had a very high regard for the 109Fs and Gs, as we had there in 1942. The Luftwaffe flew them very well." Predictably, though, he claimed his fellow Spitfire pilots wouldn't hesitate to duel with either variation of the Luftwaffe's leading fighter aircraft.

They were considerably more cautious when confronting the Focke-Wulf 190. Introduced by the Luftwaffe in 1941, the FW 190 was well-armed, agile, and clearly in a class of its own. Pilots flying the Spitfire V were badly mauled in their early meetings with the "Butcher Bird," as it was called. During the Allied raid on Dieppe in August 1942, a mixed force of FW 190s and Me 109s shot down Allied aircraft at a rate of almost two to one.

To counter this new threat, the British launched an emergency program to improve their principal fighter aircraft. As a result, the Spitfire IX was introduced. It was the first major variant to exceed a top speed of 400 mph. Among its many other virtues was that in appearance it was not so radically different from the well-known Spitfire V. Said Lucas, remembering how this was used to their advantage against the Luftwaffe: "They saw these aircraft, the Spitfire IXs—they didn't know they were IXs; they thought they were Vs—and they thought they were going to have another field day. And

Johnnie Johnson with all these fellows, the Canadians in the IXs, simply took the pants off them! They never knew what hit them!"

Lucas was referring to Wing Commander (later Air Vice-Marshal) J E "Johnnie" Johnson, arguably the RAF's greatest Second World War ace. In March 1943, at age twenty-seven and newly promoted, he was given command of the RCAF's 127 Airfield at Kenley. There, he was to mold the unruly Canadian pilots into a professional fighter wing. "The Canadians had a reputation for toughness," he wrote afterwards, "and they required a firm hand on the reins." Tough and decisive, Johnson proved the right sort of individual to accomplish this seemingly difficult task.

Part of his success was due undoubtedly to the new Spitfire. It inspired confidence. But Johnson had also the benefit of his vast experience. He was surprised, for example, when he discovered the Canadian squadrons were still flying their sections in the old-fashioned line-astern formation (squadrons consisted usually of a dozen aircraft operating in sections of three or four), which along with the line-abreast and v-shaped, or "Vic" formation, had been abandoned by seasoned veterans. Such formations were found to be easy targets. Moreover, pilots were continually dividing their attention between maintaining their position and watching for enemy aircraft. Practised squadrons had since adopted the "finger four," so-called in that it loosely resembled the outstretched fingertips of a hand. It had evolved from observation of a Luftwaffe tactic known as the "*Schwarm.*" Aircraft flew about 200 yards apart and at different altitudes, the pilots of each pair looking inward at the other to cover his "blind spot" behind and to scan a wider area of the sky. The "finger four" not only reduced the chances of mid-air collisions, but more importantly it reduced the likelihood of Allied fighters being "bounced" by marauding enemy aircraft. As an offensive weapon, it had certain advantages as well. Pilots now attacked in pairs, one leading and the other, called a "wingman," watching the leader's tail. Positioning and range were important factors, also. Often they came diving out of the sun to attack. But the best, and safest approach was from above and astern of a target. Early in the war, pilots used a reflector sight with horizontal bars adjusted to the wingspan, measured in feet, of their adversary (if attacking an Me 109, the bars were set at 32), and when the silhouette filled the space between the bars, their adversary was in firing range—usually three hundred yards or less. Later a gyroscopic sight was adopted. It not only gave the range to a target but calculated how much lead, referred to as "deflection," was required so that bullets would hit an aircraft in flight. The art of "deflection shooting"—the ability to determine how far ahead, and where in the sky, to shoot so that a target would fly literally *into* the gunfire—largely by instinct was a skill most pilots developed eventually. The ability to do it accurately more often than not, while in the hurly-burly of aerial combat, was more difficult.

Under Johnson's leadership, though, the pilots of 127 Airfield at Kenley were able to improve their deadly craft. Similarly, the pilots of 126 Airfield, at Redhill, were to profit from the hard-won experience of their commanding officer. Wing Commander JE "Jimmy" Walker, DFC, at twenty-four was Johnson's junior by only a few years but at least as much a veteran—as evidenced by the two bars to his Distinguished Flying Cross and record of ten-and-a-half "kills," which was more than Johnson's total. Following his enlistment in the RCAF in 1940 and basic flight training, the native of Claresholm, Alberta, had sailed for England, where he was assigned to several RAF squadrons. He had flown in winter conditions at Murmansk in 1941, and the desert campaign from 1942 until his appointment to lead the new Canadian airfield in June 1943. Most important was that he brought a familiarity with the sort of tactical support operations expected of the new formations associated with 2nd TAF.

The promotion of Squadron Leader B D (Dal) Russel, DFC, of Westmount, Quebec, to the more operational position of Wing Commander Flying seemed equally sensible. Russel had flown with the RCAF's first fighter squadron overseas during the Battle of Britain. He was highly regarded for both his character and his professionalism in combat.

The pilots at Redhill were a mixed lot. Some undoubtedly were recent graduates of the British Commonwealth Air Training Plan in Canada, and had yet to be tested. Most had experienced some action and knew first-hand of Rhubarbs (low-level fighter attacks against enemy installations, including airfields, and ground movements by rail and motorised transport), Ramrods (a short-range bomber raid), Rodeos (fighter sweeps), and Circuses (bomber support and cover, intended to wreak havoc as well as draw the Luftwaffe into the air for a good scrap). There were even a few "old men" who had flown over Malta or North Africa, with either RAF or RCAF squadrons.

The squadrons, in their histories and nicknames, were equally colourful. The oldest was 401 (City of Westmount) Squadron, also known as "Ram" Squadron. Formed in Canada as No 1 (Fighter) Squadron in May 1937, it had sailed for England in June 1940, arriving just in time to participate in the Battle of Britain. In the next eight weeks, the squadron won credit for the destruction of thirty enemy aircraft, with as many as thirty-five more damaged. In March 1941, following a general reorganisation that reserved the "400-Block" for RCAF squadrons serving in conjunction with the Royal Air Force, the unit was renamed. Later that year the squadron had exchanged its Hurricane IIs for Spitfire VBs while stationed at Digby in Lincolnshire. The squadron's unit code, painted on the sides of its aircraft, was YO. Usually another letter followed after the RAF/RCAF rondel, which, in the case of Flight Lieutenant Harry Furniss of Montreal, was the letter "Y." Furniss, who was shot down over Germany in March 1945, was fond of interpreting his callsign as "Why oh why?"

Squadron Leader E L Neal, DFC, commanded 401. As a flying officer in 1941, he had recorded the redesignated squadron's first victory when he damaged a Ju 88 over the North Sea during a patrol off Skegness, Lincolnshire. Neal's own aircraft was hit during the action, forcing him to crash land in a wheat field near Horncastle while returning to Digby.

Neal's counterpart commanding 411 "Grizzly Bear" Squadron was G C (Charlie) Semple, who had succeeded Russel on his appointment as Winco Flying. The squadron itself was relatively new. Formed at Digby in June 1941, it was the RCAF's fourth fighter squadron overseas. Its unit code was DB.

Twenty-two-year-old G C "George" Keefer, DFC, originally from New York City, commanded 412 "Falcon" Squadron (unit code VZ), which had joined the airfield from an armament practice camp at

Fairwood Common, South Wales. It, too, had been formed at Digby in 1941 as the RCAF's fifth fighter squadron in England and had since flown in various patrols and offensive operations over occupied France.

Keefer's background consisted of private schools in the United States and summers with his mother's family in Prince Edward Island, where he enlisted with the RCAF in 1940. His flying instructor at Cap de la Madeleine in Quebec wrote of Keefer, who had soloed after only four hours of instruction, "Exceedingly keen; no cockiness; absolutely no fear... He has a lot of dash and pep." Not surprisingly, he graduated at the head of his class and was posted overseas almost immediately. By September 1941, Keefer was in North Africa with the RAF's 274 Squadron, flying Hurricane IIs. In eleven months, he crammed 179 sorties into his logbook. Each flight was different, and usually dangerous—although the only "war wound" he received occurred when a scorpion crept into his uniform one night and stung him.

In June 1943, when Keefer assumed command of 412 Squadron, his record was a modest four enemy aircraft destroyed, one probable and six damaged. However, his coolness and discipline both in the air and on the ground, which could not be measured, and not so much his scores, were the leadership qualities needed to lead 412 Squadron. Much depended on the RCAF formations, as each would contribute to the overall success of 2nd TAF in Europe. There was also the RCAF's prestige overseas to consider. In recent years it had become a sensitive issue, as had "Canadianisation," a term which will undoubtedly ring familiar to contemporary readers accustomed to debates concerning culture, constitutions and national unity. Previously, the RAF had agreed to create and pay for as many as twenty-five new RCAF squadrons. By 1943, Canada had at least assumed the cost of its own squadrons overseas, but within a year sixty per cent of Canadian airmen in Europe still flew with the RAF. The matter had become confusing, with promotions and the advancement of experienced aircrew within the RCAF at stake. Morale, both overseas and on the homefront, were also factors. As historian Desmond Morton has pointed out, "Pilots and navigators might be obscenely contemptuous of such issues but even they grumbled at

British policies such as the inexplicable rules that made some flying personnel into officers while others remained as sergeants." Pay, uniforms, discipline (or lack of it)—all were deemed better in the RCAF. For the most part, though, airmen and ground crews were relatively content as long as they were occupied.

By the end of July 1943, the new formation had begun to take shape at Redhill. Already the pilots of 126 Airfield had participated in a number of Ramrods, providing close escort during a bombing raid, and one fighter sweep, or Rodeo. Flight Lieutenant D R (Doug) Matheson of 411 Squadron was credited with the airfield's first operational score when he damaged a Me 109 during a dogfight over Amiens, France, on July 4th. Several weeks later, four pilots with 401 Squadron shared in the destruction of one FW 190. That pretty well summed up the month's tally. It was discouraging inasmuch as they all realised a few good scraps with the enemy were needed to establish a sense of esprit de corps. Moreover, effective teamwork would come only with practice—on the ground, as much as in the air. This pointed to the importance of administration, which was certainly a less glamorous role, but vital nonetheless considering the components of each airfield. To maintain a dozen serviceable aircraft, each squadron had an establishment of eighteen Spitfires, either Vs or IXs. The number of pilots allotted to a squadron was also based on a fixed establishment, which was usually twenty-seven, as each aircraft had a pilot assigned to it and occasionally a second who alternated. Each aircraft also had an air engine and airframe mechanic—fitters and riggers, if they came from the RAF. Armourers, photographers, radio and oxygen specialists, and electricians serviced several aircraft. From such complements of ground crew were built up servicing echelons comprised of more than a hundred trades personnel for each squadron. In addition, various other units were required to provide support and the degree of mobility expected of 2nd TAF formations. Altogether, even in its earliest development, the airfield's personnel numbered more than seven hundred.

In early August, they were ordered to new surroundings. Leaving behind a good runway and taxi tracks, well-built hangers and dispersal huts, their convoy of sixty vehicles wound and jogged along rutted, dusty roads from Surrey to Kent. From Redhill to the more rough-hewn facilities at Staplehurst was only sixty-four kilometres, yet the journey took more than three hours.

Their Spitfires flew in the next day and were soon dispersed around the grassy fields at their new location. The airstrip itself was situated on low-lying farmland, and left much to be desired. Mechanics were kept busy repairing tailwheels that were torn from their Spitfires after getting jammed in the badly laid metal runway tracking. In many other respects, the "era of the makeshift had begun," according to one member of the airfield's establishment. Pilots and groundcrew lived under canvas in a nearby orchard, where they were often victimised by—of all things—a goat named Heniker.

"If Heniker wasn't getting into trouble of some sort," remembered Sergeant Robbie Morton of the wing's maintenance section, "he just wasn't happy. It used to be his favourite practice to vault over the tents at night—usually late—and ten times out of ten he never quite got over. Often the boys would be wakened from blessed slumber to find the tent trembling or collapsing under the strain of Heniker perched on top and bawling the 'nanny goat blues' at the top of his lungs."

Within days of settling at Staplehurst, pilots were sent out on Ramrods as part of 2nd TAF's systematic attack on targets in France and the Low Countries. According to Michael Ewasyshyn, an airframe mechanic with 412 "Falcon" Squadron, August 1943 soon found everyone growing weary of the constant escort duties. The result was an increased number of incidents arising from visits to the local pubs, and general mischief on the station itself. To illustrate, Ewasyshyn recalled observing several pilots who had gathered one day at a stump behind the squadron's dispersal. The furtive activity of Sergeant H A "Tall" Heacock, Pilot Officer J H "Mac" MacLean and Flight Sergeant H W "Bud" Bowker soon attracted the attention of several other erks, who ambled over to see what was going on. "As they neared the merry trio," said Ewasyshyn, "Heacock was seen pouring gasoline down a rabbit hole. Bowker then quickly stepped forward with an oxygen cylinder sending gushes of this gas into the hole. The explosives expert, MacLean, motioned the lads back and boldly threw a flaming rag into the hole. A thunderous explosion took place, shooting tongues of flame out of many little holes." Ewasyshyn noted that the conspirators had obviously neglected to take this possibility into account, with the result that another officer on the scene was instantly dispatched across the airfield in search of a fire tender to put out the flames.

There were other incidents that month, as well as a change of command. On the 27th, Wing Commander K L B (Keith) Hodson, DFC and Bar, took over from Walker, whose tour had expired. By an interesting coincidence, Hodson had once been Walker's instructor at the Uplands air base in Ottawa. It would be his job now to cure the prankish restlessness afflicting the airmen at Staplehurst.

In this, Hodson wasted no time at all. "Hod," as he became known, did not easily suffer fools, misfits or malcontents. Moreover, he bluntly declared that if anyone didn't like the way he ran things he was quite willing to forget rank and settle matters any other way suggested. It was just the sort of tonic the men needed. They soon began to appreciate his firm leadership, recognising that it was for their benefit, and he became well liked.

Hodson also had some unexpected help soon after his arrival. On September 8th, Staplehurst was cut off from outside contact and all personnel were confined to the station. The reason for this virtual quarantine was 126's involvement in Operation "Starkey," which was intended to test various elements that would be involved in the actual invasion of France in 1944. The operation barely rates mentioning today in most historical texts, which is a reflection of its inconclusive outcome and the almost farcical ineptitude with which it was executed. But at the time, it loomed significantly. Group Captain "Iron Bill" McBrien, commanding 17 Fighter Wing, had visited already to personally brief the airmen. In short, "Starkey" called for a sizeable force of landing craft with suitable navy escort to sail most of the way across the English Channel. The intention was to simulate the first wave of an invasion force. Large numbers of medium and heavy bombers would carpet-bomb Boulogne as though to indicate a landing in that area. Meanwhile, countless fighter aircraft—including the Spitfires of 126 Airfield—were to maintain standing patrols inland to intercept enemy fighters coming to the defence. It was hoped the Luftwaffe would be sufficiently alarmed that a good number of its aircraft could be engaged.

It might have sounded good as a plan, but the results were more in keeping with Count Helmuth von Moltke's famous dictum, "Nothing is certain in war." Heavy mist at Staplehurst prevented the Canadians from getting off the ground until 0900. Then, inexplicably, they discovered most of the bomber force failed to show up at all. Nor did the Luftwaffe respond as hoped. The only engagement occurred when a number of FW 190s bounced an Allied patrol off the French coast. The ensuing dogfight ended with no losses to either side. Allied planners took some consolation in concluding that their advanced landing grounds, including Staplehurst, could indeed support intensive air operations mounted against occupied Europe. Nevertheless, "Starkey" left the pilots of 126 Airfield bitterly disillusioned.

Foul weather, which continued to play havoc with scheduled operations, further dampened their spirits. Not a single victory was recorded in the entire month. On September 19th, Flying Officer V A Haw of 411 Squadron went missing during a Rodeo over France. He was later reported captured. Mindful of the possibility that others might experience a similar fate as a result of their sweeps over occupied territory, the air force brass devised exercises to educate pilots in escape and evasion techniques. Every so often, particularly when operations were grounded by inclement skies, airmen would be rounded up and driven to locations throughout southeastern Kent, where they were left without food or money (except two pence for an emergency telephone call), and wearing civilian clothes. Their objective was to return to Staplehurst forthwith, without getting caught. Their identity cards were confiscated prior to the exercise, and they were permitted to reply to any questions asked of them using only "yes" or "no." To complicate matters, Home Guard and other military units in the surrounding area were alerted with instructions to apprehend the "downed airmen."

Here was an opportunity for real mayhem. The Canadians made

the most of it, too. Eight of twenty men sent out on one exercise returned triumphantly to the station with a catalogue of stories to tell
concerning their escapades en route. But none would match the
boldness of several pilots left stranded for the purpose of a similar
"do" in mid-October. Flying Officer J T Murchison and Pilot Officer R W Davenport, DFC—both of 401 Squadron—stole a couple
of unattended Spitfires from 129 Airfield at Ashford, while Flying
Officer D P Kelly of 401 took off in a Tiger Moth from the same
landing strip. No less imaginative were Flight Lieutenant W R
McRae and Flying Officer T Koch, who eventually returned to Staplehurst in a bus that had been liberated from a camp at nearby
Headcorn! As well, a number of bicycles were reported missing
throughout the area, which left the local constabulary both unhappy
and embarrassed. Air force officials, equally red-faced by the whole
affair, promptly tightened up the rules of their escape exercises in the
hope of curtailing such antics. The result was the Canadians had
something else to complain about in addition to their lack of operational flying and the generally dreary conditions at Staplehurst.

Two days later, they received word that winter quarters were waiting
for them at Biggin Hill. The announcement's effect on morale was
swift, as well as predictable, for even by the autumn of 1943 Biggin
Hill was known as one of the RAF's best and most prestigious advanced landing grounds. Situated on a vast level plot amidst the
patchwork North Downs, the airfield had its roots in the First World
War as a station occupied by a Radio Signals Unit of the Royal Flying
Corps and, later, several fighter squadrons. Expansion during the interwar years, including the addition of modern runways, taxi strips
and maintenance facilities—as well as comparatively lavish accommodations for pilots and groundcrew—merely added to its lustre.
For some, moving to Biggin Hill also meant a return to familiar
haunts. But then it wouldn't take long even for newcomers to learn
that officers frequented such popular pubs as the White Hart at
Brasted, run by motherly Kath Preston, while NCOs and airmen
preferred The Jail in Jailhouse Lane.

They arrived on October 13th. Spirits sagged somewhat as their relative inactivity, even at Biggin Hill, continued. Heavy air raids over London became a nightly diversion. It was not unusual to find airmen standing outside in their pyjamas, or less, watching the spectacle. There was even an element of risk involved. Sergeant Morton remembers stepping out one night and being greeted by the sight of what appeared to be a flaming meteor hurtling out of the sky toward him. It was in fact a Dornier bomber that had been hit by flak. It missed Morton, crashing instead into some houses not far from the airfield.

By the end of the month, though, pilots finally were able to put something on the scoreboard. Flight Sergeant Bowker of 412 Squadron shot down a FW 190 over the English Channel, and later sent another crashing into a house on the beach at Ault on the French coast. In the same engagement, Flight Lieutenant M D (Dave) Boyd, also with 412, damaged a Me 109. Still, the airfield's score remained somewhat meagre. It would be weeks, too, before any similar opportunity for action presented itself.

In the meantime, their experience at Biggin Hill was enlivened by the arrival in early November of Canada's most celebrated—and notoriously difficult—fighter pilot, Flight Lieutenant George "Buzz" Beurling, DSO, DFC, DFM and Bar, the so-called "Falcon of Malta," otherwise revered (or reviled) as "Screwball" Beurling. The lanky ace from Verdun, Quebec, had joined the nominal roll of 412 Squadron while in the midst of yet another scandal. He was, in a word, grounded. Earlier, he had been under open arrest for refusing to end his stunt flying in a Tiger Moth belonging to his squadron, but the idea of Beurling being court martialled was too much for the Liberal government of Prime Minister Mackenzie King. Persuasion was exercised, with the result that the RCAF withdrew its charges.

Beurling was with 403 Squadron, part of 127 Airfield, when the controversial incident occurred. In fact, he had been with the squadron since his much-publicised transfer in September 1943 from the RAF to the Royal Canadian Air Force. The RCAF was never entirely sure they wanted him in the first place given his unorthodox approach to discipline and reputation as a loner, but they could hardly refuse to accept someone who had become a living legend. So, Beurling was duly sworn in. Then began the difficult process of deciding where and how his talents could be best used (with the least potential for embarrassment to the RCAF, no doubt). Eventually, Beurling was sent to 403 at the request of its commanding officer. Squadron Leader Hugh Godefroy had been persuaded by one of his intelligence officers that Beurling could be an asset provided they were willing to "take their chances on the discipline side." Godefroy "chewed on it for a while," the officer recalled, before he finally agreed.

The young intelligence officer who quietly played his part behind the scenes was Monty Berger.

As early as May 1940, Monty had tried to enlist in the RCAF as an aircrew candidate but was rejected on medical grounds. Frustrated but undeterred, he signed on with the Canadian Officers Training Corps at McGill University in Montreal. Later, when he moved to Quebec City, he resumed his military training at Université Laval, where he qualified (in French) as an artillery second lieutenant. But again he was disappointed. Notwithstanding a number of Allied set-backs in the war, his prospects of being called up as an officer were, in his words, "at least a year or two away." In the meantime, one of his boyhood chums was scheduled to be sent overseas immediately upon completion of his training as an air observer. It seemed that if you wanted to get into the war in a hurry the way to do it was in air force blues, after all, and not army khaki.

Then, unexpectedly, came the RCAF's call for radar technicians. If nothing else, the job had the virtue of being considered vital to the defence of Britain—and, consequently, the defeat of Nazi Germany. This had further meaning to Monty inasmuch as he was the son of Rabbi Julius Berger of Montreal.

Still, the advertisement presented him with something of a dilemma. He had joined the *Chronicle-Telegraph* (with the help of an uncle, who had spoken to one of the owners) at a salary of thirteen dollars a week. This was after Monty had told the esteemed editor of

the Montreal *Star* to "go to hell" when a reporter's job he was offered—at the sum of twenty dollars a week—was delayed a fourth
time.

In Quebec City, where he was born on July 26, 1918, Monty had
lodgings less than a block from the Chateau Frontenac and about a
minute's walk from the *Chronicle-Telegraph* building. In many ways
he was well placed to enjoy a successful association with North
America's oldest newspaper.

Instead, in the spring of 1941, the young editor answered the
RCAF's advertisement.

Following his enlistment and a stint at St Hubert Manning
Depot in Montreal, where he endured the customary "square-
bashing" experienced by a new recruit, Monty was sent off to a radar
training course at McGill University. The surroundings, at least,
were familiar. And, while he did not profess to be at all scientifically
inclined, the curriculum proved not too difficult. Meanwhile, his
natural urge to record events around him emerged in the form of a
newsletter he produced, fittingly called "The Amplifier." Several
issues were brought out before the course ended.

By September 1941, Monty was in England, landing at Bournemouth where he stayed for several days before moving to Cranwell.
There he was assigned to a four-week course in advanced radar training, while at the same time he was transferred to the RAF as a newly
minted Leading Aircraftsman, paid what was called a "shadow corporal's salary" in the RCAF, which was considerably more than his
RAF colleagues received. He carefully avoided this subject when he
went to his first posting at No 85 RAF (Night Fighter) Squadron,
based at Hunsdon-near-Ware, north of London. Now flying
Mosquitos, No 85's original claim to fame was that it had been
Canadian ace Billy Bishop's squadron during the First World War.
To Monty's surprise, he discovered also that the squadron's current
commanding officer was a Canadian originally from Quebec City.

After a few months at Hunsdon-near-Ware, Monty received his
corporal's stripes. It was gratifying, given that many of his fellow
workers were skilled craftsmen, having worked at His Majesty's
Voice—a leading record-making company with an emerging interest

in manufacturing television sets—prior to the war. Still, it is difficult to picture Monty tinkering with radar sets and enjoying it for long. Several of his friends in London, particularly a few ex-journalists working in public relations for the RCAF, shared this disbelief. They urged him to find another line of work. It was, as Monty said, "an interesting theory." But after the better part of a year nothing had happened to alter his situation.

Then, in the spring of 1943, an item appeared in Daily Routine Orders noting immediate vacancies for intelligence officers. For the second time in Monty's war, an advertisement (of sorts) played a crucial role in determining his fate.

The notice indicated that applicants should have an ability to interview officers and other ranks; be experienced in gathering and collating information; and, finally, be able to get on well with people. Here, at last, was an opportunity for which he was suited. His skills as a journalist would undoubtedly prove helpful meeting the first and second requirements. So, too, would the fact that he was bilingual, having grown up in Montreal. He could claim as well the benefits of a job he worked at briefly following his studies at Columbia in 1940; he was an analyst with Industries Research Incorporated in New York. There he had prepared long reports on such subjects as the practical aspects of automobile financing (on behalf of a potential competitor to General Motors Acceptance Corporation, at that time the only firm offering such financing), and the relative merits of mass-producing glass in the United States at a time when, according to Monty, "much of the glass used by industry was manufactured in South America."

The final requirement, as Monty recalls—an ability to "get on well with people"—was an exercise in subjective judgement. For this, he could only hope to make the best impression possible when he appeared before the selection board in London.

"I was terribly nervous; and after being asked some questions, which I guess were not too difficult, I forgot to salute on the way out! I was sure that I was a dead duck. However, a few weeks later I was notified that I had been recommended for entry into the intelligence course."

The selection board's willingness to take a chance on him should not have been so surprising. No more could be asked of a neophyte "spy" than to possess the skills, aptitudes and maturity that Monty had demonstrated already.

He was commissioned as a Pilot Officer within a few months. Following a brief but nonetheless thorough course at the RAF's Intelligence School at Highgate in London, he transferred back to the RCAF and was posted to 403 Squadron, based at Kenley. His immediate supervisor was the squadron's Senior Intelligence Officer, Flight Lieutenant "Birdie" Birtwhistle, a schoolteacher from England. Monty remembers him as a very precise individual, and a perfect tutor—although as a rule he spoke in bursts. Monty recalls one conversation that illustrated their different personalities.

"I'd like you to do (something or other: the exact words are forgotten)—what do you think?" Birtwhistle demanded briskly.

Monty gave the query his usual considered judgement.

"Well," he drawled reflectively, "I'll turn that over in my mind a bit."

Birtwhistle exploded with laughter. "I can just see those wheels turning over in your mind!" he roared before striding off.

"He was really very quick and I talked very slowly," Monty allowed afterwards. "However, we got on very well together. It was an exciting experience."

Monty's persevering nature and good humour stood him well during his early apprenticeship. The truth was he enjoyed the role of intelligence officer, despite the many demands made of him. Said one observer: "The spy's one of the most interesting jobs on the station and one of the most responsible. His hours are long and his problems detailed. He is compiling reports at his desk long after the men ... have knocked off for supper. And often he's up again early in the morning to prepare for another do." Briefing and debriefing pilots was only part of an intelligence officer's duties. The rest of the time he was an impresario of sorts, arranging activities to boost morale or generally keep pilots from dwelling on the sordidness of their jobs. By all accounts, Monty excelled in fulfilling this aspect of the IO's job description. His arguments in favour of soliciting the transfer of

Pilot Officer "Buzz" Beurling to 403 Squadron were an example.

"He was really very personable and keen on helping," Monty insists. "Many of our pilots who were so effective in shooting down enemy aircraft owed at least part of their success to Beurling's instruction."

As a squadron IO, Monty frequently briefed and debriefed the famous ace. He remembers, too, being involved in an incident that illustrated Beurling's extraordinary skills as a pilot, and his killer's instinct.

The squadron had returned one day from a mission and, during debriefing, reported all had been quiet.

"I shot down an FW 190," Beurling announced, almost in passing. This astounded everyone, but most of all Hugh Godefroy, who became visibly annoyed.

"How could you have shot down an FW, Buzz? You were flying Number Four!"

"I saw a little dot in my mirror at twelve o'clock," Beurling replied calmly. "I knew that if I said anything on the R/T the chances of our whole section turning around quickly enough weren't very good. That spot would have disappeared. So I peeled off, climbed and got behind him. I was to his left and behind, and I could see my shots going into the rear of his cockpit. The FW went down in flames."

Beurling's eyesight was legendary. It was said in Malta that he *always* spotted the enemy in the air before anyone else. Brian Nolan, who wrote the most authoritative biography of the Canadian ace, reported that Beurling's wingmates continually marvelled at his visual gift, "one for which there was no scientific explanation."

"Of all the stories about him told by his wingmates," Nolan added, "most concern his extraordinary vision. The story most repeated involved Beurling waiting around the dispersal hut at Kenley in England one day when he suddenly announced, 'Here come the Forts.' No one else could hear them, let alone see them. 'There are thirty-six,' he announced. Moments later the others heard the Flying Fortresses, and shortly the big planes began appearing in the far distance. Everyone started counting. There were thirty-six."

Notwithstanding such tales of Beurling's "super vision," his account of shooting down an enemy aircraft without anyone else realising it seemed farfetched. More importantly, without an eyewitness the only possible evidence that could be used to support his claim would be if the movie camera in his Spitfire, which operated when the machine guns were fired, had recorded the event.

"By golly," said Monty afterwards, "the film clearly showed the aircraft being shot down. He had spotted this dot, peeled off, got behind it and got back to position without anybody knowing what had happened."

Godefroy was already chafing as a result of Beurling's lone-wolf behaviour. It clearly contradicted a basic tenet that every other pilot in the squadron had come to understand, and respect, as essential. Johnnie Johnson had made a point of laying it out for Beurling the day he arrived at Kenley. "There is one rule," he said firmly, "and it is not to be broken. We always fight as a team."

The rule existed wherever Beurling went, but he didn't always follow it. Craving action in the air, and denied as much largely because of circumstances or foul weather, he seemed to distance himself from his fellow pilots, while making it difficult for Godefroy to maintain his authority. Eventually, of course, such behaviour got him into trouble—as it did in October 1943.

Shortly after the episode in which he claimed to have shot down an FW 190 without anyone seeing it, Beurling was promoted to Flight Lieutenant. He had objected initially, but changed his mind when he found out the squadron's Tiger Moth—a primary flight trainer known to thousands of Canadian airmen during the Second World War, and much loved for its wind-in-the-wires manoeuvrability—would come under his charge. Beurling's antics in the two-seater biplane eventually led to his being placed under open arrest, but not before he had invited Monty along on several of his hair-raising flights.

"To this day I feel them in my gut when I think of them," Monty says. "He would hedgehop and do all kinds of fancy turns. It was quite something."

The air force brass took a somewhat different view. Beurling, with his grounding order still in effect, ended up at 412 Squadron.

He arrived at Biggin Hill, officially, on November 7th. In a bizarre twist of fate, the new Winco Flying at 126 was another highly decorated Canadian ace, Robert Wendell "Buck" McNair, DSO, DFC and Two Bars. He had replaced Russel the previous month. McNair, a sharpshooting Westerner from Battleford, Saskatchewan, had earned his gongs in the defence of Malta, where he had openly declared his mistrust of Beurling's unorthodox ways.

November proved to be a comparatively busy month for the airfield, which added four FW 190s to its list of victories, and several more damaged. Yet almost two months passed before Beurling was credited with shooting down a FW 190. It would be his last victory in combat. Disillusioned by the air war over Europe, the "Falcon of Malta" returned to Canada within a few months, and shortly thereafter resigned from the RCAF. Beurling all but vanished into obscurity, until his mysterious death in Italy in 1949 reminded Canadians that he had been one of the Second World War's most enigmatic individuals. Interestingly, it was Monty who published for the memorial service attended by Beurling's family and friends one of the most moving tributes to the fallen ace.

Monty also ended up at Biggin Hill—newly promoted as a Flight Lieutenant occupying the position of Senior Intelligence Officer. Ironically, his arrival coincided not only with Beurling's diminishing impact but also an increase in the amount of operational activity for 126 Airfield. The last month of 1943 was the most hectic yet for the Spitfire pilots. In addition to several more FW 190s destroyed or damaged, they claimed a Ju 88 and a Dornier 217, both shot down during Ramrod operations in December.

Meanwhile, preparations for the Normandy Invasion were moving ahead. A new order of battle was drawn to reflect the creation of an Allied Expeditionary Air Force, which combined 2nd TAF and the US Ninth Air Force under the command of Air Chief Marshal Sir Trafford Leigh-Mallory. Of more interest to the pilots and groundcrew of 126 Airfield, wintering at Biggin Hill, was that by the year's end their squadrons were all equipped with versions of the Spitfire IX.

With this, and in their youthful exuberance, they were eager to greet both the coming of spring—and the promise of D-Day.

2

"WE LIVE FOR D-DAY"

S O FAR the crossing had been relatively uneventful—a good omen for the wing's advance ground party. But sometime around one o'clock in the morning, a terrific explosion erupted not far from their landing craft. Heads swung about all at once to look. There was confusion astern of their place in the convoy where another landing craft was carrying a similar party of RCAF ground personnel. Then someone called out that a torpedo had just crossed their bow from the port beam. Bloody E-boats, no doubt. The enemy's fast attack craft were doing their worst. A third torpedo sliced by—astern again. Several seconds later it rammed into a landing craft directly behind their own. There was another thundering explosion, momentarily lifting a huge fountain out of that part of the English Channel and what remained of the stricken craft, which had been cut in half. Flames shot into the night sky. For those watching this appalling scene, shock and anger were mixed with a heightened sense of their own vulnerability. They waited anxiously for the next attack, wondering how they might react if their vessel was blown up under them. But none came. Evidently the marauding E-boats, if that's what had been responsible for the damage, were satisfied with their night's work or were scared off. Undeterred by the torpedo attacks, the convoy continued to churn towards the unseen coast. Someone made tea to keep the troops awake, there being no place to sleep except in or under the vehicles packed into the landing craft. There was little conversation. Most of the men were occupied with private thoughts, of home, family, the task for which they had spent months in England preparing, and the myriad details that needed remembering.

Shortly before daybreak, the convoy hove to off the coast of Normandy. Having survived its perilous journey across the English Channel, the ground party of RCAF officers and men eagerly disembarked from its landing craft. Amidst a scene that words could barely describe, they set out almost at once to establish a forward airstrip at Ste Croix-sur-mer on the French coast.

It was early on the morning of D+1—June 7, 1944. Just twenty-four hours since the greatest invasion in history had breached the enemy's Atlantic Wall.

Half a century later, the D-Day invasion still seems beyond the scope of one's imagination. More than six thousand Allied vessels, including four thousand landing craft and hundreds of attack transports, destroyers and other warships, accompanied roughly 150,000 men who stormed the coast at Normandy at dawn along a front stretching between Caen and Valognes. They were preceded by a devastating naval bombardment of the enemy's coastal defences. More than twelve thousand aircraft, including five thousand front-line fighters, provided cover over the beaches in addition to attacking key targets inland. "The value of this air supremacy," wrote journalist and historian Chester Wilmot, "can hardly be overrated. It was undoubtedly the most important single factor in the success of the invasion, for its influence penetrated to almost every aspect of the enemy's plans and operations."

For months prior to D-Day, the Allies had played a complex game of secrecy and deception intended to suggest they would land not at Normandy, but farther north along the coast. Throughout the spring, for every bombing raid linked to the invasion plans, twice that number of sorties were flown over the Pas de Calais area, in the hope of misdirecting the enemy's attention. Meanwhile, the Luftwaffe was all but prevented from carrying out reconnaissance flights over the south of England, where the invasion fleet was assembling. Thus, as Wilmot added: "Through air power the Allies were able not only to surprise the enemy but to mislead him."

In fact, the Luftwaffe was already a spent force by June, 1944. Years of neglect had left it with a bomber strength of only 153, which was considerably less than its strength of 1,290 in September 1939. Monthly production of Luftwaffe fighters had peaked at 1,523 in May 1944, but overconfidence in the Atlantic defences, the war in the Soviet Union and the defence of Italy had left only three hundred or so to be dispersed throughout occupied France. Incredibly, only 119 serviceable fighter aircraft were available out of a total of 169 deployed on the Channel front. These flew an estimated 319 sorties against the 10,858 mounted by the Allies that historic day. The result, while frustrating to the Allied pilots keyed up for action, was hardly surprising. Not a single Allied aircraft was lost on D-Day due to the Luftwaffe's intervention. In fact, they were scarcely seen over the beaches throughout the entire day. *"This was very disappointing,"* complained 411 Squadron's diarist. The Grizzly Bears had started their first sweeps at 0810; the last touched down at 2335 without having made contact with the enemy. Not until evening did four Heinkels appear over the battlefront. They hastily scattered their bombs over part of the Canadian sector before they were jumped by another squadron of Spitfires. All four of the enemy bombers were shot down. Elsewhere, though, it was not an especially good day for the scoreboard of any Allied air formation.

But it was a magnificent outing, nonetheless. For the pilots of 126 Wing (it had assumed that designation in May), the invasion came as an enormous relief following months of bomber escort duties, exercises, and seemingly endless rehearsals. In February, while still operating out of Biggin Hill as 126 Airfield, the Canadian Spitfires were assigned to accompany Marauders and Mitchells on raids against VI launching sites at Tocqueville, Beaumont-Le Roger, and south of Dieppe in France. Further raids were mounted on

marshalling yards and airfields in Holland. Fighter sweeps in the
Ostend-Bethune-Abbeville areas were common. The Spitfires also
provided cover during heavy bomber raids on Eindhoven, and sometimes escorted Flying Fortresses returning from raids on Germany.

In March, dive-bombing was added to their list of tasks, as 2nd
TAF was ordered to aid in the softening up of France prior to the
invasion. This occurred in conjunction with a move to Tangmere,
east of Chichester in West Sussex, in mid-April. It was said the
airfield owed its existence to a First World War pilot who made a
forced landing on the site in 1916. He flew out the next day and
reported the field at Bayley's Farm would make a good landing
ground. Eventually it was requisitioned and cleared, the latter
accomplished with the assistance of a party of German PoWs. Tangmere was soon in business as an airfield used by bombers of the
United States Army Air Service. Following a period after the war
when it was declared surplus, its usefulness was rediscovered during
the Munich Crisis in 1938, when air raid shelters were hastily dug,
hangars were camouflaged and aircraft were brought to readiness. By
1944, Tangmere was one of the most important advanced landing
grounds in England. Ironically, many Allied pilots relied on the
airfield for emergency landings, as had one of their First World War
compatriots, or when diverted by foul weather.

The Canadians of 126 Airfield settled in officially on April 15,
1944. From Tangmere they continued their raids against rocket sites
and were involved in a wide range of duties, including escort patrols
for bomber attacks against Douai and Cambrai, for example, and
fighter sweeps. Attacks on rail and road communications in occupied France continued. All of it formed a part of what one observer
described as a "dreadful note of preparation" in their activities
throughout the spring.

There were few scores in the air, though. In five months only
seventeen enemy aircraft were shot down, bringing the airfield's total
to twenty-nine destroyed (and another thirteen damaged) by the end
of May. In the same period, at least half a dozen Allied pilots had
been killed or captured during Ramrods over France. Accidents, too,
claimed their victims. Early in March, the Spitfire belonging to

Flight Lieutenant L F Berryman of 412 Squadron struck another aircraft after landing at Biggin Hill. Berryman's kite swung off the runway, nosed over and burst into flames. He managed to climb out of the cockpit, but his uniform was engulfed in fire. Leading Aircraftsman Mike Ewasyshyn, who had been waiting for Berryman, immediately grabbed a blanket and ran to the scene. He wrapped the pilot and rolled him on the ground until the flames were extinguished. Berryman suffered burns to his face and hands, but was spared further injury as a result of Ewasyshyn's alert response.

Such tragedies underscored the element of risk that existed in the most routine aspects of their daily lives. The number of injuries and even fatalities that occurred in England and, later, while on the continent as a result of traffic accidents or other mishaps seemed baffling if not absurd to many pilots. Their work in the air was dangerous enough.

The enemy, however, seemed unwilling to be lured into combat. Often only light flak opposed the Canadian pilots during their sweeps. The most noteworthy episode had occurred on March 15th, when four pilots of 401 Squadron had each shot down one FW 190. Flying Officer R H (Bob) Hayward had damaged another and also shared a damaged Me 410 with Flying Officer D D "Red" Ashleigh. The wing's CO, Keith Hodson, declared the bar open that afternoon to celebrate the victories. By coincidence, Don Fairbairn, a correspondent with the CBC's overseas radio unit, was on hand. Said Monty Berger: "Eventually a very slick programme was done that starred "Doc" Arnold Jones and his fine black spaniel, 'Dinghy.' They often entertained the wing with their collection of antics." Breaking down the pilots' aversion to publicity was more difficult, but Fairbairn was able to record their yarns, too. The programme was well received when it was broadcast back in Canada.

But "hard news" involving the Canadian pilots overseas was elusive that spring. Often, when they weren't detailed to operations, the wing's squadrons were sent on exercises to sharpen their skills. In February, for example, 411 Squadron spent a week at an air firing course at Peterhead, Scotland. On another occasion, the pilots of 126 Airfield participated in an exercise to determine the amount of time required for quick briefing and take-off in response to a call for army support. The pilots assembled in their briefing rooms at Biggin Hill, where Army Liaison Officers described an imagined tactical situation and provided specific "targets." Pilots were ferried by transport to their aircraft. Each squadron was timed from the start of briefing until the last aircraft had started. Two squadrons took nine minutes, three took ten minutes and another took thirteen. It was estimated another five minutes would have been required for actual take-off.

February also featured a more elaborate exercise for the entire wing. It established the Dorking-Horsham Road as a "front" with Dorking, Guildford and Redhill as flak areas. The intention was to attack Frensham Ponds near Farnham with a succession of fighter-bomber squadrons from 17 Wing. Simulated ground strafing was carried out, as well. Ten squadrons including the Spitfires of 126 and 127 airfields were involved. The entire attack took five minutes, after which the Spitfires returned to station for a refuelling and rearming test. Such exercises were meant to examine the flying, servicing and INT/OPS organisation under conditions approximating the close army support role they would be expected to carry out on the continent. This was accomplished, although at the cost of heightening expectations and fuelling rumours concerning the coming invasion.

This naturally raised another matter. There were spies everywhere—or so it seemed given the general concern for security.

In the latter months of 1943, reports of "indiscretions both in correspondence and conversation" had reached the point that officers commanding all units within 83 Group, 2nd TAF, were mildly reproached for their inattention. One incident in particular, involving "alleged careless talk and seeking of official information by civilian driving instructors," had so alarmed Sergeant G T Mountjoy of the RAF's Intelligence Security Section that he sent a curt note to the commanding officer of 126 Wing, "Hod," himself. Mountjoy reported that civilians employed by the British School of Motoring had on several occasions "pumped" the airmen under their instruction. Later, in a pub at Maidstone, one driver had asked in a loud voice, "Are you taking all three of your squadrons with you when you move to Biggin Hill?" The matter was duly investigated—inconclusively, it seems, although it remained the sort of incident that sent chills up the backs of those charged with safeguarding the biggest Allied secret of all.

By February 1944, with planning for Operation "Overlord" well underway, such fears had intensified. The security ring around Britain tightened. Civilian travel between the United Kingdom and Ireland was stopped, for example, in the hope of limiting the flow of information to Dublin, where German diplomats had established a fertile centre of espionage, apparently unimpeded by the Irish Government. Unprecedented restrictions were later imposed on all foreign diplomats in London. They could not enter or leave the country, and their mail was subjected to censorship. Monty, as the wing's own "spy," was acutely aware of the need for such measures. There were, however, occasions when he was exasperated by the prevailing atmosphere. He advised the COs of 401, 411 and 412 squadrons of "a certain increasing laxity" with regard to the matter of security. "All pilots are asked to cooperate in putting an end to this by refraining from pressing the Duty Intelligence Officer for specific information about pending operations."

Monty also put his literary skills to the task. Numerous pamphlets were produced and circulated in mimeographed form among the wing's personnel. These featured a few requisite security slogans— *"This is your country—don't talk the enemy into it." "Whatever you do, never let it be said." "While you sip, let nothing slip." "Words with a stranger spell danger." "Think before you ink."*—along with other "words of wisdom" drawn from Eccleasiasticus, and even a few songs set to familiar melodies, such as "We ain't a-gonna talk no mo'," with instructions that it was to be sung "in mournful unison by a trio of dejected-looking erks."

There was a deliberate satirical edge to this, of course. Measures intended to ensure security were often disliked among pilots and groundcrew in normal circumstances. Some of the new regulations seemed unduly restrictive, if not absurd. In March, Sergeant G W Pierce, RCAF Service Police, reported to Monty: "The specially trained dog which has been supplied to the airfield has proved to be a great help to the police. Holes in the fence made by airmen attempting to get out of camp without booking out have been reported to the RAF Regt and in the meantime the dog is used to patrol these holes."

The security men were equally concerned by the amount of gossip that was circulating. As D-Day approached, Sergeant Mountjoy reported: "One rumour has it that the airfield is about to move to Scotland for a 'rest.'" Word was circulating that 126 Airfield would be the first to move to France when the second front was established. "Another rumour mentions seventy-five per cent casualties when the fighting starts." Mountjoy added: "However, from my observations I have been unable to detect any falling off of morale and I do not think that any undue store need be placed on these rumours."

Idle chatter among the wing's personnel was natural in the circumstances. They all knew they were preparing for the invasion. Curiosity was building.

There was some truth, too, in the propagandists' cant about enemy spies and the need to be tight-lipped. Information had reached Berlin via clandestine channels that confirmed the likelihood of an Allied invasion of France in the spring. Attempts were being made to learn the precise date and proposed site of the landings.

In the meantime, the Luftwaffe's limited activity over France even during daylight raids on vital installations was baffling. According to Chester Wilmot, this passivity "even during the most ostentatious exercises in the English Channel, seemed accountable only on the ground that Goering was husbanding his resources until the [Allied] armada put to sea."

The truth was Hitler's generals were locked in bitter disagreement regarding the coming invasion. Field Marshal Erwin Rommel, who had put an end to the cosy life experienced by the occupation troops on his arrival at the front early in 1944, had at least predicted that Allied superiority in the air had the potential of being a deciding factor. He was convinced the Allies would use their air power to frustrate the movement of German troops to the front, wherever it was established. Consequently, Rommel argued that the invasion had to be stopped at once, before a foothold was gained on the continent. He was right—but only in retrospect. Swamped with information, much of it deliberately planted by the British, and bereft of hard facts to reveal the truth of the Allied plan, the enemy remained largely unprepared. The Luftwaffe's inability, or unwillingness, to penetrate the formidable aerial defences over England merely added to Rommel's frustration. As late as May 21st, in his weekly report, Rommel complained: "There are *no* results of air reconnaissance of the island for the entire period!"

Thus, in effect, a major Allied victory was achieved even before the landings occurred. Yet few Allied strategists were willing to take the odds in their favour for granted. Exercises continued in the months prior to the invasion, so that pilots could hone their skills.

Such exercises highlighted a number of deficiencies in the original organisation and administration of the airfields assigned to 2nd TAF. They lacked much of the equipment needed to be truly mobile. The intelligence staff in particular were worried they might not be able to keep up once they had landed in France. Their facilities were inadequate and uncomfortable, particularly in cold weather. Said Monty: "The men carried out all of the briefings and interrogations in little ridge tents with maps scattered about, and an easel placed strategically to catch the precious rays of sunlight—when there was sun and it wasn't too windy. We discovered to our dismay after a number of moves the maps were torn and dog-eared, and the secret documents had become tangled among various other forms of equipment and papers."

To compensate, the intelligence staff were granted the use of a three-ton lorry, but that quickly proved just as inadequate. Following a heated "battle of the bumph" with the brass at 83 Group and further appeals, Monty and his cohorts received two Austin office tenders. "These," he said, "were constructed with comfort and every space-saving device in mind."

Monty adds:

They were used in pairs, and so they became known as the 'Siamese Twins.' The idea was that wherever the wing set up camp, the two tenders were drawn up alongside each other. The equipment inside was unloaded, and wings folded out from the sides, much like a camper trailer. These wings became floors of an office that was able to hold a great number of people and the mounting piles of paperwork, or bumph. After the floors were secured, canvas coverings were erected to form a protective ceiling, and sides for the offices. Then a large tent was set up in between the two trucks. This formed the main briefing room for the pilots. Cocoa matting was added to keep the truck bottoms dry and the sides of the newly formed offices were covered with maps, posters and important bulletins. It really was an ingenious arrangement.

The tenders were delivered to the wing in May 1944, by which time documents marked "SECRET" were arriving in great numbers and "hush-hush" meetings were commonplace. Men vanished from the scene for days or weeks at a time, Monty reported. Special driving courses were given, in which men battled with huge vans, driving backwards onto small landing craft, and driving them off into several feet of murky water. Others were trained in camouflage and decoy, and a great deal of advice was given in laying out airfields, which, they understood, were to be constructed in Normandy.

There had also been yet another change in the position of Wing Commander Flying. In mid-April, Squadron Leader George Keefer replaced "Buck" McNair. The new CO of 412 was Squadron Leader J E (Jack) Sheppard, DFC, of Dollarton, British Columbia.

In the meantime, the rumour mill was working overtime. In London, Canadian diplomat Charles Ritchie wrote in his diary, "Perhaps it is the invasion. We live for D-Day."

The sense that something was about to happen was palpable.

Most of May 1944 saw ideal conditions in southern England, with gentle spring days leaving the channel itself calm and sunlit.

"Weather for poets," said Chester Wilmot. The invasion was imminent.

In France, Rommel dictated to his secretary: "I am more confident than ever before. If the British give us just two more weeks, I won't have any more doubt about it." His confidence is hard to understand, particularly in light of the many misgivings he voiced previously and his complaints on the eve of the invasion regarding the Luftwaffe's inability to provide reconnaissance photographs. Nevertheless, Rommel got his wish.

In England, the Allies made their final preparations. This included a new order of battle that affected the Canadian fighter pilots and groundcrews at Tangmere. On May 15th, 126 Airfield became known officially as 126 Wing, part of 17 (RCAF) Sector, under the direction of 83 (Composite) Group, 2nd TAF. The new designation shed the static connotation they had lived with for almost a year, and reflected an expectation of the formation's mobility following the invasion.

So it was that as members of a full-fledged wing, the airmen received Eisenhower's now-famous leaflet prior to the invasion, which he called "the Great Crusade."

"The eyes of the world are upon you," said the Supreme Allied Commander. "Your task will not be an easy one. Your enemy is well trained, well equipped and battle-hardened. He will fight savagely. But this is the year 1944!... The tide has turned! The free men of the world are marching together to Victory!"

Heady stuff—and typically American in its cheerleader's confidence. By comparison, a memorandum marked "SECRET" that arrived at Tangmere for immediate distribution among all personnel was filled with sage advice in the form of sardonic one-liners and humorous verbal pratfalls. "Invasion without Tears," issued by 83 Group Headquarters, was subtitled "How to get to the Second Front in Comfort (for all those NOT going by Air—particularly Unit Commanders)." The document contained a somewhat phlegmatic introduction by Air Vice-Marshal Harry Broadhurst, AOC 83 Group:

The invasion of the Continent is a vast undertaking, requiring organisation of the most intricate detail. Yours may be a very small job but if it is not done smoothly and accurately the machine will creak, and too many creaks might cause a disaster.

This information is given to help you do your part towards making a success of the biggest military operation the World has ever known.

Having dispensed the official line, whoever composed the remaining text provided a few additional introductory items—with a hint of the more down-to-earth style that would characterise much of the document. It is worth quoting in some detail.

"You will go to a large and very comfortable camp called the CONCENTRATION AREA," said the anonymous author. "There your vehicles will be waterproofed so that you can successfully drive ashore on the other side. After about two days you will go to a similar but smaller camp called the MARSHALLING AREA, where you will be formed up in parties ready for shipment and a spot more waterproofing will be done. A day or so later, you will go to the "HARDS" [stretches of open beach paved with concrete or stone to permit tanks and vehicles to back straight into landing craft], where you will do a little more waterproofing and embark. Next your ship or craft will join others to form a convoy. Then off you go to do your stuff."

This process, according to the author, was properly known as "Going through the SAUSAGE MACHINE, and you may be some six days in it." He added hopefully, "There is no reason why everyone shouldn't find the Sausage Machine quite comfortable and even enjoyable, provided certain simple directions are followed."

Thereafter, the document reviewed the process. For this, the author adopted a Spike Milligan-like voice. In the section entitled "GETTING READY," under "KIT (Cut it down)," he advised: "Sorry about the fishing tackle and the baby grand, but there just isn't room." For "SPECIAL ITEMS TO TAKE," readers were advised to remember Robinson Crusoe. Books and playing cards were recommended.

"Drivers, take a piece of chalk. Why? See paragraph 26." Flipping ahead, one discovers the chalk was for the various "cabalistic symbols" personnel would scribble on the vehicles as they passed through stages of the waterproofing process. "You must always have a tow rope or chain," the document added with heavy emphasis, "otherwise if you stick in the water while landing, you may be left stranded or blown up by some ignorant bystanders."

Everyone was to take a haversack ration to feed themselves on their way to the concentration area. These contained a special cooker. "You'll have to light it. Now, one way of making a fire is to rub two Boy Scouts together. But in case there are no Boy Scouts available, better take matches."

Under DOCUMENTS: "Yes, you need documents to get to the Second Front... There are only two." These were the Nominal Roll, and Form 1178, identified as "the blue thing in large letters." It gave the dimensions and weight of each vehicle. "Fill it in, truthfully ... (gas companies and railway stations have weight machines) and then stick it on the windscreen." Form 1178, it seems, was every driver's ticket to the front.

Pets, on the other hand, would not be allowed on the journey. "Park them," said the document. "Several pet dogs, large and small, have insisted on accompanying master on Invasion Exercises. We appeal to all TAF dogs, whether posted or attached, to make other arrangements for the real show, and to make them NOW." Police dogs were excepted.

The second part of "Invasion without Tears" examined the procedures established for travelling to the concentration area. Punctuality ("obviously convoys shouldn't arrive late... But also, convoys should not be early: it upsets the works if you are ... so try to arrive at the exact time detailed on the Movement Order), routes ("stick to them ... so you know a better route: just this once, however, go the way RAF Movements have routed you), and special information for officers commanding units, were outlined.

On arriving at the concentration area, personnel were requested not to leap from their vehicles. "Wait for the word," the document advised. Hotel accommodations would be provided while the men attended briefings and vehicles underwent the initial stage of their waterproofing. Similar procedures were to be followed at the marshalling area and hards.

"Well, you're afloat now," the document proclaimed following a brief word on the subject of "GOING UP THE RAMP" into the landing craft. "Bon voyage."

The crossing itself was given relatively short attention. Under "ON THE HIGH SEAS (not very high, we hope!)," the author cautioned all personnel: "The Captain's word is law. He can tell anyone or everyone what to do or where to go...He can even marry you (though we don't recommend it on this trip). Relax, and do what he says. Even if he's just a Leading Seaman, he is still the Captain."

Then, France. "ASHORE (at last!)" Drivers were told to follow the signs posted, making sure "the Army has cleared the enemy out first."

"Keep your fingers crossed and get to work," the document concluded.

Within hours of the document's distribution, its contents were put to the test. On May 22, the 126 Wing's diarist noted that Keith Hodson and his party had left Tangmere for "parts unknown." In fact, they were en route to the concentration area at Old' Sarum, north of Salisbury. By all accounts they were well catered to while their transportation underwent its prerequisite waterproofing routine. Three days later, eighty-eight vehicles rolled off the "assembly line" and travelled to a marshalling area established at Purfleet, near Tilbury Docks. There, the men were confined to camp, with very little to do apart from attending the odd briefing.

Yet another change of camp was necessary as part of the gradual formation of convoys destined to board ships for the cross-channel journey. Traffic was so heavy that several hours elapsed before the advance party reached its destination. Several small towns en route were congested by crowds of spectators who turned out to witness the pre-invasion spectacle. More delays were experienced at the docks, where a huge traffic jam had to be sorted out. It wasn't until the morning of June 2nd that men and vehicles finally made it aboard their US Navy landing craft. These proceeded down the Thames, now hushed in anticipation, then dropped anchor off the Nets at Southend, where they remained until the afternoon of June

5th. Then, along with innumerable other ships of all types, they sailed around the coast at Dover and almost to the Isle of Wight. Following a small change of course, the ships steered across the channel. They dropped anchor a few miles off the coast of Normandy and remained there until 1400 hours on June 8th, when they received word they could proceed.

The landing proved to be uneventful. They headed for an improvised assembly area, where the vehicles were partially de-waterproofed. Hodson and his party moved on to Ver-sur-Mer, where they were surprised to find, due to the constantly shifting plans that preceded the invasion, that the others in the increment to the wing's so-called "A" Party—which included nine officers, among them Monty Berger—had arrived already.

Monty's trip to France was not without its share of comic absurdity, and genuine danger. He had left Tangmere at 0700 on Wednesday, May 31st—almost a week after Hodson and his party—and arrived at the assembly area at Old' Sarum later the same day. While the vehicles were waterproofed, Monty and his cohorts ate, slept, and played softball against the staff of 127 Wing. "The games were keenly contested and would have been doubly memorable had 126 won them," Monty wrote afterwards.

By Monday, June 4th, the party received word they would be moving out soon. New identity cards were issued, and without explanation each man also received a pound note in advance pay. They departed Old' Sarum shortly after noon on June 5th, and arrived at Camp A19 in the dark, gloomy and filthy concentration area near Druxford at 1700 hours. A pre-invasion conference scheduled for 2130 hours was postponed until 0330 hours on June 6th. Moreover, it lasted a scant twenty minutes or so, rather than the hour and a half originally anticipated. Nor was there any hard information to emerge from this conference. Monty had expected stirring words and a lot of inside "gen." Instead, he and his party were shown maps covered with codenames that nobody bothered to explain.

Fortunately, the stay at A19 was brief. The men received their overnight packs and life belts. They drew blankets and palliasses, changed their English money—including the pound note they had

received—into francs, and, according to Monty, "topped it all off
with a good stiff drink."

They were scheduled to leave A19 at 0430 on D-Day. It was not
until 0730 that they moved to Portsmouth, where they boarded their
LCTs. The ships began to assemble in a convoy at 1300. Soon they
were steering towards the embattled coast of France.

"The weather was dull with a little drizzle, the sky overcast, the sea
choppy," Monty recorded. Partway across the channel, he opened the
sealed map he had received prior to leaving, and found out for the
first time precisely where he would be landing. There was little else to
do. Each LCT carried a dozen or so vehicles, which made conditions
somewhat cramped. "Everywhere you looked were lines and lines of
these little craft," said Monty. "Off in the distance one would occasionally see an escorting naval vessel." For a while, the odd stream of
red tracer climbing into the night sky or a star shell illuminating the
distant shore provided the only indication they were heading towards
the battlefront. Then the convoy was attacked, resulting in the loss of
several landing craft including one carrying the advanced ground
personnel of 127 Wing. It was a horrifying scene to watch from the
craft carrying Monty and his group. The rest of the convoy, having
survived the marauding enemy torpedo boats, pressed on towards
the coast. Flight Lieutenant Dave Ambrose, a flying control officer
who travelled in the same party with Monty, remembered: "It was
quite amazing how the convoy split up, and each craft was directed
by a control ship.... The channels were well marked with buoys and
we passed through warships and landing craft of all types and sizes."

At about 0730, Monty's LCT anchored about a hundred yards
off the beach and dropped its ramp. By now the wind had picked up
and was blowing the landing craft into the channel. Two attempts
were made to run aground after several lorries were swept away while
disembarking. Ideally, no more than three or four feet of water
should have been under the landing craft. No matter. Monty, behind
the wheel of an RAF jeep, and his companion, a Canadian army intelligence officer, were given the signal.

"Up until the very last second we were exchanging light banter," Monty recalled. Then they hit the water—and promptly sank. With his gift for understatement, Monty recalled: "We weren't as close as the textbook said we should be. I know because I was submerged up to my neck!"

Nevertheless, like a scene out of an old Laurel and Hardy film, they calmly drove the next hundred yards or so with water swirling under their chins most of the way. Finally, as though to vindicate the expert waterproofing job done in England, they pulled up on the beach and came to a halt. Monty's first words in France are not known, but he and his companion must have been relieved that they had landed safely in spite of their preposterous method of travel.

Monty has, however, recorded his earliest impressions of the incredible scene around him that morning:

> There was a relatively narrow cleared area of sand, and there was a lot of barbed wire rolled up tight alongside, which presumably the army had cut clear to make a path. I remember there were minefields on both sides of us, which one could see. And there were vehicles and remains of vehicles. Tanks. We couldn't see very far, as it was still a bleak, grey day. It had been heavily overcast and something of a wispy fog remained.

Thus Monty Berger became the first RCAF ground officer to land in France, at Ver-sur-mer at 0815 hours on the morning of D+1. His mood was tempered somewhat by the loss of his personal kit, which had floated away into one of the neighbouring minefields during his hundred-yard "dash" to the beach. For several days afterwards he endured the shame of having to wear a borrowed army uniform. There was no greater indignity to an air force officer than to be forced to muster in "brown jobs." However, this was insignificant compared to the historic moment they were enjoying. Said Flight Lieutenant Ambrose: "I was amazed at the complete lack of confusion on the beach. The engineers and sappers were hard at work clearing the barbed wire and other obstacles. Bulldozers were pulling stalled vehicles from the sea."

There was no RAF assembly or transit area operating yet, so Monty and his small party set off almost at once for Ste Croix-sur-mer, where construction of an advanced landing ground, known as B3, had been proposed. It did not take long to realise they were very much in a battle area still.

"As I was leading our little convoy along a country road soon after leaving the beach, I was vaguely aware of this odd splattering on the stone walls at my right," said Monty. "Then I realised we were targets of snipers in some trees not far off on our left."

Two miles farther along the road, as they were about to round a corner, a despatch rider on a motorcycle zipped toward him and braked suddenly, shouting, "Stop, sir!"

"What do you mean, 'stop'?" Monty demanded. "I have to get to our airstrip in a hurry."

"Well, sir," the rider answered, "the ground isn't captured yet. As a matter of fact, they're having a pitched tank battle around the corner."

Sure enough, added Dave Ambrose, a column of tanks "churning and snorting and obviously looking for trouble" hove into sight at that moment.

Monty, armed only with a pistol, was in no position to argue with either the despatch rider or the enemy.

"Here we were, minimally trained for combat and in France long before many of the crack army units," he explained afterwards. "Had we got into a real knock-down, drag-out fight, I don't know what would have happened. We were virtually defenceless. But we didn't think about that. Our concentrated attention was on the fact that we had to be at a certain place at a certain time, and we were running behind schedule."

The party quickly retraced its steps towards Ver-sur-mer and set up camp in an orchard on the outskirts of the village along with the men of two RAF commando units that had accompanied them across the channel. There was still no sign of the main "A" party. In the circumstances, it seemed the only thing to do was to make a start on the new airfield. In the meantime, "Doc" Lindsay, the Senior Medical Officer, went into the village to see if he could be of any assistance. Later he reported that the doctors at a field dressing station he had found were utterly exhausted, having operated for twenty-four hours without a break.

"Our first night in Normandy was comparatively quiet," recalled Ambrose. "Maybe we were so tired we heard very little. Most of us had been tensed up and had slept hardly at all the two previous nights."

Monty added his own assessment. "Hardly anybody in blue had come near anything before that smacked of fighting, and each man kind of wondered whether he would be more or less numbed, either mentally or physically, by suddenly coming pretty well into the thick of it. However, everyone was so busy and so intent on doing the things that had been drilled into him that he didn't realise he was working at such a high pitch."

The pilots, too, while not yet based in France, were doing their part. Indeed, June 7th had been significantly more eventful in the air than D-Day itself. Four patrols over the Normandy beachhead were carried out by the Spitfires of 126 Wing. To the surprise of the Canadians, they finally met up again with Luftwaffe aircraft which had rallied in support of the beleaguered coastal defences. But they were no match for the Spitfires. Wing Commander Keefer destroyed a Ju 88, while 401 Squadron Leader G D (Greg) Cameron, DFC, of Toronto, shot down two. There was plenty of action throughout the day. Seventeen of the wing's pilots had a hand in bringing down a total of thirteen enemy aircraft, with another probable and four left damaged. The combat report filed by Flight Lieutenant G W (George) Johnson, DFC, of Hamilton, Ontario, was typical inasmuch as it revealed the determination with which the Canadian pilots pursued the enemy. Johnson had claimed one Me 109 destroyed. He wrote:

[I] went down with Red Leader on 2 e/a chasing a Thunderbolt on the deck. They split and I took the port one. First burst from 600 yards dead astern knocked small pieces off. Fired several bursts during a steep turn without seeing results. E/a straightened and I noticed strikes on cockpit and engine. Smoke poured out from e/a and it crashed into a farmhouse.

The Canadian pilots returned to Tangmere in a jubilant mood. They had given more than their share in support of the ground troops still fighting to expand the bridgehead at Normandy.

The next logical step was to begin operations from the continent itself. Work was well underway on the proposed airstrip between Ste Croix and Ver-sur-mer despite an enemy strongpoint holding out in a small woods to the north. With the arrival of Hodson's party on the evening of June 8th, the wing's "A" party now comprised a total of fifty-one bodies. They set up camp on the morning of D+3 in a wooded field across from a former German officer's mess, where a series of elaborate dug-outs, partly completed, offered ideal shelter. The CO's directive that everyone should take cover at night was hardly necessary, as everyone was exhausted from working non-stop on the airfield.

By the afternoon of June 9th, D+3, sufficient clearance had been made in the battle area to take in aircraft. It was an historic moment—or so everyone hoped. The AOC of 83 Group planned an appearance, but his arrival was delayed. That night enemy bombs damaged a nearby village. Casualties resulting from this raid included a number of men in a RAF regiment working on another airfield.

The morning of June 10th dawned bright and clear at B3. At 0535 hours a Spitfire V made a forced landing with his landing gear up. Fortunately the pilot was uninjured. This might have been an auspicious beginning nonetheless but for the fact that in crashing the pilot had missed the runway! So it was that the first *official* "landing" at B3 was recorded at 0620 hours, when a Flying Officer Smith of the RAF's 245 Squadron touched down. He, too, landed in somewhat poor condition after his Typhoon had been hit by enemy flak. But at least he stayed on the hastily constructed tracking.

Throughout the day, a total of 128 sorties were flown from the new airfield—an impressive achievement in the circumstances. In fact, B3 was soon almost overwhelmed with air traffic. By June 11th, when the airfield was deemed to be working at full capacity, 146 sorties were mounted. Two pilots of 411 Squadron shared in the destruction of a FW 190 that day, the wing's only score on D+4. There was tragedy, too. Pilot Officer T W Tuttle was killed when his Spit-fire burst into flames and crashed after being hit by ground fire northwest of Caen. It was only his third operational flight.

That the Canadian airmen were actually operating from the con-tinent so soon after the invasion was front-page material. Stan Helleur, a public relations officer with the RCAF, churned out the details for newspapers back in Canada. "Canadian Spitfires Fly from First Base on French Soil," screamed one headline. Helleur related that British army engineers had transformed a vast stretch of knee-high grass and clover at the site of B3 into an "exceptionally fine air-field" within the span of only two days.

Helleur also found a fitting description of the wing's travails so far when he quoted Squadron Leader Edison, the wing's Senior Flying Control Officer. Edison remarked with appropriate aplomb—and some accuracy: "It's a dusty step forward. But it's a big one."

3

FIGHTER WING
ON THE
CONTINENT

THE NEWS from the other side of the front was much less encouraging. On June 12th, Rommel signalled Field Marshal Wilhelm Keitel, Chief of the Wehrmacht Supreme Command: "The enemy is strengthening himself visibly on land under cover of very strong aircraft formations." He added, "Our own operations are rendered extraordinarily difficult and in part impossible to carry out." The situation, Rommel explained, was due primarily to "the exceptionally strong, and in some cases overwhelming, superiority of the enemy air force." He concluded gloomily: "Neither our flak nor the Luftwaffe seem capable of putting a stop to this crippling and destructive operation."

Like a bitter refrain, Rommel pointed repeatedly to the devastating impact of Allied air power following the D-Day landings. It extended from the battle zone in France to roughly a hundred kilometres inland. The result was all traffic behind the front was virtually impossible by day, which added to his difficulties resupplying units defending the coast. Even troops on the battlefield itself were severely prevented from manoeuvring as they wished, Rommel insisted, while the Allied armies operated virtually as they pleased.

The Field Marshal's latter point was overstated. The Allies undoubtedly were consolidating their foothold on the coast, but not without meeting stiff resistance by the enemy. By June 10th, when most of the second wave of Allied troops was ashore, fighting still raged around several key points on the Cotentin peninsula. British and Canadian forces were involved in particularly heavy action at Caen.

Moreover, while aircraft of the 2nd TAF *were* operating from improvised airfields in France, even this remained tentative. Leading Aircraftsman Wally Twigg, an armourer with 412 Squadron who flew over on June 10th aboard a DC3, saw for himself how perilous the conditions were on the coast. "The Limey pilot landed on an airfield that was still under shell fire," Twigg recalled with evident horror. "We dodged shell holes to take off and landed in a wheat field at Beny-sur-mer." There, Twigg and his armament section set up in a hurry. Spits landed throughout the daylight hours and returned to Tangmere for the night.

By June 12th, when Rommel signalled Berlin, the third wave of Allied forces was ashore to press the attack. More than 325,000 men, 104,000 tons of supplies and 54,000 vehicles were in France on D+6. The initial phase of Operation "Overlord" had concluded with the bridgehead firmly established (although fighting would continue at Caen for some time yet), but still hazardous. That night a stick of bombs landed on the airfield at Ste Croix, resulting in casualties to a number of RAF personnel. An army engineering vehicle and a searchlight battery were knocked out as well.

Spitfires belonging to 126 Wing finally put in an appearance on the 13th, each carrying a gift in the form of fuel tanks filled with beer. Wing Commander Hodson ordered one tank to be delivered to each of the RAF servicing units attached to 126, in recognition of their hard work, and a third was sent over to the men of 127 Wing. They had performed brilliantly, according to Monty, despite the loss of most of their equipment during their harrowing cross-channel journey on D+1.

Conditions generally soon began to improve at B3. Bread and newspapers were being dropped regularly by pilots, while eggs, butter, fresh vegetables and potatoes bartered or purchased from the local inhabitants frequently appeared on the menu. Such items relieved the wing's overworked cooks.

The airfield continued to draw the enemy's attention during the next few days. One night while eating supper under a tree, Wing Commander Hodson and his party were startled when a shot rang out. It was followed quickly by another. Then the guard standing at a gate not far away shouted: "Snipers!"

The officers looked at each other. Monty, who had been appointed acting Camp Commandant, "with a do-or-die look in his eye," according to Hodson, announced in a low voice, "I'll look into it."

Monty strapped his pistol around his waist, pulled out the gun and strode towards the gate. There he found the guard hiding behind a tree, and soldiers crouching in the ditch along a nearby road. According to the guard, the first shot had come from the direction of a small building in a field on the other side of the road and smacked into a wall a few feet from his position. He had promptly fired back into the darkness. Monty rounded up a party of erks and spaced them along the edge of the field, while two Army Liaison Officers who had arrived on the scene were sent to throw a couple of their souvenir German grenades towards the building. The erks were ordered to fire at any movement they saw.

"The ALOs threw the grenades, which went off," Monty reported. "There was no movement. A brief huddle was held. All erks were to stand fast, fire at any movement, while I crawled right around the field to the other side to see what I could see. I did this, and found a similar force of Tommies on guard in the ditch there. Nobody had seen the sniper, but the Tommies insisted there definitely was one—somewhere."

Monty, having been on both sides of the field by now, was less certain. He decided to walk back.

"I must have passed a gap in a hedge, for a shot literally whistled by my head," Monty recalled. "I crouched pretty quickly after that." He realised at once that the erks had fired, as ordered, at the first movement they had seen. The mistake was Monty's, although he might be forgiven if he had uttered a few expletives when he made it back to his men. There, with the assistance of the Tommies on the other side of the field, Monty organised a search of all the houses in the neighbourhood. Nothing was found. The incident was recalled with some hilarity afterwards by Wing Commander Hodson and his men, although they would admit, too, that it had shown how keyed up everyone was at B3. Few were willing to take anything for granted.

Group Control Centre (GCC), which detailed operations to 126 Wing, became operational on D+8. That day word came down that 144 Wing would take over B3, and the "A" party of 126 Wing would move to a new airfield at Beny-sur-mer, just five kilometres from Juno Beach, where the Canadians had landed on D-Day. Hodson and his party left early the next morning and found the airstrip, known as B4, still under construction. Nevertheless, four aircraft circling at dusk were brought in, with only one "piling up mildly" after overshooting the runway. The next day, however, the airstrip was fully operational—even if it seemed a bit crude by contemporary standards. Methods of airfield construction on the continent varied. Initially, the most common material used was Sommerfeld Mat (also known as Summer Field Tracking). It came as narrow seventy-five foot rolls of three-inch wire mesh netting—glorified chicken wire. A steel linking bar connected the netting, which was held to the ground by pickets every two feet. Rigid steel mats were used also, but they required more hands to assemble. Each one-by-twelve foot mat weighed 130 pounds. Another system, known as Bar and Rod Type Track, was used occasionally. Eventually, though, the preferred material was American-built Perforated Steel Planking. PSP, as it was commonly known, was the simplest to assemble while offering the best characteristics in varying field conditions. Each unit was sixteen inches wide by almost ten feet long, weighing sixty-five pounds. Large holes ran in three rows down the length of each panel, which was indented between rows to provide additional strength. Tabs and slots on either side provided a quick and easy means of connecting panels. The durability of PSP is evident in the odd piece that still turns up in a farmer's field in Belgium or Holland to this day.

In all likelihood, though, the RAF engineers used rolls of Somerfeld Mat when they constructed B4 at Beny-sur-mer. This would account for the many complaints from airmen and ground personnel concerning the amount of dust that swirled in great choking clouds whenever the wing's Spitfires started up or took off. Hundreds of vehicles, and almost a thousand ground personnel who had survived "the sausage machine" ordeal in England, soon added to the crowded and dusty conditions at B4. By June 18th (D+12), a Sunday, the airfield was pretty well established.

Monty was particularly relieved when his INT/OPS vans were safely delivered—along with their contents, much of which was highly secret. The wing's intelligence staff were already working at full speed, briefing and debriefing pilots. The vans made their jobs a lot easier.

It helped, too, that the wing's IOs got along well as friends, even if they were different personalities. Flight Lieutenant Donald Stewart, six months short of thirty, was the oldest of the staff, and the most gregarious. "He was a cheery, outgoing, clap-on-the-back kind of person," Monty recalled. Originally from Paris, Ontario, Stewart was working as an insurance salesman with Canada Life, "and doing very well," when he enlisted in the RCAF at Hamilton in July 1941. The glamour and excitement of flying appealed to him, so he applied for pilot training. He was sent to a Manning Depot at St Hubert's, south of Montreal. "One day a sergeant asked if anyone was interested in music," Stewart recalled. Picturing a soft job in the depot's library "or somewhere else," Stewart volunteered. "Fine," the sergeant barked, "report to the gym at seven o'clock. We're moving the piano." Thus Stewart was introduced to a fundamental rule of service life. "I never volunteered for anything again!" he declared.

Nevertheless, Stewart's interest in music was genuine. His "original Spitfire band," as he called it (not to be confused with the popular orchestra started by former Spitfire pilot Jackie Rae in the early 1980s), was a hit with service personnel when Stewart went overseas in 1943. He had "washed out" of pilot training in Canada but was commissioned as an administration officer before being reclassified to intelligence. Stewart served his apprenticeship as a "spy" with other

RCAF formations in England before joining the staff of 126 Wing.

Another member of the INT/OPS staff was Pilot Officer Gord Panchuk—"Pan," to his wingmates. He was short but had a deceptively muscular build on his stocky frame. Of Ukrainian descent, Panchuk hailed from somewhere in Saskatchewan where prior to the war he was employed as a school teacher. "He was a great worker," said Stewart, "and meticulous."

Complementing the IOs were several Army Liaison Officers, or ALOs, attached to 126 Wing. Their duties included the collection of information to enable squadrons to carry out their tasks to the best advantage, briefing pilots to provide detailed military intelligence, and debriefing (often referred to as "interrogation"). The ALOs were a vital link in view of the ground support role often carried out by the wing's Spitfires.

The medical staff, too, while not directly involved in operations, were essential to the wing's well-being. They shared the hardships of establishing advanced airfields on the continent. Corporal George Killen of Lloydminster, Saskatchewan, a medical orderly attached to 126 Wing, says that for the first few months in France they lived like moles. Hospital tents were half-buried to protect patients from ground blast. "Our sleeping tents were dug down as well," says Killen, "a routine that promised lots of exercise every time the wing moved."

Killen remembers also that at Beny-sur-mer the army cemetery was adjacent to the airfield. "Casualties from the fighting around Caen were coming in so fast we used to go over in the evenings to dig graves," he said. "Pretty sad."

According to Killen, the medical unit's supplies were "pretty basic." They consisted mainly of sulpha drugs and penicillin. Serious infections or injuries were referred to an RCAF mobile field hospital nearby. Apart from the usual coughs and colds, Killen added the most afflictions they encountered were boils, scabies, dysentery, and VD.

The section consisted of four medical officers, or MOs, one for each squadron, and one Senior Medical Officer (SMO). The remaining staff consisted of a sergeant, two corporals, as many as eight orderlies and four ambulance drivers. The ingenuity of one medical corporal, Art Richardson, was such that the medical section was never without hot water, according to Killen. "In all I think we kept the wing in quite good health considering some of the 'not-quite-perfect' living conditions."

In fact, the section was designed for field work. Immediately after D-Day, as operational flying continued with sorties flown to cover the Normandy beachhead, the staff observed a increase in fatigue among the pilots. This was to be expected. However, others were deemed unfit for life on the continent, and were quietly moved out.

The medical staff also initiated an inoculation program in the hope of preventing more serious physical harm to the pilots and groundcrew. Medical complications resulting from the amount of dust at B4 proved more difficult to prevent. They could hardly stop operations. The dust was so thick it discoloured uniforms—to the point where air force blues soon resembled the dull grey of German army kit. Airmen were ordered into army khaki to avoid any unfortunate incidents. A warning on the briefing board in the INT/OPS vans reminded personnel "not to go near the American lines" in their air force blues: they risked being shot (the same board announced in bold lettering that together the Allies were "making the world SHAEF for democracy!").*

The wing's airfield controller earned his meagre pay, too. He worked in conjunction with the Flying Control Officer, who was in direct contact with the aircraft. Together they coordinated hundreds of takeoffs and landings, as well as handling the odd emergency. Sometimes, for example, aircraft would return with an unusable or damaged R/T. The pilot would buzz the control van while waggling his wings to let the controller know he wanted to land. On duff days, the controller inspected runways and taxi strips.

The truth was there was seldom a let-up in anyone's routine once the wing moved to the continent. Life was made more difficult by an outbreak of diarrhea and dysentery. Surprisingly few airmen became complete casualties, but many subsisted on a mixture of chalk and opium while continuing their flying duties. More worrisome were

---

* The pun referred to the Supreme Headquarters, Allied Expeditionary Force—commonly known as SHAEF.

the number of casualties with accidental gunshot wounds, which the medical section attributed to the frequent handling of firearms by individuals untrained in their use.

Then, for several days in mid-June, a period of heavy rain and generally abominable weather virtually shut down the airfield. The erks began to refer to the sea of mud surrounding them as "Flounder's Field." Matting was put down in their slit trenches in a largely futile effort to stay comfortable. On good days, the ground being low and flat at B4, it was possible to see shipping activity still going on every day in the English Channel, and to hear the mighty roar of shells fired from Allied vessels. Until recently, too, a favourite target was an enemy radar station that was still holding out at Douvres, southeast of the airstrip. It was from this strongpoint that the occasional mortar round had landed in the area of B4. By June 18th, the same day the Spitfires of 126 Wing occupied the airfield for the first time, Marine Commandos had decided to eliminate the strongpoint. It was knocked out after several hours of fighting.

The extent to which the enemy station had irritated the Canadians was evident in their rush, after its fall, to collect souvenirs from the site. "Our erks lost no opportunity to get into this natural haven," recalled Monty. "The last of the two hundred Germans left there were barely out the door when our boys were into the amazing underground structure at the station." In fact, Monty said that a number of erks from the wing's Motor Transport, or MT, section slept the night there. "Fair quantities of champagne and wine, which they discovered, had their effect in due course. Other souvenirs included bicycles, emblems, field telephones, cushions and—most useful—a number of beds with mattresses. The spoils did not last long, however, for the next day a guard arrived and large signs warned all comers to keep out because the area hadn't been checked for mines and booby traps!"

The speed with which the Canadians had descended upon the site reminded Monty of an expression that was often associated with his countrymen. "I hope it was originated by a Canadian," he said. "It went: 'The Yanks fight for glory, the English to defend themselves, and the Canucks for souvenirs!'"

The return of good flying weather meant a resumption of operations—and the return of the dust at B4. Flying Control, with its van located right beside the strip, caught the worst of it. According to Monty, the technical and equipment "wallahs" on the southeast side of the field were not much better off. "The armament staff went nearly out of their minds figuring out ways to keep dust out of the Spitfire's cannons," he recalls. Monty remembers also a sergeant in one squadron's armament section who claimed the dust of B4 was worse than anything he'd seen during the North African campaign.

"The armament people invented some pretty crafty tricks to cope in those days," Monty added. "I remember, for example, they collected hundreds of pounds of old putty-like waterproofing from the vehicles and used it on the panel joints of the gun bays."

The equipment personnel were just as resourceful. Every take-off left a film of dust over their spare parts and instruments. "They had to dust every single piece of technical equipment in stock—and there were thousands of such items—at least once a day. Finally, they hit on the brilliant notion of wrapping every piece individually in waxed paper. The section also obtained a large steel bin to use as storage for their wireless spares. Electric lights were installed in the bins and left burning to keep the instruments dry and at a constant temperature."

Monty and his staff had their own difficulties with the dust, even though the intelligence vans were parked in a small field several hundred yards west of Flying Control. Between them were the wing's Spitfires. The CO's office tender was positioned in another field that ran roughly parallel to the strip, which was laid out north to south. Tents ran along the perimeter next to low hedges, leaving the centre of the field wide open. It wasn't long before the wing's personnel realised they had a ready-made site for a baseball diamond.

"Our team often played three five-inning games a night against different Canadian army units that were hauled out of the front for a twenty-four hour rest," said Monty. "They always wanted a bit of a game to relax." The wing won a long string of about forty games, he added. Nevertheless, they were humbled by the stories they heard from their opponents on the field. "It smartened a lot of our fellows up to hear how the Canadian soldiers up ahead, on that Caen salient, were taking real punishment in battle," Monty explained.

The truth was few escaped the hardships of being in France after D-Day. The wing had seen its share of action. It had experienced losses of its own, too. Nor was it uncommon to see aircraft return to B4 so badly damaged it was almost as though they had been piloted by willpower alone. The airfield itself resembled an arms bazaar. "All around, virtually as far as the eye could see on the flat ground between the airfield and the ocean, was a vast ammunition dump with all kinds of cases and crates and shells and rockets and bombs," said Monty. The sound of war was unrelenting, too, no less at night, mostly from artillery and ack-ack. Monty remembered how often duty officers ran out to take cover under the protective cover of the wing's vans, more from falling shrapnel than bombs. "The pilots would come into the bullpen the next day and tell me how much they were fed up with sleeping in slit trenches and so had gone up to their tents, only to find it was so noisy they couldn't sleep. They ended up back in their slit trenches."

The rest of the time the wing's personnel were almost prisoners of the campsite. "It was a while before the fellows could go off the strip very far," said Monty. "Then, swims in the sea nearby were popular, and welcome relief from the dust."

The war's proximity was evident, too, in the occasional alarm everyone experienced at B4. One night a driver reported to the MT section that enemy troops had broken through to the sea. Allied troops, he said, and transport were retreating in disorder. "He himself had seen it," Monty recalled. "This spread through the camp like wild fire, and nearly caused a panic." Captain Lines, one of the ALOs, was promptly consulted. "Our positions appeared firm and showed no cause for alarm, according to the latest gen. So, without a second's delay, a message was Tannoyed throughout the station giving the exact situation." The driver was summoned to INT/OPS, where he explained he had heard the news from a military policeman at a nearby crossroad. Under further questioning concerning the Allied "retreat," the driver insisted he had seen lots of traffic.

"In disorder?" Monty asked.

"Well, no sir, not in disorder," the driver confessed. He was sent off with a stern reprimand, yet the incident was hardly forgotten.

"For quite a period," said Monty afterwards, "in fact, until the breakout from the beachhead, tension was great for fear of a military reverse, although the army always appeared confident. On the other hand, many people showed no reaction or fear or worry in the most surprising situations."

Monty remembers also that innocence was sometimes the cause of near disaster, as an episode involving one of the wing's armament assistants illustrated. Manhandling the 500-pound bombs used by the wing's Spitfires was arduous work, even with the two-wheeled trollies they used to lug the bombs around the airfield. An order had gone out to scrounge enough materials to make more of the trollies, which were needed in large numbers during rush periods. A small party, including the unnamed armament assistant, went in search of material for wheels in the neighbourhood of the fortress at Douvres. There, the young lad emerged from a patch of woods with what appeared to be the proper article under each arm. "These all right, Sarge?" he hollered, holding out two round objects.

According to Monty, the sergeant took one look and started to run backwards, shouting: "Get rid of them, you clot! They're Teller Mines!"

Thus, one way or another, either by contact with frontline soldiers or near-disaster of their own making, the wing's personnel were sharpened to the potential for calamity in their midst. If there was any consolation in their circumstances it was that so far casualties among the wing's pilots were relatively modest. Flight Sergeant L W Love of 412 Squadron was lost on June 17th. Four days later, Flying Officer H E Fenwick, DFC, from Sioux Lookout, Ontario, was shot down during a patrol by 401.

Nevertheless, the Canadian Spitfires had proven they were capable of performing the all-out tactical support assignments expected of the wing. Getting stuff on the ground was their principal duty. Consequently, while the pages recording their air victories sometimes went days without an entry, the sheets listing "enemy ground casualties" were crammed with statistics showing the number of trains, buses, barges, armoured cars, half-tracks, fuel bowsers, staff cars, trucks, light vans, and even ferry boats the wing's pilots had destroyed—or,

in the case of enemy personnel, killed. By the last week of June the
wing's pilots were dropping bombs on special targets, shooting up
road and rail traffic, and, almost as an afterthought, knocking enemy
aircraft out of the sky, with regularity. This led to some crowing at
Beny-sur-mer, where 126 Wing had adopted as its motto (always present on the chalkboard in the INT/OPS van): B4 is Never B-hind.

On June 27th, the same day the Americans captured the port of
Cherbourg, the Luftwaffe came out in force for the first time in
weeks. Their appearance coincided with an Allied offensive intended
to capture Caen, which had stubbornly held out since D-Day. Ordered to support the offensive, the Spitfires of 126 Wing took off in
shifts. For its part, 411 Squadron was off the ground at 1255 hours
on an armed recce south of Caen, and soon encountered more than
fifteen FW 190s. Squadron Leader G D (Graham) Robertson destroyed one, Flight Lieutenant G W (George) Johnson damaged
two, while Warrant Officer J A (Jim) Kerr scored hits on another.
Flying Officer Phil Wallace went missing in the day's action, although he later turned up safely. Flight Lieutenant H J (Harold)
Nixon had to bail out over the Allied lines when his aircraft was rid-
dled with flak over Bayeux.*

The next day was even more eventful. The Luftwaffe threw still
more aircraft into the air, partly in support of a tank battle that raged
around Caen. But again they were outmatched. Thirty-four of their
aircraft were shot down over Normandy, of which as many as
twenty-six were destroyed by 83 Group Spitfires. Thirteen of those
were claimed by pilots of 126 Wing. Flight Lieutenant R H (Bob)
Hayward of 411 Squadron destroyed two FW 190s and damaged
another, while Flight Lieutenant H C (Charlie) Trainor claimed one
Me 109 and one FW 190 of his own. The Grizzly Bears had put on a
fine show, matched only by the six enemy aircraft claimed that day
by pilots of 401 Squadron (two pilots of 412 Squadron, Flight Lieutenant C W Fox and Flying Officer W J Banks, shared in the destruction of one Me 109F). It had been one of the busiest and most

---

* Nixon's downed Spitfire Mk IX was salvaged by a team of enthusiasts in the late-1980s.

successful days for the Canadian pilots since D-Day. Monty estimated the Canadian wings "paid the cost of their formation" with
their share of the totals. Moreover, the wing had showed how timely
its intervention could be in support of ground operations. According
to Monty, foul weather in England had grounded much of the air
support intended to cover the push around Caen. "The Hun were
trying to take full advantage of this to strafe and bomb our troops,"
he explained. "However, the three Canadian wings did their part.
Our pilots flew almost into the ground to cover the Allied troops. It
was one of the most glorious days in the wing's history."

Flying Officer Tom Wheler of 411 Squadron, one of six Grizzly
Bears who claimed an enemy aircraft destroyed that day, recorded his
part in the action:

> I was flying Red 4. The squadron was SW of Caen when Huns
> were reported south of Le Havre by Blue 2. My R/T was partially
> u/s. The squadron broke port and dove with wide-open throttles,
> leaving me far behind. I climbed alone to 8,000 ft above cloud,
> sighting 15 a/c that turned out to be FW 190s and Me 109s.
> They turned toward me to port still at 6000 ft. I dove out of the
> sun and attacked the last FW 190 on the starboard side of the
> formation. At 300 to 400 yds I fired a burst from line astern and
> saw hits on cockpit and wing. The e/a caught fire, flicked over,
> crashed into the deck and blew up. I turned starboard and fired at
> another FW 190, range about 100 yds, angle off about 60°, and
> saw hits on starboard wing. FW 190 broke hard towards me and
> disappeared into cloud. I took a cine shot of burning wreckage of
> first FW 190. Returned to base with four gallons of petrol.

Charlie Trainor's claim of two enemy aircraft destroyed put him into
the scoring column for the first time. Incredibly, within only a week
the native of Bedford, Prince Edward Island, would become an "ace,"
increasing his total by seven and a half. "Almost every time he went
out, he scored," said Monty. Trainor deservedly earned a wide reputation for his remarkable number of victories in such a short span.

Other pilots, too, made names for themselves that June 28th. Bill

Banks, who had contributed to 412 Squadron's appearance on the day's tally, soon became known as "Sharpshooter." Said Monty: "His aim was deadly."

Yet the day was not a complete success. The BBC lavishly described the victories, but for the most part gave credit to a squadron of RAF Typhoons instead of the Canadian Spitfires! "We were always sensitive about this sort of thing," Monty allowed, "but it was exasperating and disappointing because it was the first time 126 Wing had done anything to really crow about."

The wing's record for the month of June was impressive, even without the BBC's acclaim. It had logged more than 3,000 hours while flying a total of 1,648 operational sorties. For this, the wing's scoreboard showed thirty-three enemy aircraft destroyed, one probable and eleven damaged. By itself, 411 Squadron, for example, contributed 1,029 hours, or an average of almost 1.8 hours per pilot per day. No matter how they were cut, the figures were pretty good for twenty-five men during the twenty-three flyable days that month.

By July 1st, conditions at B4 were deemed sufficiently secure that half-days off for some of the wing's personnel were resumed. Erks started drifting into Bayeux, thirty kilometres away, for a spot of sightseeing and other forms of relaxation. There, as at the airfield itself, the Canadians were often besieged by children pleading, "*cigarettes pour papa.*" Camembert cheese, a speciality throughout Normandy, had become popular among the men, who brought it back in vast quantities from their day trips. French wines, eggs, and Calvados were also in good supply.

On July 2nd, a total of seven enemy aircraft were destroyed, and another five damaged. The first, a FW 190, was claimed during a patrol by 411 Squadron. Then, while providing cover to ground operations, 412 Squadron got into a scrap. Flying Officer D C (Don) Laubman, who had just returned from a course in England, no doubt gratified his instructors by shooting down two FW 190s, the start of a sensational run of victories. The day ended with Me 109s claimed by both Flight Lieutenant I F ("Hap") Kennedy and

Pilot Officer W T (Bill) Klersy of 401 Squadron, who had been sent out on a dive-bombing mission.

No scores in the air were added the next day, despite an armed recce by 401 Squadron. However, at least eight motorised transports were left as "flamers." Less encouraging was the news that Squadron Leader Cameron was missing after the action. *Promptus ad vindictam*—"Swift to avenge"—was the motto of 412, but it was with that spirit that the pilots of 411 (*Inimicus inimico*, "Hostile to an enemy") dealt a return blow to the enemy. The Grizzly Bears claimed virtually every one of the six enemy aircraft shot down on July 4th. Charlie Trainor continued his streak by shooting down two Me 109s and sharing a Dornier 217 with the Squadron's CO, Graham Robertson. Fittingly, the latter action finished up over the airfield at Beny and was witnessed by most of the wing's personnel.

Three days later, on July 7th, the Canadian pilots ran their scores even higher during several armed recces and patrols over the battlefront. Nine enemy aircraft were destroyed, and three others damaged. That evening, too, while the whole of Normandy watched, they accompanied wave upon wave of Lancasters that bombed Caen so heavily that fire and smoke rose thousands of feet into the air and the earth quivered at Beny-sur-mer, sixteen kilometres away.

And so it went. Aircraft flew four and five times a day. Turnaround had to be fast. Refuelling and rearming were top priorities. Meals were gulped down or not had at all by pilots and erks alike. Pilots were running through their allotted time on operations in double-quick time. Changes to the wing's nominal roll were frequent, although its character maintained an indomitable spirit.

On July 8th, Wing Commander Keefer was grounded after an unusually long and successful third tour. He had seen action in England, North Africa and now the continent, preserving the spark kindled by Buck McNair. His record included four enemy aircraft destroyed in the month of June. He had flown unceasingly, as well as guiding the policy for all of the squadrons in the wing.

In honour of Keefer, a grand dinner was laid on in the officer's mess at B4. Although under canvas, white tablecloths appeared for the first time during the wing's time in Normandy. Champagne and wine flowed, and—incredibly—the menu included real steak. Monty was likely not alone in remarking it was blessed relief from the compo rations they had endured since D-Day.*

Wing Commander Dal Russel, who had dropped a rank to Squadron Leader to return on his third tour of operations as CO of 442 Squadron, 144 Wing, was promoted again and returned to replace Keefer. "Dal was a superb organiser, a fine pilot, and a great leader," remembered Bill Olmsted in his autobiography, *Blue Skies*. Olmsted was a young flight lieutenant when he joined 442 Squadron in early July 1944, shortly before Russel left to command 126 Wing. "I admired his understanding of human nature and how his personality inspired confidence and cooperation in every man who served under him." Olmsted added: "He had an infectious laugh and a great sense of humour, which we came to know well because he was constantly mingling with the pilots."

The new CO's exceptional qualities were all the more appreciated when it became known that only recently his brother Hugh had been shot down and killed, which, Olmsted added, "explained the dark circles" around Russel's eyes. Olmsted said that Russel kept his grief bottled up inside. "Time and time again I was to observe and even experience his compassion and understanding."

Less than a week after Russel's appointment, 2nd TAF was reorganised, in the course of which 17 Sector was abolished. The new structure was intended to make 83 Group more compact while increasing the size of the wings. To that end, 144 Wing was disbanded and each of its squadrons was added to the strength of the other Spitfire wings in 83 Group. Thus, from July 15th, 126 Wing was composed of 442 "Caribou" Squadron in addition to its three original members. Formed at Rockcliffe (Ottawa) in January 1942 as No 14 (Fighter) Squadron, it had served in the Aleutians before it transferred to England early in 1944. The squadron was renumbered to conform with the "400-block" reserved for Canadian fighter units overseas.

---

* In Monty's personal archives is a receipt from Squadron Leader H W (Ted) Edwards, the wing's adjutant, for five bottles of Pétillant André Lainé at 150 francs each, purchased for the dinner in honour of Wing Commander Keefer. The receipt is marked "paid."

According to Bill Olmsted, the squadron had eighteen Spitfire IXs for twenty-six pilots, and perhaps another one hundred and twenty ground personnel when it joined 126 Wing. Pilots worked in shifts, from noon one day to noon the next, and were assigned a specific aircraft, which they sometimes shared. Each aircraft had its own rigger, fitter and armourer, who each carried out his own regular daily maintenance and inspections. More extensive work was done by mechanics attached to the wing. Pilots also drew on the expertise of squadron photographers, wireless experts, electricians and, added Olmsted, "chaps who ensured that the oxygen bottles were always full." Olmsted's praise for the outstanding work performed by the erks was both lavish and unending.

The addition of 442 Squadron justified an upgrade in the wing's establishment for CO. Five days later, Wing Commander Keith Hodson welcomed Group Captain G E (Gordon) McGregor, OBE, DFC, who had been on the staff at 83 Group Headquarters for several months. McGregor, originally from Montreal, was an experienced pilot as well as an excellent administrator.* "He was an ideal teammate for Dal and the wing," said Olmsted. But, added Monty, it was a sad parting for Hodson, who had nursed the wing through the difficult days of 1943 and all the pre-invasion headaches. In doing so, he had come to know many of the men personally. At his farewell dinner, he was presented with an elaborate scroll and a sterling silver tray inscribed with the signatures of each officer who had served under him. Emotion ran high when Squadron Leader Edwards spoke briefly at a private gathering of the officers before Hodson left. Hodson said his final farewell to the wing over the Tannoy.

"These could not have been easy days for Group Captain McGregor," Monty noted, "but he quickly showed a happy faculty for maintaining things as efficiently as ever. The wing continued on its course with increasing success. McGregor and Winco Dal Russel had been together in No 1 Fighter Squadron during the Battle of Britain, and they were among the first Canadians to be awarded the

---

* Gordon McGregor put the same skills to good use after the war, when he joined Trans Canada Air Lines—the forerunner of Air Canada—and eventually became its president.

Distinguished Flying Cross." Already one of the oldest pilots in 1940, McGregor had nevertheless attained a score of seven and a half destroyed, five probables and twelve damaged. He was the first CO of 401 Squadron and had been assigned the task of forming 402 Squadron. "His wide experience and first-hand knowledge of 83 Group Headquarters were to be valuable assets to the Wing in days to come," Monty predicted.

Both McGregor and Russel, who were to add further lustre to their already distinguished careers while serving with 126 Wing, would be equally quick to give credit where it was most due: to the high calibre of airmen under their command, whose courage and determination, particularly that July, was truly astonishing. Indeed, the month was crammed with activity: so much that it would be impossible to chronicle each and every incident. On July 20th, for example, an armed recce by 442 Squadron—only days after joining the wing—had been "absolutely uneventful" but for the sighting of a number of small groups of civilians with carts moving south. Soon after this, however, the Canadian pilots ran into forty-plus FW 190s over St Lo at 23,000 feet. In the ensuing combat, Bill Olmsted, commanding the squadron's "B" Flight, destroyed two of the enemy fighters. The first broke into flames and the other exploded violently in mid-air, leaving much flying debris hitting his aircraft. Flying Officer G R (Gerald) Blair of Vancouver, also with 442 Squadron, added one more to the scoreboard, while three pilots from 401 and 412 claimed as many FW 190s for their squadrons.

The next day was even more profitable. Three FW 190s and four Me 109s were shot down by four pilots who had set out ostensibly to do a weather recce. The wing's Intelligence Diary recorded the action, the historical importance of which seemed to inspire an unusually picturesque description:

> Four aircraft of 412 Squadron led by Flight Lieutenant Linton carried out a weather recce from 1437 to 1550 hours. They ran into 40 plus 109s and 190s over Lisieux at 10,000 feet, going south-west. Seven were destroyed: one 190 and two 109s by Flying Officer Banks, two 109s by Pilot Officer Jamieson, two 190s

by Flight Lieutenant Linton. Flight Lieutenant "Tex" Phillips had a good 'squirt' at a 190 but had to break before results could be observed as he had four enemy aircraft on his tail, all firing like mad.

Outnumbered at least ten to one, the pilots had not hesitated to initiate the attack. Monty suggested it was incidents like this that evoked such utter terror among the German pilots when they heard *"Achtung, Spitfire"* over their own R/T. "And it was the skill and ability so many of the wing's pilots possessed that allowed them to take on such extraordinary odds with confidence, and to so often come out unscathed," he insisted.

There was, however, more to Monty's enthusiasm than simply the extraordinary accomplishment of shooting down so many enemy aircraft in a single outing. The FW 190 claimed by "Sharpshooter" Banks marked the 100th Hun destroyed since the wing's formation—an event that had been anticipated in the form of a raffle with prize money to be awarded and fine silver mugs to be distributed to the pilots who claimed the 98th, 99th and 100th victories. That Banks personally ran the score to 102 during the same sortie was all the more remarkable. Word was sent down that Air Vice Marshal Harry Broadhurst, AOC 83 Group, was particularly pleased.

Ironically, that same day a huge explosion at the armament park at B4 almost resulted in tragedy for the wing. Monty was in the INT/OPS van with Eric Clark, an ALO who had just joined the staff, when the blast sent them both flying headlong to the ground. A corporal working on a belt feed mechanism in the armament section's repair hut suddenly had the roof crash down on him violently. Donald Stewart and Frank Nobbs, another ALO, were "blown some distance" while walking along a nearby road. "But a little dazed and dusty, we got up—scared—none the worse and feeling plain lucky," Stewart remembered. Similar incidents occurred elsewhere around the airfield.

"The strangest sight of all was on the ball diamond," said Monty, "when like a pack of cards the team in the field fell forward to the ground."

Then a second blast erupted from the armament park. Most of the players had scrambled to find whatever cover they could when a third explosion echoed across the airfield. Monty said that with this, the umpire called the game. He added that Stan Helleur, the wing's public relations officer, dryly announced he'd heard of games called on account of rain or dust, "but never on account of noise."

Humour aside, it was fortunate the explosions were as much as several hundred metres away from the Spitfires parked in their dispersals. Any closer, said one of the armament officers, and they might have caused sympathetic explosions among the bombs lying around the aircraft.

Three days later, on July 27th, the wing celebrated yet another brilliant outing. An armed recce by 401 Squadron resulted in a pitched dogfight with a mixed force of FW 190s and Me 109s south of Caen. Eight of the enemy fighters were shot down, one was damaged. This was in addition to several motorised transports the pilots claimed. The pilots of 411 Squadron left fourteen vehicles as "flamers" or "smokers," as well as two tanks and several armoured personnel carriers and troop buses. Later, an armed recce by 442 Squadron added six more vehicles to the scoreboard. Mixing it up with a number of enemy fighters over the battlefront, the squadron's pilots got away after damaging three Me 109s and leaving another as a probable, the latter claimed by Bill Olmsted. Then, during a patrol at the end of the day by 401 Squadron, Flight Lieutenant R R Bouskill of Toronto shot down one FW 190, while Flight Lieutenant T P Jarvis of West Vancouver damaged another in the same action. It was the wing's last aerial combat in July, although several days of good hunting for ground targets remained.

Indeed, it had been the wing's best month so far. Throughout July, almost four thousand hours were logged on operational duties. The number of sorties had more than doubled to 3,429 since the previous month, for which the wing's pilots claimed fifty-six enemy aircraft destroyed, one probable and twenty-six damaged.

Their own losses since D-Day were comparatively modest: eighteen pilots had been listed as missing, not-yet-returned or killed.

4

POUR LA
LIBERATION

T OWARDS the end of July, a conviction held by some in the German High Command, and by Hitler especially, that the Normandy landings were merely a feint and that the real invasion would fall on the Pas de Calais, was finally dispelled. Considerable effort had been spent inculcating this notion in the first place; and in the weeks following D-Day the Allies had maintained their diversionary tactics in the hope of preserving the idea that a "second invasion" might yet materialise. Their real purpose, of course, as they established a colossal amount of men and material on the Normandy bridgehead, was a planned breakout into France and the Low Countries.

By early August, however, the Germans did what they should have done two months earlier. They began moving their armoured divisions and infantry south from the Pas de Calais, while reinforcements were brought in from other points to begin preparations for a large-scale counter-offensive. But even then, as Rommel had already pointed out, manoeuvrability was severely restricted. The 9th and 10th SS Panzer divisions, for example, sent from Poland, took four days to cross Germany and a further eleven to reach Normandy from the French frontier. The difficulties were almost entirely a result of

Allied air attacks. In the same period, Allied reinforcements were moving from southern England to Normandy in less than twenty-four hours, and were virtually unhindered in their continuing mobility across the Channel by either the Luftwaffe or, for that matter, the German Navy.

To a lesser but still meaningful extent, the Allies faced difficulties of their own. Their original plan for the invasion anticipated the capture of Caen on D-Day. British and Canadian troops fell somewhat short of this objective and, throughout the following weeks, were repeatedly thrown back in their efforts to take the city. For Field Marshal Sir Bernard Montgomery, commanding the land forces in Normandy, Caen became the focal point of the battle in France. The enemy, too, had come to regard the city as key to their overall strategy, and therefore defended it vigorously. But they could not match the air supremacy enjoyed by the Allies. The RAF mercilessly bombed Caen, virtually obliterating William the Conqueror's ancient capital. The outskirts were occupied after much hard and bloody fighting, in which the Canadians played a principal role, but the centre held. Both Eisenhower, as Supreme Allied Commander, and British Prime Minister Winston Churchill were growing impatient with the generally slow pace of progress inland since D-Day. They had to be persuaded by Montgomery that his "grand design" of a wide envelopment of the Germans, reaching as far south as the Loire, still possessed logic and would soon produce results.

In fact, operations aimed at taking Caen had succeeded in drawing the enemy's armoured reserves towards the British front and away from the Americans, who were preparing an assault south of the Cotentin. This in itself favoured Allied prospects. Hitler, who had insisted that the crumbling defences on the Normandy front must be restored, now wanted a strategic reversal in the west. In early August he approved a commitment of eight armoured divisions to an operation intended to encircle the invaders. Thus the stage was set for one of the greatest tank battles during the Second World War—and one of Germany's costliest defeats.

Everything went badly for them almost from the outset. Their assault began on the night of August 6th, when two hundred tanks

advanced—without artillery support—on either side of the river
Sée. Americans dug in on high ground repelled the initial assault and
calmly waited for daylight to call in tactical support aircraft, which
proved devastating to the enemy's vanguard. Along with rocket-
firing Typhoons of the 2nd TAF, which flew 294 sorties on August
7th, they reduced one Panzer division's tank strength to thirty that
day. Hitler had demanded that the attack be prosecuted "daringly
and recklessly" to achieve victory, but he seemed to be getting only
part of his wish.

The German offensive also suffered in its timing. It coincided
with a new drive by the Allies at the opposite end of the Normandy
bridgehead, aimed at Falaise. Code-named Operation "Totalise," the
push was carried out mainly by Canadians along with an émigré 1st
Polish Armoured Division. As the British-Canadian 21st Army
Group drove south to cut off the German line of retreat to the Seine,
the American 12th Army Group hurried eastward. The result was
the Germans, and not the Allies, were placed in imminent peril of
encirclement. During a telephone conversation with General Omar
Bradley, commanding the US First Army, Montgomery agreed that
"the prospective prize was great." Later he explained with typical English understatement: "If we can close the gap completely, we shall
have put the enemy in the most awkward predicament."

Thus the Allies were committed to sealing the narrow gap. On
the ground, the task devolved mainly to the Canadian and Polish
armoured divisions that were ordered in the direction of a road junction eighteen kilometres east of Falaise. Meanwhile, the enemy withdrawal had "assumed the aspect of desperation," observed Canadian
military historian Charles Stacey. "The enemy's dire circumstances
were driving him to attempt something which our superiority in the
air had not allowed him to think of for months past: mass road
movement in daylight." The result was predictable. "[O]ur fighter-
bombers struck at the packed roads hour after hour, turning the
whole area of the Gap into a gigantic shambles; while our artillery,
moving up within range, poured thousands of shells into the killing
ground. In that seething bloody cauldron which the Germans were
to remember as 'der Kessel von Falaise' one of the haughty armies

that had terrorized Europe was perishing miserably." The Canadian pilots of 126 Wing contributed substantially to the enemy's predicament. Scores against ground targets mounted each day from the 9th, until they reached a crescendo on August 18th, when over six hundred vehicles were shot up. The wing's total for the month would reach an incredible two thousand vehicles—so many, in fact, that 83 Group Headquarters asked for verification. But according to Monty, who interrogated the pilots, the figures were accurate. Moreover, he said, they were corroborated by the army's own assessments.

> The pilots were pretty excited, I remember. They'd come rushing into the bullpen, vying with each other to relate what they had done and eager to find out if they'd beaten the other squadrons. Then they'd hustle out to have another go at the Jerries. How they marvelled at Charlie Trainor's combat films, in which each round or shell seemed right on target, never a wasted shot too short or too long. Batting in the same league were "Goodie" Goodwin and Bill Olmsted of 442 Squadron, and Charlie Fox of 412. Golly, they were intrepid lads. Nothing could beat their spirit—ever.

To take the pilots even closer to the action, the wing had moved to a new airfield, B18, at Cristot on August 8th. By all accounts it was a dismal, depressing change. Cristot was flat and sandy, which in itself was a letdown after the bucolic setting they had enjoyed at B4. The sand, in particular, made life uncomfortable. "It seemed to pour down on you wherever you were," Monty recalled. He had come upon this dreadful moonscape the day before and parked the Siamese Twins in anticipation of the wing's arrival. "Not many people realised before we got there that the fighting had been so heavy just a couple of days earlier. Soldiers were hardly buried. Occasionally you would see a hand sticking out of a soft mound of earth, and some Jerries were found unburied—and smelling pretty high—in a patch of woods on the other side of the airfield." The scene not only produced a most disagreeable olfactory effect, but formed a very attractive enticement to swarms of flies. In no time, almost everyone in the wing soon suffered from dysentery again, with a few cases requiring hospitalisation.

"But worst of all," said Monty, "after we'd been there a week or so, was the plague of wasps that started. You couldn't leave sugar or jam uncovered on a table or in seconds it would be teeming with hundreds of wasps. We had to check every bit of food to make sure we didn't swallow them. Lots of fellows were stung inside their mouths."

To their credit, the pilots managed to run up their scores almost in spite of the circumstances at Cristot. Mostly they took their chances during ground strafing missions, which Bill Olmsted described as "dangerous and thrilling" because of the risk of enemy flak over the battlefront. Flying Officer T R (Tom) Wheler of 411 Squadron became a victim of one well-aimed burst of flak on August 7th, while returning to base after an armed recce in the area of Lisieux. His was the only Spitfire with any ammunition left when his squadron spotted a truck on a road below. Unfortunately for Wheler, he had already committed himself to attacking it before he realised that an anti-aircraft battery was also hidden in a nearby orchard. Flak poured in the direction of Wheler's aircraft, soon disabling it. Wheler bailed out safely, only to find himself started on "an adventure-packed three-week journey," according to 411 Squadron's official history, "that ultimately put the MBE ribbon up alongside the DFC he had won in air combat and ground attacks."

Wheler, an American whose Canadian parents resided in Georgia, hid for several days after, leaving a false trail for his pursuers. He lived "like a native" on a diet of vegetables and frogs' legs while making his escape. Several days later, though, he was captured and taken to Pont l'Eveque, where he was put in a truck that was driving to Paris. En route, Wheler wriggled out of a small window in the truck. He was contemplating how to finish his disappearing act when an Allied air raid closed a part of the road immediately ahead, and forced the vehicle to stop. In the confusion, Wheler slipped away. He walked all night. Early the next morning, north of Livarot, he begged food from a French farmer who also gave him a leather tunic, a map of the area and information that British troops were only a few kilometres away to the west, near St. Pierre. Wheler set out, making good progress on foot under the cover of darkness and resting during daylight. He also was able to inflict some damage on enemy installations as he went. His first act of sabotage occurred when he came upon a number of rail cars left unguarded on a small rise. He disconnected the cars, released the brakes and, after wedging himself into position, physically pushed the cars in motion—enough to get them rolling down the hill until they derailed on a curve. Later he came upon a V1 launching site in some woods. He waited until all was quiet, then crept into the compound and cut as many wires, cables and hoses he could find to effectively put the facility out of commission. Wheler was captured again a few days later, but fortunately the Germans had no inkling he was responsible for the sabotage. He escaped again and eventually found sanctuary with a French family near St. Etienne l'Allier, where he stayed until British forces arrived in the area at the end of August.

Extracts from the Wing's Summary of Operations give an indication of what had transpired while Tom Wheler was gallavanting about the French countryside.

August 5th: "Although the weather was none too good, Flight Lieutenant Olmsted and Flight Lieutenant Hume scored one jeep flamer, one DR (despatch rider), one truck and trailer damaged, and two half-tracks, with troops, damaged."

August 10th: "There was considerable ground movement seen and 401 Squadron claimed twelve destroyed, a smoker and a damaged, as well as three tents shot up. Squadron Leader Trainor accounted for six destroyed and the damaged vehicle of the total."

August 12th: "The morning dawned duff as usual and the sun took longer than it generally does to burn the ground haze up and make the weather suitable for armed recces. The 'blitz' of the Hun started properly at 1042 when twelve aircraft of 412 were airborne to do an armed recce in sections covering the side roads between Flers and Argentan. They returned with a score of twenty-seven destroyed or damaged and one troop-carrying vehicle damaged."

The Diary also reported: "Everyone was happy to welcome Flight Lieutenant Scotty Murray, DFC,* of 401, who made his way back through enemy lines after having bailed out some weeks ago. He told of meeting Squadron Leader Cameron, who went missing on July 3rd, in the hayloft of a barn, so we're hoping to see him shortly, too."

Later: "Twelve aircraft of 411 did another dive-bombing show against a jetty on the Seine river. One direct hit and three near misses were seen and then the squadron hunted up some more Jerry transport to the tune of eight destroyed and damaged."

As well as ground casualties, the wing's pilots had shot up a respectable number of enemy aircraft. During a patrol by 412 Squadron on August 10th, Wing Commander Russel claimed a Me 109 as damaged. Flying Officer Laubman shot down one and shared another with Flying Officer M C Saunderson. One destroyed and one damaged were claimed by Flying Officer C R Symons and Squadron Leader D H Dover respectively. The next day 411 Squadron returned from a fighter sweep and claimed four Me 109s destroyed and one FW 190 damaged. Then, on August 17th: "All patrols were uneventful except one by 401 Squadron, which took off at 1859. Thirty-plus FW 190s were seen dogfighting with Typhoons and Spitfires so our pilots got into the fray." Flight Lieutenant Russ Bouskill destroyed one FW 190, while Flight Lieutenant Dick Cull of Sebabeach, Alberta, and Flight Lieutenant George Hardy of Bladworth, Saskatchewan, each claimed one damaged. The Diary added: "Flying Officer Teddy Sheehy, after being shot up by a 190 and having a blown tire, landed safely and unhurt at B4." That same day, information reached the wing's intelligence staff that Flight Lieutenant Barry Needham of 412 Squadron, who bailed out in enemy territory several weeks earlier, had arrived safely in England.

Then, August 18th—one of the more spectacular days in the wing's history. "Another fine day set the Wing off to an early start," the Diary recorded. "Operations which started much the same as any others in the past few days soon reach unprecedented heights

---

* Flight Lieutenant G B "Scotty" Murray, DFC of Halifax, not to be confused with St John, New Brunswick's Flight Lieutenant F T (Fred) Murray, DFC. Both served with 401 Squadron.

and resulted in the highest score of enemy transport yet reached by this Wing and perhaps any other."

The list of enemy ground casualties for the day was almost incredible. "Squadron Leader Dover and Flight Lieutenant Fox of 412 went on a special mission to spot some enemy transport and located at least a thousand to fifteen hundred vehicles in a large wooded area near Argentan," noted the diarist. "Most of the area was just jammed with traffic, bumper to bumper. In addition, they located some tanks as well as many horse-drawn guns and vehicles. The real blitz on Jerry started at 1437 when 442 started a series of eleven armed recces to the area northeast of Vimoutiers where large concentrations of five hundred-plus and three thousand or more transport were seen."

Monty said the wing's Spitfires carried out almost two hundred sorties, each of which accounted for itself in the scoring column. By the day's end, Monty reported the wing had claimed "220 enemy vehicles destroyed, 151 left smoking and 292 damaged." He added: "Four tanks were left in flames, five smoking and 15 damaged. Eight armoured fighting vehicles were destroyed, two probable and six damaged as well as a troop carrier and seventy troops and an ammo dump."

The intelligence staff could barely keep up with the activity. In his memoirs, Bill Olmsted, who was always one of the first to arrive at the briefing room in the mornings, had described Monty as "excitable and energetic" in normal circumstances. He was also methodical, not least of all in his ritual of greeting pilots as they returned from sorties and, almost before they could climb out of their cockpits, cheerily interrogating them with, "Well, how many troops did you kill this trip?"

The armament staff, too, was working at full speed. And not surprisingly, the amount of activity took its toll on aircraft. The Intelligence Diary reveals: "It was suggested by Wing Commander Russel that the squadrons do their armed recces with eight aircraft instead of twelve in order to keep up a reasonably high percentage of serviceability."

Nor were the victories without a cost to the wing in personnel. On August 18th, the Diary reported: "Squadron Leader Trainor was last seen at two thousand feet heading south, believed hit by enemy flak." Several weeks would pass before word filtered back that Trainor was captured. Two other pilots were downed as well during the day's search-and-destroy activity over Falaise, including Flight Lieutenant A F (Sandy) Halcrow of 401 Squadron. The element of risk was ever-present, but so were the dividends—even if occasionally they were unexpected: "Flying Officer Middleton attacked a vehicle and overshot, striking the edge of some woods on the roadside, causing large explosions and flames. On a later armed recce, this area was again flown over, and F/O Middleton reported about one acre burned out. Many petrol drums and five burned out vehicles were seen. In view of this, his claims were raised by five flamers."

August 19th found the pilots back in the air and claiming numbers almost as great as the day before. But again, there were losses. Flight Lieutenant McDuff of 442 Squadron bailed out when his aircraft was disabled, and was listed as NYR—"not yet returned." Flying Officer J A "Jock" Swan was wounded in the leg, but landed safely. However, Flying Officer C R Symons was killed after attacking a vehicle. Hit by flak, "he flicked to the deck and burst into flames." By August 24th, Monty would report that as many as thirty pilots were missing since D-Day, including nine in the last ten days. Search and rescue operations were carried out when circumstances warranted—usually when pilots were reported missing over the English Channel. On August 18th, for example, Flying Officer Jack Lumsden of Hamilton, Ontario, was hit by flak and bailed out over the Channel. "In those days pilots weren't carrying dinghies any more," Monty recalled, "but Lumsden was managing to stay afloat, although he wouldn't have lasted much longer. His squadron mates orbited but had no dinghies themselves to drop, so a rush call was sent to 127 Wing, which sent up a pilot who dropped a dinghy within a few yards of Jack. Soon after a rescue launch arrived and picked up Lumsden."

The pilot who dropped the dinghy was Flight Lieutenant E S Smith, who turned out to be one of Lumsden's childhood friends. "I didn't know it was Jack until a couple of days afterwards," Smith said. "We used to go to the same summer camp on Georgian Bay.

Hell, he didn't need a Mae West. He could have swum to the English coast!"

Pilots shot down over the continent were not always as fortunate. Many were captured. Most had hair-raising experiences to relate if they were fortunate enough to make it back to the airfield. No wonder the Intelligence Diary jubilantly marked the return of pilots who had been previously listed as lost in action. "Many happy returns last night when Flight Commander "Duke" Halcrow of 411 Squadron returned after having escaped from the Germans. News also came that Bill Tew of 401 is safe with some US troops, and Warrant Officer Jeffrey was seen in Bayeux by Halcrow. Then, today, Dave Evans of 411 got back after many exciting experiences and to make everyone completely happy who should walk in before dark but Squadron Leader 'Hap' Kennedy of 401 Squadron."

Each of the pilots was interrogated by Monty, who provided in the Intelligence Diary a glimpse of the ordeals they had experienced. Evans, for example, who had bailed out on July 15th, related: "I landed quite easily in an orchard on the side of a hill and was immediately taken prisoner. I was stripped of my Mae West, and they attempted to take my watch and lighter but I made such a row about that they gave them back. I was moved under the care of two guards to a PoW camp. On the way, Flying Fortresses passed overhead, which were being engaged by flak. Shrapnel was starting to fall and I made a whistling noise as if a bomb was falling. Both the guards dived into ditches either side of the road, while I attempted to hop over a gate in the hedge. A guard shouted, 'Halt!' and I looked back to find myself covered by a rifle."

"Hap" Kennedy, who was hit by heavy flak on July 26th and bailed out, got off to a better start. He ran and crawled about a kilometre from where he landed until he met three young boys. "They told me to hide where I was, and they would fetch me civilian clothes. After an hour they returned with a jacket and pants."

Warrant Officer J S Jeffrey of 411 Squadron, who was making a short burst on one of the FW 190s, was jumped by two others from behind. Smoke and oil covered the windscreen, the engine cut, and so at 3,500 feet he bailed out. "One FW 190 followed me right down to the deck taking pictures of me, I think to confirm the kill. I made a really smooth landing in an orchard ... [and] immediately put my parachute harness and Mae West under a hedge." Jeffrey marched straight up to a farmer he had seen standing outside the door of his house. "I asked him for a change of clothing, which he fetched without hesitation. I told him to burn my battledress and all my equipment. I learned later that he had dyed my uniform so he could wear it himself."

Jeffrey was asked if he had a photograph of himself. He did. "In less than half an hour my identity card was stamped, my photograph affixed and everything in apple-pie order."

Scotty Murray, who was hit on June 27th, had quite a time getting back with a number of interesting experiences along the way. Incredibly, he ran into Squadron Leader Cameron and a British paratrooper. They were on their way to Spain, they said. They had French papers but no photographs." Murray, who had an extra photograph of himself, pasted it on Cameron's document. The resemblance was good enough.

Flight Lieutenant Sandy Halcrow's account was perhaps the most dramatic. Hit by cannon fire during the wing's outing on August 18th, his aircraft was in danger of bursting into flames. At only eight hundred feet—which was dangerously low—he bailed out.

"I noticed someone running to where I was going to land," Halcrow told Monty. "My first impression was that he was a civilian. No sooner had I landed, I released my harness and called out, *'Anglais!'* This was nearly fatal. The "civilian" turned out to be a German soldier pointing a rifle at Halcrow. He was soon joined by another soldier toting a machine gun.

"They signalled me to walk towards a hedge, where an officer and twenty men were standing. They started to take off my Mae West and helped themselves to chocolate, cigarettes and compass. They handed the money back to me. While they were disrobing and robbing me, one of them asked in English, "Have you been shooting up Red Cross wagons?" Halcrow said he hadn't. "They then went into a huddle and started to share their booty."

The English-speaking soldier asked Halcrow his rank. Halcrow said he was a Captain. Following a brief consultation with his officer, the soldier told Halcrow he would have to see the Kommandant. He wanted to know if Halcrow was in the RAF. He nodded. Then his escort led him to a spot some thirty yards away, where Halcrow found five Americans, a Pole and a Russian.

"I asked them what type of fellows the guards were. They said they were mixed: Rumanians, Greeks, Italians, Poles and Russians. I reckoned that a little morale-breaking was indicated. We got the Russian and Pole working on them, and with my limited French explained to them that the Luftwaffe was finished and that they were completely surrounded. Out came the "Safe Conduct" passes which had been dropped by the RAF—they each had one in their possession. One of the Italians came up to me and said: 'Tomorrow I your prisoner.'"

However, a German was added to the unit of guards. That night the Kommandant sent for Halcrow's papers. He wondered what this meant. The papers were returned shortly afterwards without comment.

"Along with seven cows, we slept the night in the stables," recalled Halcrow. "The next day for breakfast we were given a piece of bread each. About 0900 hours, the Kommandant came to tell us that there was no more food to be had, only a three-pound bag of granulated sugar which he left for us. Guards were changed hourly. They always put a German in charge." That afternoon intermittent shelling went on for about two hours, only a few hundred metres away. They passed another night in the stable.

Then, Halcrow said, they were awakened at 0200 and told they were to get moving. "The Germans wore their camouflaged smocks. As I approached the stable door both my arms were grabbed and in this manner I was marched to a truck hidden under some trees. Four of us (a Russian, two Americans and myself) were put in one truck and a Pole and three Americans in the other. There were twenty guards to each truck.

"For about two hours we drove through congested roads, and without lights. We passed a lot of horse-drawn artillery on the way. The convoy eventually stopped short of a village. The reason for this was that the convoy was being shelled… We were taken across fields, with about six or seven thousand infantry, to join up with the convoy south of the town.

"British shelling was amazingly accurate," said Halcrow. "Piles of destroyed vehicles and dead horses—and German soldiers—littered the area. Shortly after, British tanks appeared from out of the woods. Throwing their arms away, the Germans went hell-for-leather towards the village. I followed suit." Said Halcrow: "In the melee only one American and myself kept together. About forty Germans and ourselves took shelter in a basement. We were joined shortly by another dozen Jerries."

The next morning—it was August 20th—they went into the adjoining house, which had been set up as a First Aid post. Halcrow and the American were welcomed by two German doctors and four orderlies, with open arms. "They gave us food, drink, tobacco and cigarette papers to roll our own. One of the orderlies who spoke a bit of English impressed on me that, when we were rescued, we should explain to the troops how well we had been treated."

That afternoon, the village was dive-bombed by American Thunderbolts. Halcrow said the German soldiers were pretty shaken by the attack. A young SS-type hobbled in, hit in the foot by a shell. Halcrow was told that the soldier was eighteen years old, but had been in the army a year already. "Tough and arrogant," Halcrow said of him. Nevertheless, Halcrow suggested they surrender. "Little by little, the SS boy gave way. I told him he would be well looked after in a hospital and, if he insisted on staying on, gangrene would set in and he would lose his leg. Finally, he was won over."

Halcrow and a German stretcher bearer set out down the road soon after this, carrying a large Red Cross flag. They met the local curé, who pointed out where the Allied lines could be found. Halcrow had a note from one of the Germans, which stated that many in the village wanted to surrender. Eventually he met a Major Peterson of the Glengarry Highlanders, and gave him the note. "He said he could not spare any men to go and fetch the b——. Already he had seven hundred that had surrendered to him, including two generals!"

Halcrow had witnessed first-hand the devastating effect on morale during the German withdrawal at Falaise. Fighting to close the Gap had virtually ceased by the morning of August 22nd. The Canadians had captured as many as 12,000 enemy troops over the past few days. Said Charles Stacey: "Uncounted thousands of other Germans had met death in the blind and desperate combats of these days of slaughter... The whole vicinity of St Lambert was covered with the human and material debris of an army which had suffered the greatest disaster in modern military history." It is difficult now to comprehend the extent of the devastation wrought upon the escaping German army; images of the so-called "Highway of Death" outside Kuwait at the end of the recent Gulf War are perhaps the closest comparison.

In the aftermath of the slaughter at Falaise, Allied troops began to make up for their comparatively slow progress since D-Day, rapidly advancing in pursuit of the retreating enemy. The French capital fell in a matter of days. The "breakout" from the Normandy bridgehead had been accomplished. Now that "the chase" had begun, the men at Cristot were in a celebratory mood.

According to Monty, several marquee tents were raised at the airfield and a special dance floor was built using wood from packing crates seized at the Caen aerodrome, which had at last fallen to the Canadians. The wing's catering officer and several others rustled up salads, cheeses, chicken and turkey, and a variety of liquid refreshments. Air Marshal L S Breadner, the RCAF's Air Officer Commander-in-Chief in London, was among several high-ranking guests during the occasion. "The Air Marshal seemed to have a real good time and wandered around talking to an endless stream of people," said Monty. "He particularly enjoyed Bob Hyndman's sketches on the tent walls."

Flight Lieutenant R S (Robert) Hyndman of 411 Squadron (he later became an official war artist and, in civilian life, a noted portrait painter), was renowned for his caricatures of various pilots and nude women. According to Monty, one of his sketches featuring "two graceful lovelies" always hung over the wing's bar no matter where it travelled.

The wing's band gave one of its better performances that night, "though any music would have sounded sweet in the cool moonlit air of Cristot," Monty suggested. And, as the Wing Diary so pleasantly recorded, "the whole affair was suitably supported by nurses from the Canadian and British hospitals, about a hundred and fifty in all. It was great to see women neatly dressed and smiling again, after more than two months of tatters and dust and the grime of Normandy. It was just great."

There was a touch of comic relief the morning after the festivities when a visiting pilot from 127 Wing and his engineering officer were preparing to leave Cristot. No one was around to crank the propeller of their Auster, so the pilot got out to do it himself, leaving the engineering officer at the controls. The engine started, the pilot shouted to throttle back, and the EO by mistake or in his excitement pushed the throttle the wrong way. The Auster leapt forward like a startled steer and went straight into the AOC's aircraft, which, Monty said, "had been minding its own business some distance away."

Duff weather towards the end of August and Cristot's distance from the rapidly moving front after the action at Falaise meant a brief respite for the overworked pilots and groundcrew. Still, the ALO's "gen talks" continued every morning at ten o'clock in the Briefing Room. The BBC's "News at Dictation Speed," broadcast at 0900 every day, was carefully copied out, typed and distributed in mimeographed form. The ALOs also posted a General Information Situation Board for all the ranks. Don Stewart, representing the intelligence staff, added his own news items and latest bulletins, usually accompanied by his seemingly endless supply of corny puns. At Cristot, 126 Wing's inclusion in the British West European Forces (or BWEF) was ended with the creation of the British Liberation Armies, or BLA, which Stewart wryly interpreted—to everyone's amusement—as "Burma Looms Ahead."

"There was always some good joke going around the camp, or else some pet bind, or excitement," Monty recalled. Flying Officer Leonard Hardie Wilson of Stratford, Ontario, remembers that during one dull day the pilots gathered in a tent to view the latest cine-gun footage. One pilot seemed to have had a particularly busy outing. His film showed a few trucks, and later an ambulance being attacked. "This received some hoots of derision," said Wilson, as the shooting of ambulances, identified by the red crosses on top, was officially *verboten*. He explained that he only shot at them if they appeared to be heading toward the front, in which case they would not be carrying wounded, and given the desperate circumstances the Germans found themselves in, were probably being used to ferry ammunition and supplies. This argument seemed to mollify his critics. However, shortly after that his film showed him firing briefly at an aircraft. There was silence, then somebody piped up, "Hey, that's a Spitfire!" The audience erupted in an outburst of loud, derisive catcalls. "Our hero fell silent for a minute," said Wilson, "then he brought the house down with this classic line: 'Yeah, I thought he was one of ours, so I only gave him a short burst.'"

The airmen, at least, were enjoying the comparative lull in activity—even though everyone realised it would be shortlived. Each day put Cristot farther from the battlefront. Already, word had begun to circulate that they would be leaving B18 soon for a new airfield.

Monty was one of the first to receive definite orders to pack up. By the early hours of August 28th, he and the others who comprised the wing's "A" Party were on their way. Ahead was a gruelling ten-hour trip to the new airfield at Evreux. "It was an awful trip," remembered Monty. The utter destruction of Laigle, Flers, and Argentan seemed particularly unnerving. "Refugees in countless numbers were dazedly making their way back towards whatever might be left of their homes, pushing little carts or leading donkeys laden with salvaged articles," he said. "It was a pathetic sight, although it sobered people up for the trials later in the day. The heavy traffic and wreckage closely followed by our own armoured columns had taken their toll of the roads, which were pitted and worn through and very bumpy for such a long journey. That was bad enough, but halfway to Evreux the jarring must have had its effect, for one of the van's rear wheels rolled off completely. That put me out of the running for a while and gave the MT officers a few anxious moments. If operations were to start at Evreux-Fauville the next day, as we planned, it would be embarrassing without me and my contents on hand. Some fast organising was done and a repair unit came along and did a fine job."

Somewhere beyond Argentan, their convoy of thirty or so vehicles (including some from another RAF unit) met a British armoured division that was forming up along an intersecting road. "They were preparing for one long dash right across the Seine and straight north from Rouen into Belgium as quick as they could go. Of course, none of us knew about the urgency of their move. We just knew we had to get through but the MPs wouldn't let us go at all, and were even shoving our vehicles off the road into fields. They even said we might not be able to get moving until the next day."

Monty's temper, which seldom rose but was considerable when ignited, got hold of him. He ordered the vehicles turned around, which was accomplished despite the interference of the Military Police. "One way or another we got the bulk of the convoy to Evreux," he said, with little indication of the extent to which his determination was responsible. They pulled in to the airfield, known as B28, before dark.

It was perhaps just as well that the journey had been so difficult, for, as Monty said afterwards, their new home "was a dreadful sight," relieved only by the fact that for better or worse they had arrived. "It had been a key German aerodrome in France, used first to launch bombers against England and more recently as a base for many of the Luftwaffe fighters defending Paris. It had always been a happy hunting ground for our Spits back in England. But what Allied bombing raids hadn't knocked out, the Germans had demolished. Every building had been reduced to a skeleton framework, if anything at all. Every few yards there were craters down the main runways and perimeter tracks. Loose boarding, with nails of all shapes and sizes, covered all the roads. Several dozen flat tires had the MT section in a flap. This last-minute sabotage by the Germans proved to be an effective nuisance."

It seemed an interesting comment, too, on the character of the airfield's previous inhabitants, to find all the roads at B28 marked *Coventrystrasse, Sheffieldstrasse,* and so on, in neat signposts that were left behind, no doubt deliberately.

Over the next few days, Monty observed that the local inhabitants wasted little time "mopping up" after the area's liberation. Sweeping and rebuilding were part of Evreux's rehabilitation, but there was a darker urgency as well. Men and women accused of collaborating with the enemy were summarily rounded up by the local citizenry and marched down the streets, their heads shaved and marked with swastikas. Monty added that several kilometres from the airfield was a large prison where hundreds of them were incarcerated.

The situation at the airfield remained depressing. For one thing, said Monty, "the weather was so bad the prospects of a grass landing strip being made serviceable seemed dim." In the circumstances, few could resist making a quick day trip to the French capital. "It was a little awkward when the CO came over from the old site and wanted to see somebody, and found he had gone to Paris for the day. Ted Edwards, the senior administrative officer, finally had to clamp down and forbid anyone else from going." The order elicited groans of disappointment, for it meant an end to the wild abandonment many had experienced. "The delirium with which the Parisians welcomed the Allies was unbelievable," Monty remembered. "Champagne flowed, you couldn't spend a *sou*, and it was almost as much as your life was worth to produce a package of cigarettes. You were besieged by countless outstretched hands. Invitations to dinner were countless, even though food was scarce. Many of the fellows accepted only so they could bring their own rations—and extra, if they could wangle it."

Such hospitality was extended, and wherever possible reciprocated, with simple but nonetheless heartfelt explanations that it was "pour la liberation." Little else needed to be said.

The holiday mood in Paris contrasted sharply with the atmosphere at either Cristot, where many of the wing's aircraft were still based, or Evreux. Pilots managed to log a few armed recces. The weather was so wet, however, that operations were pretty well washed out. On September 1st, all four of the wing's squadrons flew to B24 at St Andre, about sixteen kilometres south of Evreux. The move seemed to make little sense. Two other wings were established there already. More important, Monty noted, was that "83 Group HQ had visions of the wily Hun making a nasty dart and knocking out nearly half the Allied strength in one swoop." Consequently, the wing's squadrons moved the next day to B26 at Illiers, only a few kilometres away. "It was a small, uneven and awkward strip," Monty remembered with obvious disappointment. Nor did it seem, for the moment anyway, that they might escape the cramped conditions they had left behind. The personnel of 127 Wing were based at B26, and, said Monty, they were "none too happy" about it. Fortunately, almost as soon as they arrived new orders followed. Monty was informed they would be moving up to Poix, near Amiens, where B44 was situated. "No time was to be lost on this," he explained. Part of the urgency arose from the fact that 126 Wing had been out of effective fighting range for almost a week. "We who had just pulled in were to remain packed and bed down for the night, leaving first thing in the morning."

They travelled almost the entire next day. After crossing the Seine near Rouen, it started to rain. Foul weather continued throughout the night. "Everyone in jeeps and open vehicles was drenched and not very pleased," Monty recalled. "The clerks travelling inside the INT/OPS vans, however, were comfortable enough. The rest of us arrived at B44 in the pitch dark, soaking wet. We seemed to be in the midst of an entire army—actually it was only a corps. Our convoy's vehicles were almost lost in a vast traffic jam. There had been no time to put up signs to tell our people where to turn off." Monty, who was leading the convoy, and Don Stewart stood on a road next to the airfield, waving a torch while shouting: "126 vehicles turn here!" He admitted by the end of the night he was in an "awful rage." At one point he had asked an officer who had driven in "a nice, comfortable closed-in captured Jerry car" to stop and help direct the convoy, and was told, "It's nothing to do with me." Following several gasps of amazement, Monty retorted, "Well, what more in hell do you think it has to do with me?" The officer sped away, hotly pursued by even more purple expletives from Monty.

Eventually, the convoy was settled in for the night, parked alongside what appeared to be a wide perimeter track. It could have been

the runway for all anyone could see. Those that felt up to it made a
hot snack. Others just curled up in their trucks, where it was dry, and
slept. They had completed two long trips in as many days, covering
more than 640 kilometres. Much of that had been impressive for the
number of dead horses and cows along the road, smashed enemy artillery and casualties. Fighting had passed down the road so recently,
said Monty, that the dead had barely had time to start swelling yet.

Monty and his staff rose early the next morning. Telephone communications and wireless were not yet established, which was unusual.
Like the cooks, signals were the last section to pack up on a move and
the first to become operational at any new airfield, maintaining a
skeleton establishment at both old and new sites during the transition.
But it was early, yet. Nor was any aviation fuel stocked, so flying out of
Poix did not get underway until 1100 the next day. Then, several uneventful patrols were carried out in the Brussels-Antwerp area. The
wing's "B" Party arrived on the night of September 3rd, under somewhat happier conditions. The men reported they were conducted by
cheering crowds of civilians as they had passed through a number of
villages. However, their mood may have changed after surveying the
new airfield. "Poix was a barren, desolate area with destruction visible
on all sides," Monty said. "Like Evreux, what had not been bombed
was demolished just before the Allies swept in."

Compared to Illiers, though, B44 at least offered a usable grass
airstrip. By September 5th, operations resumed. But late in the day
orders arrived from 83 Group that the "A" Party should be on the
road again for their next stop forward. "The air force called this
'leap-frogging,'" Monty noted. This time, though, he was cheered
somewhat by their destination. Service Police from Group HQ
would meet his party at the outskirts of the Belgian capital. The orders said they were to depart *within the hour*, which left little time to
pack up. In the meantime, Group Captain McGregor and his interpreter, Flight Lieutenant Gustave Bédard, set out ahead of the "A"
party to await its arrival at Brussels early the next morning.

Bédard's account of their journey is rich in detail. Moreover, it
benefits from relating some of Bédard's own background and a description of his duties as an interpreter and liaison officer. Prior to

joining the RCAF in 1942, Bédard was employed as superintendent of *Parc national des Laurentides* and active in sports in Quebec City, where he was born. After putting in a stint as a recruiting officer in Montreal, he went overseas in 1944 and landed in Normandy as a liaison officer to the CO of 144 Wing. Bédard transferred to 126 Wing in July when 2nd TAF was reorganised. His duties were varied. They included, he said, acting as a surrogate CO and "scrounging officer," depending on the circumstances. "In the latter capacity," he explained, "I was asked to find a French saddle for a very high-ranking RAF officer who had been entertained at a luncheon. I produced the saddle to the satisfaction of all. Later, in Holland, I arranged with the attendants of a US Food dump an exchange of bottles of Scotch for large cans of delicious chicken in olive oil. As we moved on with the campaign, I would come down to Paris to buy French liquor, cognac, and so on, for the officers' mess."

There is a touch of cynicism in his portraits of whimsical masters and pandering to the need of many for perks. But for Group Captain McGregor, Bédard expressed unreserved respect and admiration. "Gordon McGregor was a man of character," he said. "Always in complete command of himself, he knew how to inspire confidence in his men. He was fearless, and a man of strong determination."

Bédard's case for the latter point is found in his description of their journey ahead of the "A" Party. As they approached Arras, it occurred to both Bédard and McGregor that traffic was standing idle on the side of the road. They proceeded anyway until a Military Policeman flashed a light and ordered them to stop.

"The MP informed us we could not drive any farther because the Germans were retreating from Calais and Boulogne without delay and would stand no interference from us."

McGregor and Bédard were asked for their identity cards. Giving the MP his right, McGregor declared his intention to carry on regardless of the situation. "His determination won the day," said Bédard, "and we were permitted to proceed at our own risk. The magnificent fighter that he was in the air was no less formidable on the ground." McGregor and Bédard resumed their journey and arrived unharmed at B56, the airfield at Brussels-Evere on the northeast outskirts of the city, where they awaited the "A" Party.

Back at Poix, rumours had begun to circulate that the wing might in fact be moving to Brussels. This had created some excitement as personnel began to anticipate a joyous reception by the city's inhabitants.

Monty was more concerned by the need to get his convoy formed up and on its way as ordered. It wasn't until 2200—two hours late—that the first section left Poix. An hour later, Frank Nobbs, one of the ALOs, started out with the next lot on the all-night trip of more than two hundred kilometres. "As usual, it was quite a journey in the dark," Monty recalled. "The route was poorly marked, bridges were out, wrong turns were made, big vehicles got trapped in narrow roads, and a water bowser that broke down disappeared (a repair party got to it a couple of days later)."

As always, Monty also recalled several amusing moments. Gord Panchuk had a little stove going in the jeep and was cooking noodle soup to feed Monty and himself during the trip. "It's a wonder we didn't set ourselves on fire. People were brewing tea and munching in the back of trucks all through the night." There were enough enforced stops to check the route and to allow everyone an opportunity to relieve themselves. By six o'clock on the morning of September 6th, the first section passed 121 Airfield at Douai and declared a stop for breakfast. "The catering officer not only had to be awakened but persuaded to serve up over two hundred quick meals." It began to rain shortly after they resumed their journey. By ten o'clock, the convoy reached the outskirts of the Belgian capital—and their hard-going was amply rewarded.

"I'll never forget that triumphant entry into Brussels," said Monty, "for the roads were lined with cheering, waving people. We were showered with fruit and flowers. The airmen in their enthusiasm threw every cigarette they possessed. People ran up to us with bottles of wine and champagne, poured out glasses and ran along with the vehicles until the glasses were emptied. There was shouting, singing, laughing, tears, kissing—much kissing. There were to be six days of celebration *"pour la liberation,"* and we were there at the start!"

As hoped, the convoys were directed to the airfield at Brussels-Evere, although Monty ventured that their headquarters would be established in the city itself. "In those days cafes and clubs were allowed to stay open as long as they wished, with dancing all the time."

Nor was there a shortage of booze. Hidden cellars and virtually entire warehouses were ransacked before any military or other police authority could intervene. "An airman in the Meterological Section who had been attached to the Army met some of the lads in a cafe and asked them to partake of a *case* of champagne he had just carried in intact. 'I'll get another one when we finish this,' he boasted."

"Parties, dinners, receptions—all were the order in every home, from the poorest to the wealthiest. Soldiers and airmen were collared and brought into these affairs regardless of their rank. There was no refusing."

To mark the wing's arrival, on September 16th a dance was held at the school hall of Schaerbeck, a suburb of Brussels. The event was organised by the town's burgomaster, just one of many quaint aspects recorded by Canadian newspapers that carried the story. The variety of food was even more noteworthy. "For the majority of the Canucks," said one item, "ice cream has been a thing of the corner drug store back home since they departed for overseas. But not since they came to Belgium. Raison pie and ice cream, strictly a four-colour magazine advertisement since 1940, became a reality on the mess tables. And strawberry flavoured at that." There was even food in the vast amount of war booty the Canadians had claimed. "In the past, the Canucks had picked up quite a supply of Hitler's vehicles, rifles, revolvers, belts, steel and cloth hats. This time they hit the jackpot—a sizeable supply of Hun food rations, from steaks and pork chops to margarine and hard tack." The impression was that the wing was living in luxury, which was not far from the truth, compared to what they'd been used to. Having lived under canvas since D-Day, the Canadians had at last found buildings for their quarters. The officers enjoyed a real mess "with its ultra-smart ante room," the highlight of which was its bar. Corporal Lloyd Leight of Orillia, Ontario, the mess steward, claimed it was the longest bar he had ever seen.

Of course, the airfield at Evere was not quite as posh as the newspapers suggested. Almost all of the buildings had incurred some damage. Its runways and perimeter tracks showed signs of being bombed. But the grass strip was usable. The first patrols from B56 on September 7th marked the start of a two-week period that Monty said would be remembered as nightmarish.

"Being so near to Brussels and, at first, the most forward Allied airfield, countless dignitaries dropped in to visit. This was in addition to the variety of bombers and fighters who got into trouble over enemy territory, and needed an airfield to land. It was quite common to have generals and admirals in conference on the grass beside the flying control van while all this air activity was going on. The Flying Control Officer, John Edison, and his staff had to be polite and answer hundreds of questions a day. They were not set up to handle so much traffic, but to their credit they coped, without incident."

Among the more notable visitors were General Eisenhower, General Montgomery, Prince Bernhard of the Netherlands, General Crerar of the 1st Canadian Army, General Dempsey of the Second British Army, Admiral Bertram Ramsay, and the American generals, Simpson and Bradley.

"The visitors, on their own, were only a small problem. But they arrived when Flying Control was responsible for five hundred Dakotas a day, as well as the fighters." As many as forty aircraft were in the circuit at once, and five on the runway after landing. This was in addition to 126 Wing's own operations, at a time when "pickings were good against the enemy on the ground."

The pace could not be maintained for long. It was too dangerous. The CO and Winco Russel petitioned Group Headquarters, declaring that either the Dakotas or the Spitfires had to quit flying out of the airfield. "Nothing happened for a day or so," Monty recalled. "The mayhem continued. Then, literally out of the blue, the AOC hove into the circuit one day in his Fieseler Storch, a captured Jerry communications kite, and found forty other aircraft waiting to touch down. Within seconds of landing he ordered 126 Wing grounded until further notice."

5

EPIC DAYS

THE DAKOTAS WON.

On September 20th, the wing's "A" Party left their luxurious quarters at B56 and moved to Le Culot, south of Louvain—an hour's drive. The new airfield, B68, had been recently liberated from the Luftwaffe. The barracks were badly damaged. In further contrast to Evere, their new quarters were damp, unheated and overcrowded. The lack of indoor plumbing and flush toilets, which they had enjoyed during their brief stay outside the Belgian capital, was also keenly felt. Pilots drove sixteen kilometres to a nearby town just to bathe. Conditions generally were so poor that respiratory afflictions increased, and morale was affected.

Yet, despite inconsistent weather and the move, the wing maintained a steady pace of operations—which, during the week of September 17th to the 24th, were mainly in support of a daring though largely unsuccessful attempt by the British and Americans to catapult into Germany in one bold stroke.

In the aftermath of their decisive victory at Falaise, Allied troops had advanced at breakneck speed, retaking both the French and Belgian capitals in the process while chasing the enemy back into Holland. By early September, however, it had become painfully obvious to Allied strategists that continuance of the advance depended on the ability to keep it supplied. This meant access to ports within reach of the front. The Canadians had seized the small facility at LeTréport on September 2nd, the same day they had marched uncontested—and with some poignancy—through the streets of Dieppe. Canadian war correspondent Ross Munro said the 2nd Division's tribute to their comrades who had fallen during the disastrous 1942 raid on the French coastal town was "probably the most impressive and meaningful Canadian parade of the war." However, the Allies were still in urgent need of a usable port facility. A week later the larger port at Ostend was captured, but it had been damaged. Inland, one of Europe's best ports, at Antwerp, had fallen to the British on September 4th. This was a magnificent prize. It was estimated as many as a thousand ships could berth at Antwerp's twenty-five square kilometres of docks. Incredibly, too, both ports had been captured virtually intact. But the enemy still held the banks of the Scheldt river between Antwerp and the sea. No Allied shipping could enter until this seventy-kilometre stretch was cleared. "A speedy and victorious conclusion to the war now depends, fundamentally, upon the capture by First Canadian Army of the Channel ports," wrote General Crerar to his Corps Commanders on September 9th. Yet even as the offensive got underway, it was overshadowed by events elsewhere. Field Marshal Montgomery had sold an ambitious plan to take the bridges over a series of rivers and canals in Holland as a means of securing a swift route across the Rhine, unhindered by such natural barriers, and boldly into Germany itself. The operation, known as "Market-Garden," was approved by Eisenhower on September 10th.

In the late 1960s, while conducting aerial surveys of Holland, experts with KLM Airlines were puzzled by what appeared to be aircraft scattered about the heaths near Arnhem. Careful examination of their photographs suggested the "aircraft" were in fact ghostly silhouettes. Further research, including comparisons with aerial photographs taken of the area in September 1944, confirmed this extraordinary discovery. The images were of gliders that had crashed and burned, leaving only their profiles scorched into the soil.

They came in waves during the early afternoon of Sunday, September 17th, as part of the greatest armada of troop-carrying aircraft ever assembled. Almost five thousand fighters, bombers, transport aircraft and more than 2,500 gliders comprised "Market," the airborne phase of the operation. Virtually an entire Allied airborne army, complete with vehicles and equipment, began dropping deep into Nazi-occupied Holland. Poised along the Dutch-Belgian border, massed tank columns of the British Second Army waited to unleash the "Garden" element of the assault. At 1435, under the protective cover of rocket-firing fighter aircraft, the tanks began their dash along a route paratroopers were fighting to capture and hold open.

Montgomery's plan was based on an assumption that the enemy's armies in the west had been so decisively weakened since D-Day that they would collapse if sufficient pressure was applied. In fact, the German forces in Holland remained formidable and were to mount increasingly effective resistance to the offensive. Five main bridges were to be captured. The Americans fulfilled their end of the bargain by taking the bridges at Eindhoven and Nijmegen. The last objective, at Arnhem on the lower Rhine, was to become famous as "A Bridge Too Far." There, British airborne troops—dropped deliberately some distance away from the objective to allow time to organise before going into battle—were cut off. Their desperate situation would define much that followed in the brief campaign. Foul weather in both England and Holland added to the atmosphere of crisis and, worse, often prevented timely intervention by aircraft of the 2nd TAF—including the Canadian Spitfires of 126 Wing. They had to contend with grass strips at both Evere and Le Culot that deteriorated quickly as a result of extensive rain. Nevertheless, Flight Lieutenant R W Davenport of 401 Squadron shot down one FW 190. Lieutenant Commander Wallace, on loan from the Fleet Air Arm, damaged another during the same combat. Sadly, Wallace was killed during a patrol the next day. Thereafter, the Luftwaffe made itself scarce until the 24th, when fifty-plus enemy aircraft were reported in the vicinity of Nijmegen. But not one was spotted by pilots of 412 Squadron, which was out on patrol. More evidence of the enemy's presence surfaced later, when three RAF flight sergeants arrived at Le Culot. They had bailed out after being shot down while dropping supplies to the beleaguered paratroopers at Arnhem on the 21st, and had evaded capture for two days.

By then, the situation at Arnhem had become critical. Finally, after much gallantry, the paratroopers were ordered to withdraw across the river. Only 2,400 of the ten thousand who landed managed to escape during the night in assault boats, many of which were manned by Canadian engineers. The cost of the operation at Arnhem was high: as many as 1,100 were killed and another 6,400 or so were captured. Indeed, the British 1st Airborne Division was virtually wiped out.

The German army had meanwhile won its first decisive victory since D-Day. Less widely realised was that during the fighting at Arnhem, the enemy had also consolidated its position along the Scheldt estuary, which some had argued—and military pundits now firmly insist—should have been the focus of Allied efforts. Historians further argue that Montgomery had even ignored reliable information concerning Hitler's decision to deny the Allies use of the Channel waterways. As early as September 12th, Montgomery's own intelligence section at 21st Army Group Headquarters warned that the Germans intended to "hold out as long as possible astride the approaches to Antwerp, without which the installations of the port, though little damaged, can be of no service to us."

In retrospect it can be seen that "the chase" began to falter after the debacle at Arnhem, largely as a result of logistical difficulties. The job of clearing the Scheldt would be handed over, belatedly, to the First Canadian Army, which would suffer as many as 13,000 casualties before the muddy "land God had no hand in," as the Dutch called it, was captured.

Ironically, the pilots of 126 Wing saw more action immediately after "Market-Garden" was aborted. The morning of September 25th dawned with very low cloud and a steady rain, but by shortly before noon the weather cleared enough to permit operations. Twelve aircraft of 442 Squadron were the first off the ground on a patrol over the Arnhem-Nijmegen-Venlo area. They returned at

1530 without sighting any enemy aircraft. But a patrol by 401 Squadron sent out at 1429 intercepted thirty-plus "bandits." Flight Lieutenant Bouskill destroyed one FW 190 and damaged a Me 109. Better still was the score claimed by his squadron mate, Flight Lieutenant Johnson, who shot down two 109s and damaged another. Afterwards, Johnson and two other pilots had to land at Eindhoven, they were so low on fuel. The rest of the squadron returned to Le Culot by 1655. Eleven aircraft of 412 Squadron were in the air by then, on the next low patrol. Sighting a few stragglers, Flight Lieutenant Laubman attacked and destroyed one Me 109. By nightfall, the pilots of 442 Squadron returned from their second patrol of the day. It was uneventful. Still, the wing's tally was five enemy aircraft destroyed and two damaged in more than a hundred and seventy sorties, which was respectable.

Their next outing, on September 27th, was even better despite early difficulties. Heavy rain left the runway unserviceable. Pilots with shovels and picks helped to fill in a few of the potholes, so that by 1100 the airfield was again declared fit for use. Less than half an hour later eleven aircraft of 401 Squadron left on the first high patrol, flying at 12,000 feet over the Venlo-Nijmegen area. Shortly after, 412 Squadron's Spitfires took off on a second high patrol. Two aircraft returned early, one with technical problems and the other an escort. The remaining Spitfires proceeded to northeast of Nijmegen, where they sighted twelve-plus Me 109s and another formation of twenty-five FW 190s, both flying east along the Rhine. The wing's daily Summary of Operations declared: "After some very thrilling combats, our boys scored eight destroyed with no losses, F/L R I A Smith, DFC shooting down two Me 109s and F/O Hurtubise getting one Me 109, while F/L D C Laubman got two FW 190s, F/L W J Banks two FW 190s, and F/O P Charron one FW 190." The latter score was remarkable considering that Flying Officer Phil Charron had rejoined 126 Wing for a second tour of operations that morning.

Twelve aircraft of 411 Squadron took off on the third patrol of the day. Later, the pilots reported sighting "some smoke trails," and little else. Then 401, refuelled and ready after its earlier—and

uneventful—first outing, left on the next high patrol. Three early
returns, one with R/T difficulties, one with technical problems and
an escort, were spared the disappointment of discovering empty
skies over the battlefront. By mid-afternoon, however, when 412
Squadron was back on patrol, at 15,000 feet a gaggle of ten-plus
enemy aircraft were found in the area southeast of Nijmegen. Flight
Lieutenant Laubman scored another FW 190 destroyed in the
ensuing combat, and, continuing his extraordinary "comeback,"
Flying Officer Charron was credited with one destroyed and one
damaged. Finishing up the day's tally in the air was Flying Officer
Bollingham, who added a damaged Me 109 to the scoreboard. The
wing's total effort was ten enemy fighters destroyed, two damaged.
And the pilots of 411 Squadron had shot up a locomotive during
another patrol.

September 27th was even more dramatic. Low patrols over Nijmegen started early and continued throughout the day. The first, by
401 Squadron, was uneventful, although it returned with information that the bridge at Nijmegen was still intact with vehicles crossing over it.

The second patrol, by 412 Squadron, ran into ten-plus Me 109s
and twelve-plus FW 190s northeast of Nijmegen. These were
engaged, with the result that the Canadian Spitfire pilots came out
8-0-2 (destroyed-probable-damaged) for no losses on their side.
Then 411 Squadron left on the third patrol at 0831 and promptly
chased down fifteen-plus FW 190s, of which seven were destroyed
and three damaged—again, without a loss to the Canadians. "The
Huns were apparently about to make an attack on some target near
Nijmegen," the Intelligence Diary noted, with obvious satisfaction.
"The tanks or bombs they were carrying were jettisoned when 411
attacked, causing some explosions."

Shortly before noon, 412 took off again and proceeded to the
hotly contested area over Nijmegen. There the Canadian pilots ran
into forty FW 190s and twenty Me 109s. Outnumbered five-to-one,
the Falcons shot down two of the enemy fighters, and damaged four.
However, Pilot Officer Hurtubise was lost. Flight Lieutenant Charlie
Fox, who was credited with destroying two FW 190s and damaging

two more, had his Spitfire badly shot up. So, too, had Phil Charron, who was also slightly wounded by shrapnel. "Jock" Swan's aircraft was damaged by flak.

The pace continued into the early afternoon, when 411 Squadron left on its second patrol of the day and claimed a Me 410, a high-altitude fighter seldom seen in their sector. It was shared by Flight Lieutenant E G "Gordie" Lapp (who had already shot down two FW 190s) and Flying Officer R M Cook. Several Ju 88s were sighted east of Nijmegen, but they disappeared in a cloud before they could be engaged. The third round of patrols left B68 at 1430. Several "bogies" were reported by 401 Squadron, but they turned out to be Mustangs. Once again, though, 412 Squadron encountered enemy fighters—and scored. "This time they chased the Huns up to their base," the Intelligence Diary reported, "and shot down four and damaged one as they were going in to land." The squadron's boldness and tenacity had been rewarded, but at the cost of losing Flying Officer Clasper, who failed to return after the mission.

The last patrol of the day left at 1621 and returned, without further incident, at 1802. It had been a brilliant show, nonetheless. Twenty-two enemy aircraft were destroyed, ten damaged. The pilots of 412 Squadron alone were credited with shooting down fourteen of the enemy fighters. "In three days, 412 had knocked down twenty-six of the thirty-seven destroyed by the wing," Monty noted. "That was the hottest pace any squadron ever had."

The lust for action was not satisfied to the same extent on September 28th, but a full measure of flying was maintained nonetheless. "Today proved to be our most active day for the month ... with 120 sorties for 217 hrs 51 minutes of flying," the Intelligence Diary observed. Again, the wing's squadrons alternated on low patrols over the area of Nijmegen. First off was 411 Squadron, which left the airfield at 0615. An hour and forty minutes later the Spitfires were back, having destroyed two FW 190s and damaging two others. By 0800, 442 Squadron was airborne. It returned at 1020, claiming one FW 190 damaged. Unfortunately, Flying Officer G G Millar was missing. Hourly patrols continued until last light, but all were uneventful.

The weather on September 29th was just as favourable, with an almost predictable outcome. The first patrol was given to 401 Squadron, which left at 0621 and soon found itself involved in "a real mix-up" with thirty-plus "bandits" about sixteen kilometres southeast of Nijmegen. It ended with four Me 109s destroyed, four damaged and one FW 190 damaged. Flight Lieutenant Johnson was injured during the action, but landed safely at Eindhoven to refuel along with the other aircraft in the squadron.

"Ten aircraft of 412 Squadron took off on Low Patrol, four landing back here at 1218, the rest landing at Eindhoven and returning here after refuelling," the Summary of Operations noted. "P/O Busby was forced to crash land near Eindhoven, being out of fuel. He was unhurt. One enemy vehicle was attacked and left in flames. Fifty-plus FW 190s were encountered six miles east of Nijmegen at 8-9,000 feet. Total claims for this patrol were three destroyed. 412 did another patrol, taking off at 1546. Flight Lieutenant Banks' aircraft was shot up by flak but he landed safely at Eindhoven. The weather began to close in."

Thus ended five epic days in the wing's circus life on the continent. Fifty-one enemy aircraft were destroyed—one short of the month-end total of fifty-two—which was exactly half of the overall total for 83 Group in the same period. By comparison, the RCAF's other high-scoring Spitfire formation in Europe, 127 Wing, came second with a record of thirty-eight destroyed. Only four pilots were lost. Top squadron honours went to 412, which had chalked up an impressive twenty-nine destroyed. Twenty-three-year-old Don Laubman of Provost, Alberta, accounted for thirteen of those, making him one of the hottest "aces" on the continent. His closest rival was Flight Lieutenant R I A (Rod) "Smitty" Smith, DFC and Bar of 401 Squadron, who had blasted six enemy aircraft out of the sky in four days, bringing his total score to thirteen destroyed— although he had built up the earlier part of his record during a tour of duty in Malta. Smith was promoted to command 401 when Charlie Trainor disappeared after bailing out, for the second time over enemy territory, on September 18th. Smith left little doubt concerning his abilities. During his squadron's first patrol, on

September 29th, they ran into thirty-plus enemy aircraft, destroyed nine and damaged five.

The wing's outstanding record might have continued, too, but for the weather. By October 1st, conditions were again miserable. Word soon reached 126 Wing Headquarters that the Canadians would be moving forward to another airfield—their seventh since D-Day. Not surprisingly, they were destined for Holland, where a landing strip was reportedly nearly ready for them at de Rips, northeast of Helmond.

"The area was being fought over or around and so only a skeleton party went forward on October 1st," Monty recalled. They arrived safely at "Rips," as they called it, where B84 was established. The next day the rest of the "A" Party followed. Two squadrons flew in on October 3rd. The others stayed behind owing to weather conditions. By October 4th, however, the wing was complete at B84.

"It was typically flat, low Dutch farmland," Monty remembered. The intelligence staff chased several dozen cows and horses out of a field overlooking the airstrip, and set up the Siamese Twins. "To the northeast we heart the sharp crump of mortar fire. It didn't sound very far away at all. We soon discovered it wasn't. Machine guns stuttered from time to time. We heard the ALOs explaining—hopefully—that the situation was 'fluid' several kilometres to the southeast, where the Americans were forming up for a big push any day. There was nothing to worry about, they said."

In fact, there were to be a few anxious moments yet. An engineering officer with 412 Squadron left his tent one night with a lit cigarette in his mouth. A shot promptly whistled by. Rumours of snipers in the woods on either side of the airfield, seemingly confirmed by the engineering officer's experience, meant that not many men wandered around after dark. The situation was not much better in daylight. The CO went on a short drive one afternoon to investigate the possibility of moving to another airfield to the east, closer to the west bank of the Rhine. On the way, American troops standing at the ready in trenches and manning guns in tanks,

warned McGregor not to continue towards Overloon, a few hundred yards on, as it was still in the enemy's hands. McGregor took
another route and met several Dutch farm folk who warned him to
be careful: the roads were still mined. "And, oh yes, they said the
Germans crossed the Rhine every night and raided their farms,
stealing food and silver and anything else they could carry," Monty
recalled. Several days later, McGregor went down the same road but
not as far as before, and was greeted by shells landing dangerously
close to his vehicle. "This time a Tommy poked his head up from a
trench, and told the CO to duck out of sight." McGregor asked the
lad where the Americans had disappeared to and was told they had
pulled out when British troops were reportedly on their way—
except that they had left a bit too early, and the enemy had slipped
in quickly instead. "It was a dangerous stretch of no-man's land
worth avoiding, the CO decided."

Back at Rips, the men were left bewildered and somewhat rattled
by another episode. Two armourers from 411 Squadron, LAC D F
Jardine and LAC E A Maycock (RAF) left the camp in a truck in
search of firewood, and promptly vanished. "No one had a clue as to
what could have possibly happened to them," Monty said, "not until
many weeks later when the CO received a note from the wife of
Maycock saying he and Jardine were prisoners of war in Germany."

Later, when Jardine returned to England after the war, he said
that he and Maycock had travelled only a short distance from the
camp to a crossroad, where an American MP was directing traffic.
"We knew that the Huns often posted their men disguised that way
to misdirect our convoys," Monty allowed. The two erks asked the
MP where the enemy was, he pointed to the right and so they turned
to the left. "Hardly had they gone a few hundred yards when they
heard machine gun fire and saw figures scurrying across the fields
and road in front of them."

"My God," one of the erks blurted, incredulously, "they're Huns!"
They brought their vehicle to an abrupt halt and tried to turn it
around. "Just as they had it halfway around, a piece of shrapnel im-
planted itself in the engine and the vehicle began to smoke. They
jumped out and took cover in the ditch. Within a minute, some

(above) Erks apply stripes to a Spitfire to denote Allied aircraft, on the eve of the Normandy Invasion in June 1944.
DND PL30827

(left) Twenty-two-year-old Flight Lieutenant R I A (Rod) Smith, DFC, at Tangmere on the eve of the Normandy Invasion. The lanky ace from Regina (he stood well over six feet!) shared in the destruction of the first Me 262, the new and dreaded German twin-jet aircraft, over Holland in October 1944.   DND PL29398

Royal Army Engineers lay wire tracking on a road they have just constructed for the first RCAF airfield to become operational in Normandy. These mobile airfields were vital in providing close support to the 2nd British and 1st Canadian armies from Normandy through to Germany. Photo taken on June 16, 1944. DND PL30054

Monty discusses the situation with the local mayor and his wife soon after landing in Normandy. DND PL31071

Lunch outside the mess tent at B4, Beny-sur-mer, Normandy.
KEN PIGEON

Spitfire IXs of 412 Squadron after the wing moved to Normandy. The aircraft in the foreground, VZ-Z, is probably the one in which F/L D C Laubman scored his victories during the air battles over Nijmegen in 1944. DND PL30268

A group of 126 Wing (mostly 411 Squadron) pilots after a hard day's work in August 1944. Back row standing: F/O R M Cook, F/L A F "Sandy" Halcrow, F/L Robert Hyndman. Second row: F/O H A Crawford, F/O George Mercer, F/L Ken Robb, F/O Gord Lapp. On left, kneeling: F/O Max Portz, F/L George "Johnny" Johnson. Sitting: S/L Charlie Trainor, F/O Barney Eskow, F/O Art Tooley. DND PL31347

Flight Lieutenant Arnold "Doc" Jones of Montreal, the wing's senior medical officer, and his companion, a spaniel named "Dinghy," in Normandy. Together they performed incredible feats, a source of great entertainment to Wing personnel. DND PL30979

Monty and pilot briefing before a mission.
MONTY BERGER

Arc de Triomphe, Paris, August 31, 1944. Monty, at left, with Capt. Frank Nobbs, Senior ALO (Army Liaison Officer), attached to the INT/OPS section of 126 Wing throughout the European campaign.

Seated outside the INT/OPS tenders known as the "Siamese Twins." Monty is third from the left.   MONTY BERGER

Two of the wing's "spies," Gord "Pan" Panchuk (left) and Don Stewart, with the situation map shortly after moving to the continent in 1944. Note the comment regarding uniforms immediately in front of "Pan." DND PL46076

A German refreshment van and a three-ton lorry, both captured in Normandy. Back-to-back and camouflaged, they were used to store parachutes, as an orderly room and a dispersal for 411 Squadron at B4, Beny-sur-mer. DND PL30263

Corporal Clare Bowen of Toronto, a motor mechanic, settles in for the night at Beny-sur-mer. Not taking any chances with all the flak, bombs and shell splinters flying about, his trench has a roof made out of two wooden doors and layers of sod. DND PL30078

Hun soldiers arrived and took them prisoner. Then a shell landed close by, set the truck on fire and wounded both of the unfortunate erks, but not seriously."

A scout car drew up and took Jardine and Maycock away. Eventually Jardine ended up in Cologne, where he was taken to a building for interrogation. Outside, a guard said: "Ah, Canadian eh? I used to live in Toronto. I hope to go back there after the war, too." The guard spoke fluent English, which led Jardine to conclude he was put there deliberately in the hope of picking up information. In the interrogation itself, Jardine said he provided only his name, rank and serial number, but was "given an earful by the German interrogating officer, who related what they knew about 126 Wing— which was plenty." Jardine was sent off to a PoW camp populated mainly by captured aircrew officers. The experience was not entirely unpleasant. Jardine had been a school teacher prior to the war, so he organised classes in an effort to keep himself and the men occupied. However, in the ensuing months the Germans started their enforced marches of PoWs. Jardine lost a considerable amount of weight—almost forty pounds—yet he survived. Many others had fallen out by one roadside or another, where they died of exposure, or starvation.

His mysterious disappearance along with Maycock had at least confirmed the wisdom of not venturing outside the camp. For those at Rips, the edict was nonetheless a hardship. Living under canvas was disagreeable in itself; in the circumstances, more than a few of the wing's personnel suggested the airfield might be more suitable for amphibious operations. In no time, B84 was a soggy morass as hundreds of vehicles arrived and were unloaded.

Incredibly, though, operations continued. On October 5th, the day after the wing had settled in at Rips, 401 Squadron was sent out on another patrol over Nijmegen, in the area of a bridge that had been captured two weeks before during the battle for Arnhem. That sorties were mounted was remarkable in itself. That this would be an historic outing as well was truly extraordinary.

In the latter part of September, during the five epic days in which they had accumulated such an impressive number of scores, the

wing's Spitfire pilots had encountered for the first time the Luftwaffe's new Me 262, referred to as "jet-jobs" on the R/T by the controllers at "Kenway," the 83 Group Control Centre. Although
reports of their existence had been received long before that and they
had been chased whenever they were spotted, no one had yet heard
of a Spitfire actually catching one of the enemy's jets. "The 262s had
easily eluded our Spitfire IXBs by using their enormous speed mar-
gin—about 120 mph," said 401's Squadron Leader Rod Smith. "I
do remember, however, reading an intelligence report ... which said
that a 262 had been shot down by ack-ack some time before mid-
September, between Diest and Schaffen in Belgium." Unfortunately,
though, the prize turned out to be worthless. According to Smith,
the Me 262 was "virtually pulverised" when it crashed.

Interest in the enemy's use of jet-propelled aircraft was naturally
high among the wing's pilots. Britain's Gloster Meteor, which combined twin Rolls Royce turbojet engines with four nose-mounted
20mm cannons to provide an impressive weapon, was beset by a
number of technical difficulties, although by July 1944 it was used to
defend England against the enemy's fast-moving V1 flying bombs.
The Me 262, on the other hand, might have easily altered the course
of the war, but for the Luftwaffe's shortsightedness and Hitler's interference. With a top speed of 540 mph, the Me 262 had "complete
superiority" over the Spitfire, observed Wing Commander Johnnie
Johnson, whose few rounds fired at the enemy jet "were more an
angry gesture at our impotence than anything else." German ace
Adolf Galland said he would rather have one Messerschmidt 262
than five Me 109s. "It's like flying on the wings of an angel," he reported to Reichmarschal Göring after a test flight of a prototype in
1943. But Hitler was uninterested in a new defensive fighter aircraft.
He wanted bombers. Later, when the 262 was demonstrated for the
Fuhrer, he asked Willy Messerschmitt: "Can this aircraft carry
bombs?" The aircraft's principal designer replied, with some astonishment, that any aircraft could do so if necessary. "So," cried Hitler,
"here at last is our *blitz* bomber!" With this, the Me 262 was at last
ordered into production, although its potential for giving the Luftwaffe a renewed ascendancy over Europe had been squandered by

Hitler's absurd edict that it be weighed down with bombs. Unexpected difficulties contributed to a further delay in delivering aircraft. By August 1944, only nine 262s were ready for posting to advanced airfields. Several were lost due to faulty servicing and crash landings. There was also the incident recalled by Smith, who claimed one had been shot down by flak in Belgium.

Smith's recollection of an intelligence report concerning enemy jets came later. As the squadron set out shortly before noon on October 5th, the possibility it might actually engage one in combat must have seemed unlikely. Besides, patrols over Nijmegen were fairly routine. Afterwards, however, the pilots of 401 Squadron realised that they had been struck by at least two oddities in their mission. The first was the unusually high altitude at which the squadron was ordered to patrol. Thirteen thousand feet seemed a bit removed from where the action usually occurred. The other peculiar feature they all noticed—they couldn't help it, really—was that the sky had miraculously cleared after several weeks of low ceiling.

Smith remembers all was quiet on their patrol until Kenway called on the R/T and informed the section an aircraft was approaching from the northeast at 13,000 feet. "The squadron was in open battle formation over Nijmegen at that moment, so I turned it northeastwards, took it up another five hundred feet and levelled it off three or four miles northeast of the town. Almost immediately I spotted an aircraft dead ahead of us about five hundred feet below. It was travelling southwest towards Nijmegen, head-on to us, very fast."

Smith, flying as Red 1, immediately reported the sighting to the rest of the squadron, then swung out some distance to starboard to give himself some room to manoeuvre sharply back, all the while intending to pull in close behind the aircraft at a steep angle to its flight path. Several of the other pilots followed.

"I quickly realised it was an Me 262," Smith said afterwards. It was painted green with a yellow decoration on its long snout. Still more exhilarating was the realisation that the aircraft had not yet sighted the Spitfires, which were more or less between it and the sun. "I felt a peculiar thrill," said Smith. Here at last was a "jet-job" that had made a mistake.

Smith started his final swing back to port and around, heading southwest. Approaching the 262 he marvelled at the aircraft's "futuristic" profile, while he pulled into position behind and lined up for a perfect shot, aiming slightly ahead. His right thumb ready to press the trigger on the joystick, Smith was astounded in the next instant when a Spitfire, making a tight left turn like his own, suddenly appeared quite close in front almost in line between his aircraft and the 262. "If I fired I would risk hitting the other Spitfire. For an instant, though, I was tempted to fire a short burst anyway. I felt there was a good chance that if I aimed far enough ahead of the 262 to hit it, my shells would be just far enough ahead of the other Spitfire to miss … at least for the few seconds it would have taken for the other Spitfire and mine to become merged into the 262's path."

Smith resisted the temptation. "Having to pass up that shot was hard to swallow," he said. He was afraid that the 262 might simply carry on "and get clean away without a shot being fired at it."

Smith describes what followed:

However, a second or two after he passed through us the 262 pilot half-rolled into a fairly steep dive, then half-rolled the other way to get himself upright, and began banking and swerving from side to side, all the while keeping in the dive and crossing Nijmegen in a generally southwesterly direction. All of us dived down after him.

The Luftwaffe pilot, realising he had become a target, was attempting to escape. The chase had begun.

Smith was certain that in committing himself to the dive the Luftwaffe pilot had made a fateful second mistake. He knew that the aircraft's rolling would reduce its speed, but he was certain the pilot had also throttled back "quite a bit" as he plunged towards the earth.

"A 262 was very clean and heavy, and therefore would accelerate very quickly with its nose down," he said, "but the Spitfire that had come between it and me … managed to get within range fairly early in the dive."

For several seconds, Smith wondered why the other Spitfire

hadn't yet fired. He was overcome by a burst of impatience and called out over the R/T, "for God's sake—shoot!" Later he admitted it was poor judgement on his part, for at that moment the pilot "was doing his very best contending with the diving and swerving of the 262."

Smith again:

> The Spitfire finally opened fire. Almost immediately two or three cannon strikes appeared on the trailing edge of the 262's wing, right alongside the nacelle of one of its engines. A ... stream of strange-looking grey smoke, more like vapour, began to issue out from where the strikes had been. For a few seconds I thought that the engine might catch fire, but it didn't—at least not then.

Smith recalled that "two or three" other Spitfires somehow managed to close on the 262. Then he and another pilot, Flight Lieutenant R W "Tex" Davenport (an American from Arlington, Virginia), flying Yellow 1, had to pull out at about seven thousand feet because they were in danger of colliding. Smith lost sight of the action briefly, but he knew the other Spitfires in his squadron were still pouring cannon and machine gun fire at the enemy jet. "When I was able to look again I saw that it had pulled out of its dive and was about three thousand feet over the southwestern edge of Nijmegen, still heading southwest." The jet was no longer trailing smoke as it increased its lead over the Spitfires still chasing it.

Smith:

> I thought the action was over and that the 262 had got away with it, but, quite suddenly, it zoomed up into the most sustained vertical climb I had ever seen, leaving far behind it the Spitfires which had followed it all the way down. To my great surprise and elation its climb brought it up to where Tex and I were. As it soared up to us, still climbing almost vertically, the sweep ... of its wings became very noticeable. Its speed, though still very considerable, was beginning to fall off, and with full power on I was able to pull up in an almost vertical position to within about three hundred and fifty yards behind it, the maximum range. I

aimed at one of its engine nacelles and began to fire a burst which lasted about eight seconds, shifting my aim to the other nacelle part way through. I saw strikes around both nacelles and within two or three seconds a plume of fire began to stream from alongside one of them. The 262 was then slowing down more than I was and I was able to close the range to about two hundred yards. I did not know that Tex Davenport was behind me and was also firing!

The pilot of the 262 had made his third mistake that day—his costliest. Both he and Smith tumbled out of their ascent into stall turns to starboard at about the same time. Smith felt as though he was experiencing the episode in slow motion now. The 262 was only about a hundred yards above. He had what he later described as "a remarkable and unhurried look at it, side-on." Most striking was the jet's "shark-like nose, the triangular cross section of its fuselage and its superb cockpit canopy which gave its pilot an all-around view." Surprisingly, though, Smith was unable to see the pilot inside.

His moment of reverie ended as he realised in falling their positions would be reversed. "The 262 would close on my tail, and I would be helpless. And that is what happened. My nose went down to the right and I had no control for quite a few more seconds."

He was also blind to whatever the 262 might do next, "which was probably just as well in the circumstances," he allowed. Later, Tex Davenport insisted the 262 fired at Smith, but no one else could corroborate his claim.

Smith again:

> In any event, after what seemed an age, during which I wondered if cannon shells would come smashing into me from behind, the 262 appeared a few yards away on my right. It was diving almost vertically downwards, as I was, but it was picking up speed more quickly and the plume of fire it was streaming had grown… It plunged on down and crashed within our lines in a field just southwest of Nijmegen, sending up a billowing column of fire and smoke.

Smith immediately called Kenway on the R/T. "We've just shot down a jet-job southwest of Nijmegen!" he blurted.

"I know, we've seen it! Good show!" came the reply. Smith had forgotten that the controllers would have "watched" the action from start to finish on their radar screens.

Back at de Rips, too, everyone was jubilant. Smith said that he and his cohorts "chattered like magpies" as they compared notes. "Throughout the action we had all had the thought in the back of our minds that we might be making air fighting history, that we would be the first fighter pilots in the world to shoot down a jet plane."

For a while, a bulletin issued by 83 Group HQ confirmed their historic claim. Later, though, it was reported USAF fighters flying deep into Germany had shot down at least two already (the accuracy of this claim is not known). No matter. It was 2nd TAF's, 126's and 401 Squadron's first jet-job, and that was good enough.

Several days later, Smith learned that the pilot of the 262 had bailed out of his aircraft before it crashed. His body was found with an unopened parachute. Evidence at the crash site suggested that the pilot, Hauptmann Hans Christian Buttman, was attached to a bomber group. This surprised Smith, who had not noticed any bombs under the aircraft. Nor had any appeared in earlier combat films. Later, though, Smith learned of Hitler's order that the Me 262 be used as a bomber. "This insane decree probably cost poor Buttman his life," he added.

More immediately, Smith also discovered that a barrel from one of the cannons on the 262 had ended up with 127 Wing at Grave. He drove over and asked the CO if he could have it as a trophy for 401 Squadron. The CO graciously agreed to relinquish custody of the prize. Some time later, though, it disappeared.

The wing got off to an early start the next morning, ostensibly patrolling the area northeast of Nijmegen but alert, also, to the possibility of meeting more of the enemy's jet-jobs. First out was 442 Squadron, which shot up a locomotive and claimed one vehicle as a smoker before returning to Rips. The next two patrols were uneventful, although the pilots of 412 sighted a V-2 trail and some rail movement in the Appledorn-Deventer area. A second outing by 442 Squadron ended with several more vehicles shot up. Six trains were sighted as well, but as it was still early in the patrol the squadron saved its fuel and ammunition.

Though the weather remained perfect, three other patrols sighted little or no activity. Then, 442's last patrol of the day found some excitement. Eight kilometres northeast of Nijmegen the squadron's twelve Spitfires scattered a hundred-plus enemy aircraft at high altitude. Two Me 109s and one FW 190 were promptly despatched, and four more were damaged without a loss to 442. Inexplicably, though, the Canadians were bounced several times by unidentified Spitfires, including once in the circuit over Rips! The latter "action" resulted in damage to the Spitfire flown by Flight Lieutenant Stan McLarty, who had claimed one of the 109s shot down over Nijmegen. The episode sparked some outrage, and presented an alarming possibility. Later, during the last patrol of the day by 412 Squadron, several more Spits without identification markings and a darker camouflage than usual were sighted at roughly the same time Kenway reported enemy aircraft in the area.

Mechanical difficulties dogged operations throughout the following day, which saw a number of early returns. High patrols over the Arnhem-Nijmegen area were again the order. Most were uneventful despite the good weather. Eleven aircraft of 442 Squadron left in the mid-afternoon and soon after sighted thirty-plus FW 190s heading west. Three were shot down. It would be the wing's last action for several days, as duff weather set in again. Visibility was reduced to less than two hundred metres on October 9th. A weather recce by 401 Squadron resulted in cancellation of further activity, including scheduled rail interdiction near the battlefront. Sunshine graced the airfield on October 12th and cheered the pilots, who were chafing at their enforced idleness, but the wing was still considered to be non-operational. An airfield construction unit made some progress laying down tracking, enough anyway that 411 Squadron departed on October 13th for a ten-day Air Firing Course at

Warmwell, England. This was a chance for battle-weary pilots to rest, while at the same time sharpening their dive-bombing, strafing and air-to-air gunnery skills in less hostile circumstances.

Bright, crisp weather and a fresh southwesterly wind dried out B84 to some extent. From the air, however, it was still barely recognisable as a landing strip. A RAF pilot whose Typhoon had been disabled by flak thought he was making a wheels-up emergency landing in a field when, instead, he pancaked short of the runway. Miraculously, the pilot was unharmed even though a portion of his aircraft's tail section was completely sheared off after striking a bale of wire tracking.

"Half of the strip was covered in several inches of water, still," said Monty. "Part of it was tracked, but churned up mud and ruts went in every direction. Aircraft taxiing along the perimeter were sinking in up to their hubs. Just standing in their bays, they were sinking."

That day, October 13th, the wing's CO went to 83 Group Headquarters at Eindhoven and delivered an ultimatum. "He said if the aircraft weren't moved immediately, he wouldn't guarantee getting them off the ground before the spring." This failed to produce the result McGregor wanted. He left in a perfect rage, delivering more threats as he went. However, by the time the CO returned to B84 a movement order for the wing's "A" Party had been sent from Group HQ. They were soon on their way to B80, a large airdrome twenty-four kilometres north of Eindhoven, at a village called Volkel.

The rest of the wing followed two days later, on October 15th. "It wasn't much fun at first," Monty insisted, "although anything would have been better than the mudhole of Rips." Two other wings that were already established at B80 made as much room as they could, although everyone slept outside in tents for the first week. Then, with winter approaching, improvised billets at a school in nearby Mille were made available. These, noted the medical section's diarist, were comparatively comfortable and well heated. Electricity and running water were added, but overcrowding remained a problem and many of the wing's personnel still lived under canvas. "The latest competition is to determine whose tent has the most leaks," noted the anonymous author of one entry in the daily Summary of Operations.

"Both officers and airmen, however, are maintained by rumours that prefabricated houses are on their way."

In the meantime, the three squadrons on strength (411 was still at Warmwell) had resumed operations after nearly a week of inactivity, starting off "hammer-and-tong" on a rail interdiction programme. Armed with one 500-lb bomb under the fuselage, one 250-lb bomb under each wing, their cannons and guns, the Spitfires attacked trains and railways at junctions, bridges and embankments to inflict the greatest damage. Priorities were sent down from 2nd TAF, based on requirements worked out with ground units. On the first such outing, the squadrons logged two missions each before lunch. "Not having bombed in three months the pilots were rusty—or completely inexperienced," Monty noted in the wing's Summary of Operations. Nevertheless, he added: "The sensational show of the day went to 442 on its first job." The squadron's pilots had strafed an engine and fifteen rail cars, causing a number of explosions. Later in the day, while returning from another mission, they discovered the train was completely wrecked and still exploding fitfully.

Similar missions were carried out over the next few weeks. In fact, it was the start of a period that Bill Olmsted, now commanding 442 Squadron, felt was one of the most difficult—"and probably most glorious"—in the wing's history.

As if there hadn't been enough "epic days," already.

6

THE 200TH
HUN

THROUGHOUT the latter half of October and into November, conditions at Volkel suggested a medieval warlord's camp. In his orderly officer's report of October 30th, Gord Panchuk observed that the airmen's mess was filthy and that tables had not been scrubbed for some time. Panchuk and an orderly sergeant stayed through a noonday meal, which consisted of stew, potatoes, peas, bread, and raisin pie. "The meal, generally speaking, was good and from all reports was much better than the average," Panchuk stated. Airmen complained anyway of a lack of variety. Stew was the principal item on the menu, day after day. It was often burnt, or—pity anyone who arrived late—cold by the end of each serving. "Nor was there any variety in way it is served or prepared," Panchuk noted. "The airmen would appreciate some seasoning (eg. onions)." They also wanted hot soup at least once a day, and porridge or cereal for breakfast every morning. Panchuk observed as well that seating in the mess was insufficient. Many of the airmen had eaten while standing.

Panchuk returned to the mess at 1800 hours for "tea," which he said consisted of bully beef, beans, cheese, bread, butter and jam. "This seemed to be above-average again. We sampled the food and the tea and found it satisfactory." Shortly after the meal started, however, the lighting failed and so the men ate in the dark, or left. "Lack of sufficient seating capacity and inclement weather was the cause of many airmen taking their food to the living tents," Panchuk said.

Still accompanied by the orderly sergeant, Panchuk inspected the airfield to ensure that blackouts were observed. He found the water tank in the airmen's living quarters had not been filled even though a water bowser passed regularly. Inside, most airmen were stoking improvised fires for heating water, "for which hundred-octane petrol seems to be the chief source of fuel." At the main guard house, he found on the books one defaulter, who was said to be reporting regularly, seven under open arrest (also reporting regularly), one under open arrest at a hospital in Eindhoven, and two under close arrest who were in custody at Brussels. His report concluded with a reference to facilities for recreation, which were minimal, and the spirits of the wing's personnel. Two items seemed to be on the minds of many he had interviewed: the case of LAC Snazel and the sugar, and Sergeant Henry. No further details are available, yet Panchuk ended his report: "It is felt that the two concerned have a marked effect on the morale of the men in general."

In the circumstances, it seems extraordinary that he was not concerned by the possibility of open revolt. Living in tents that were often blown down at night, in flooded conditions (one erk who had snapped a photograph of the airfield added as a caption: "more Coastal Command"), and the monotonous diet added up to considerable hardship. Fortunately, though, the wing's personnel were imbued by a hardy measure of esprit de corps. They were, after all, the top-scoring wing in the 2nd TAF. They were also closer to the front than any other Allied air formation, a fact to which a sign posted outside the campsite proudly testified, "Through these portals pass the fastest mortals."

And, even in non-flying weather, the daily routine of airmen and erks provided sufficient diversion from the dreariness of their existence. Maintenance crews especially had their hands full. Pilots attended briefings or watched the latest cine-gun films, from which they derived equal amounts of entertainment and professional enlightenment. The wing's ALOs and intelligence staff were seldom without something to do. The Duty Intelligence Officer, or DIO, crawled out of his sodden tent before daybreak and, as i/c of the watch, handled all telephone calls, correlated operational flashes from Group HQ, prepared an operational summary for the day, and responded to the many queries that were directed to INT/OPS. The amount of paperwork, or bumph, that entered and left the intelligence section's vans during the course of a normal day was staggering. The staff was overworked and occasionally grew weary of the paperburden. Monty's frustration was exorcised in part by preparing satirical memoranda, which included such phrases as "due consideration and deliberation has been made in the proper high places (no low places being available for the purpose, unfortunately)," and: "Attached herewith is a plan to do away with all plans, for your consideration, deliberation and APPROVAL." One such memo concluded: "Yours on bended knee, etc."

Duff weather also provided an opportunity to ensure that pilots were properly "genned up." Geography quizzes and aircraft recognition tests were common. So-called "welcome talks" were given to new pilots. Monty's instructions were to find out not only the pilot's name but also his nickname, both of which were to be written on a blackboard. "It makes him feel he is operational," Monty explained. The talk started in the office, where the new pilot was introduced to all the other IOs, ALOs and "dead-beat" orderly officers. "Find out where he came from prior to reaching GSU," Monty added, referring to Group Supply Unit, a station where large numbers of pilots and aircraft were kept in readiness to replace squadron losses with a minimum of delay. Pilots were briefed concerning the types of operations in which they would be expected to participate, with an emphasis on armed recces and dive-bombing. They were further briefed on callsigns, codes and R/T discipline. Flak maps, the enemy's disposition and order of battle, and aircraft recognition were also detailed. Methods of escape and evasion in Holland and Germany were discussed. "If by this time he hasn't walked out on you or has managed to refrain from doing you bodily harm or physical injury, blast him with the bombline," Monty declared in his instructions to IOs. He was referring to the vital line maintained just ahead of Allied ground forces. Bombs were to be dropped no less than five miles (eight kilometres) on either side of it. "Serve the guy a cup of 'compo' tea while you are giving him the griff," he added. "It will keep him from falling asleep." Monty concluded: "He'll never forget you as long as he lives, and probably will steer clear of you for the duration of his stay with the wing. If we should some day find you mauled to bits, it's probably the last pilot you 'genned up.'"

Following their session with the INT/OPS staff, new pilots were handed over to the duty ALO, who provided an overview of the military situation. Dal Russel also wanted new pilots to visit Repair and Inspection, Armament, Flying Control, Signals, Accounts, and the Wing Adjutant. They met the Winco Flying at the end of their briefings.

Such procedures for indoctrinating new pilots were called upon with greater regularity that month, owing to a depressing rise in losses to the wing. Early in October, Flight Lieutenant Bouskill of 401 Squadron, who had appeared in so many of the wing's combat reports, was killed during a patrol. Flak encountered during various rail interdiction and dive-bombing missions soon claimed more pilots. The survivors grieved silently for their lost friends or sought vengeance with a determination that bordered on recklessness and occasionally resulted in further losses. No squadron was exempted from tragedy, although for a while it seemed that 442 experienced more than its share. Bill Olmsted recalled leaving Volkel on October 28th for a low-level Rhubarb along the northern edge of the Ruhr— a mission that ended in tragedy. "Rhubarbs were rarely flown, but I felt we might be able to surprise an enemy aircraft or perhaps locate some unusual target," said Olmsted. "At zero feet we skimmed over the woods of Germany, along tree-lined roads, by peaceful farms, and over minute villages without seeing a solitary person. Other than thin wisps of smoke seeping upward from isolated dwellings, there was no sign of life, although we were nearly one hundred miles behind enemy lines."

With Olmsted were Flight Lieutenant W B "Steve" Randall and Flying Officer Jack Lumsden. Both were experienced pilots who had also had their share of close calls. Lumsden, of course, had been fished out of the English Channel once after ditching, while Randall had survived a crash landing in Allied territory when his aircraft was disabled by flak. Randall and Olmsted were friends who had served together in North Africa. "Steve was a very different breed of fighter pilot," recalled Olmsted. "Stocky and well built, with a craggy face usually lit up in a smile, hair which grew straight up, a soft, raspy voice, and a marvellous sense of humour, he loved to play his battered guitar as he sang his own witty compositions. He enjoyed life, loved people, and was easily the most popular man on the squadron." Olmsted remarked that the other pilots preferred Randall's leadership "over that of most of the rest of us," a compliment he said was "richly deserved."

Their inability to find any sign of life during the Rhubarb was puzzling. Eventually, though, they sighted a locomotive below, which they attacked. "Another and yet another came into view and fell to our guns," said Olmsted. Attacking a third train, Randall spotted some aircraft tied down to several flat cars and attacked from less than a hundred feet. "Satisfied with the destruction we had created, we turned away to attack another locomotive. Then Steve reported that his engine temperature was rising alarmingly. I immediately ordered him to head for base with Jack and me acting as escorts. Steve knew he would never make our lines, yet his voice was calm and cool as he talked over the radio." In minutes, a "large white blast of glycol" left Randall's Spitfire, and he announced on the R/T that he had "had it." Olmsted and Lumsden watched as he glided over a wooded area toward Wesel. "Over the R/T came his last message in an unperturbed voice. 'Thanks a lot, Bill. I'll be seeing you. So long, fellas.'" Randall bailed out. "Tears came to my eyes as I watched him float earthward. Then sorrow changed to anger and I was ready to do almost anything to avenge the loss of my friend, my ablest flight commander, and one of the best-liked men in the wing." Olmsted said he was "deeply touched" by Randall's calmness and perfect procedure on the R/T.

Yet:

In a queer sort of way, Steve had actually shot himself down. The coolant radiators on the Spit were large air scoops located on the underside of the fuselage, positioned to allow our speed to force cooling air through the light grillwork. During a strafing attack bullets could strike a hard surface in such a manner that the bullet fragments ricochetted in random directions, often colliding with our fast-moving aircraft. When the vulnerable glycol cooling radiator was struck, the liquid coolant poured out, usually in the form of white smoke, and a Spitfire so damaged could not stay aloft for long. The flying time left an aircraft depended on the size of the hole in the radiator, but when the coolant was gone, the engine ceased to function and generally burst into flames from overheating.

The wing's Summary of Operations that day agreed with Olmsted's assessment concerning the cause of his friend's mishap. "F/L Randall was hit either by flak *or his own fire* [italics added] and was forced to bail out near DARSTEN," read the official version. Randall had escaped his aircraft before it exploded, but his luck had run out anyway, "doubly so, as we learned later," added Olmsted, "for the Germans were waiting in the woods and denied him any opportunity to escape."

That same day, Flying Officer Costello of 442 Squadron—another of Olmsted's friends—bailed out after his aircraft was hit by flak north of Haltern, in Germany. He landed safely by parachute and was last seen running into a small wooded area. Losses were mounting. Earlier in the month, Flying Officer G G (Glen) Millar, originally from Winnipeg, was killed by ground troops while descending by parachute. "Nearly everyone was hit by flak," Olmsted recorded. His own logbook noted that by the end of October he had gone through seven Spitfires in as many weeks. None was destroyed, but they were damaged seriously enough that "in each case a replacement was required."

The most recent incident in which Olmsted had encountered some "tough luck" had occurred on October 29th, the day after Randall was lost. "I was leading the squadron to dive-bomb a large railway bridge on the southern fringe of Münster," he recalled. It was his second outing of the day. "As I peeled off the target in a gradual turn to port, I saw a string of large tractor-trailer trucks proceeding south on the auto-bahn paralleling the Dortmund-Emms Canal. I decided to attack."

In *Blue Skies*, Olmsted described how everything came apart for him:

> My rule had been that after each bombing attack, all aircraft should be checked for bomb hangups before further action was considered. I broke my own rule, this time unaware that the 500-pound belly bomb had not released. Our bomb racks were originally designed for bombs to be dropped from level flight, and since nothing else was available, we had to use them for dive-bombing. In a dive speed of 450 mph, the force exerted by speed and pressure on the rack was often too strong for the electrical system and the release hook would fail to open. Hangups or the bomb's failing to drop would result. This happened to me. I failed to notice the weight since my speed and a good pullout, combined with a turn without skidding or slipping, fooled me into thinking the aircraft was bomb-free.

Olmsted attacked the first truck, opening fire a few hundred metres from his target while diving. "The vibration of my guns shook the bomb free, so that it struck the truck when I was less than fifty feet above the vehicle. It blew the truck to smithereens, knocked me unconscious, and blasted my aircraft several hundred feet upward. My Spit slowly rolled onto its back, and when I regained consciousness two or three seconds later, I was heading for the ground upside down."

Too dazed to think, Olmsted instinctively yanked the control column hard, which righted his aircraft in the nick of time and pulled him out of the dive at treetop level. He wondered if he should bail out or attempt to return to Volkel, then realised he had little choice: the canopy was jammed shut. He set course for Volkel while surveying the damage to his Spitfire. It was dramatic, to say the least.

Olmsted:

> Both wings were badly buckled from the force of the explosion and had been blown or bent upward an extra foot and a half.

Every panel in the aircraft had been blown off, with the ground clearly visible through great empty holes in the wings. Pieces of brown canvas from the covering protecting the truck cargo were streaming from the jagged metal pieces of my aircraft, and the fuselage was buckled and twisted while the tail unit fluttered and vibrated, threatening to break off. Both ailerons were sticking almost straight up in the air. While I was consciously recovering from the dive, Providence had made me move the control column the only way it would work. The cockpit had been badly stove in and none of the cockpit instruments read correctly... Some of the control cables had been completely severed; there was no elevator control, and the rudder remained the only control which worked normally. It took both my hands, one foot, and all my strength on the control column just to prolong what little flying capability remained.

Olmsted said that from Münster to safety was roughly a hundred and sixty kilometres. He staggered along at 140 mph until miraculously he made it back to Volkel. There, however, he was presented with the potential hazards of landing his stricken aircraft. He tried once again to free the canopy, and was able to get it unstuck so that it blew away. He was considering how best to exit the aircraft when the engine "apparently ran out of oil" and began making noises "indicating that it might blow up at any moment." His situation became truly desperate when the Spitfire entered into a steep dive. Olmsted pushed himself out the small doorway and to his horror found himself stuck to the side of the aircraft. Eventually, though, the increasing wind pressure ripped him loose, and after dropping several thousand feet he pulled the cord on his parachute. "I was completely drained," he wrote afterwards. "I watched with no emotion as my aircraft crashed in a tiny Dutch field, but later I would thank that remarkable aircraft for lasting long enough to bring me safely home."

Within a few days of his return, Olmsted claimed he began to feel "quite strongly" that his incredible good luck was starting to run out. "In over 490 operational hours I had never been nicked by a bullet fired from an enemy aircraft, and my kites had received relatively few flak hits until recently. Now my aircraft were being hit on nearly every sortie."

The same day Olmsted had his closest brush with disaster, Flying Officer T F "Dutch" Kinsler of 411 Squadron was lost. He had reported his aircraft was on fire after attacking a train, and was not seen afterwards. Such losses were hard enough for the wing, but at the same time a number of the more experienced pilots were being posted as "tour expired." Said Olmsted: "We were like a football team which had been deprived of a dozen of its first-string players."

Fortunately, a number of experienced pilots had arrived at Volkel to bolster the wing's dwindling roster. Among the new faces assigned to 442 were Flight Lieutenant N A Keene, DFC, and Flight Lieutenant M E (Milton) Jowsey, DFC of Ottawa. Jowsey had flown in North Africa. Both pilots contributed early to the wing's scoreboard of enemy aircraft destroyed, in addition to showing their skills during armed recces and rail interdiction sorties. They arrived just as the poor weather had prompted the wing to send out flights of four, and sometimes six aircraft. It was felt such groups were more manageable in the prevailing circumstances and yet, as Olmsted noted, "sufficiently strong to combat successfully any enemy fighters [that] might be encountered." Left unsaid was that pilots sent out in such small groups needed to be battle-hardened. "Our days were long, starting with the predawn armed weather recce and ending with a late show at dusk," Olmsted added. "Each trip tried the nerves of the pilots as they had never been tried before, taking on a danger and grimness that had been unknown in the past."

Nevertheless, Olmsted insisted:

It was at Volkel that the true temperament and grim determination of the pilots was revealed. Flying an aircraft that was never built for dive-bombing, an aircraft that would stand very little punishment from flak, attacking the most heavily defended targets in the world, operating under the worst possible weather conditions, but displaying an inexpressible keenness and a desire to do a successful job, they never failed to earn frequent commendations from Air Vice-Marshal Harry Broadhurst, Air Chief Marshal Sir Arthur Tedder, and other Allied commanders… Daily [the wing] recorded more motor transport demolished, and more locomotives and railway cars destroyed and damaged than any other [in 2nd TAF]. Anything that walked or moved in Germany was a target for our guns and did not escape our eyes or our aim. Wherever we went, wherever we attacked, death and destruction to the enemy always resulted.

The facts support Olmsted's proud tribute to the wing. Indeed, the only rest they gave the enemy occurred when flying conditions kept the wing's aircraft grounded.

The month ended with more duff weather. However, as the wing's Summary of Operations concluded: "The slack period was a welcome respite to the hardpressed groundcrew who had put forward an all-out effort the previous two days to keep the new four-man bombing shows on the production line."

Persistently bad weather was the outstanding feature of November, as well. Conditions were seldom cut-and-dried, however; invariably, a promised change meant pilots remained in a state of constant readiness, awaiting either the order to take off or to stand down. In the course of several modest operations on November 1st (only eighteen sorties were mounted, due to weather conditions), the squadron's new pilots were at least given a bird's eye view of the battlefront. The next day saw some improvement over the airfield at Volkel, but cloud covered many of the target areas. On November 2nd, during the final outing of the day by 442 Squadron, Flight Lieutenant Jowsey and Flying Officer J P W Francis each bagged a FW 190 after successfully attacking a rail junction near Winterswijk, in Holland. The score by Francis, a native of Battleford, Saskatchewan, made his first operational sortie a real triumph.

November 4th saw more action. Fair weather in the morning allowed 411 to get away early on its divebombing assignments. The squadron's first target was a road-rail crossover and bridge about thirteen kilometres west of Wesel. A section led by Flight Lieutenant Crawford needed only thirty-seven minutes to deliver its bombs and cut the railway. Flight Lieutenant Portz's section logged forty-five minutes while scoring another direct hit and two probables on a fly-over east of Bocholt (confirmation that the railway was cut followed later in the day). Flight Lieutenant K I Robb, leading a third section, spent less than half an hour dive-bombing an ammunition dump east of Barnveld in Holland. "They could not locate the target due to 10/10 cloud, so they pranged a railway running into Ede," the Summary of Operations noted. Four aircraft led by Flight Lieutenant Mercer went after another ammo dump near Hilversum, but again the target was obscured. So they bombed a railway leading into Utrecht, scoring three direct hits on a marshalling yard. Throughout the day, each section returned to Volkel to refuel and rearm, then took off again for similar targets.

Elsewhere, the pilots of 442 Squadron had lived up to their reputation as the wing's leading "train busters." Flight Lieutenant Jowsey had led his section to a flyover south of Coesfeld, where they caused considerable destruction. "The next show was the one that produced long-hoped-for results," the Summary of Operations noted. This was led by Bill Olmsted, whose section had cut the flyover at Dulmen and had blasted a marshalling yard at Münster. In his memoirs, Olmsted recalled attacking a locomotive with Flying Officer F B "Frosty" Young:

> I had attacked first, my cannon shells causing great clouds of steam to erupt from the boiler. Frosty, eager and confident, was immediately behind me. He gave a long, accurate burst with every bullet striking telling blows to the engine. Even from a few hundred feet away, I could see a massive fire building beneath the boiler and shouted a warning to Frosty over the R/T, but I was too late. Just as he was over the engine, it exploded in a cloud of flying debris, carrying his aircraft five hundred feet up in the air as if it had been a feather. The Spit immediately began to pour black and white smoke as a long, wicked-looking flame sprouted from the engine cowling. The plane slowly started nosing toward the ground. I yelled frantically over the R/T, "Frosty, Frosty, get the hell out. Hurry. Hurry."

Somehow, Young got out of his aircraft but at a dangerously low altitude. He came down hard in the midst of an enemy anti-aircraft battery defending the marshalling yard. His stricken Spitfire crashed, according to Olmsted, within thirty metres of where he landed. Olmsted was naturally concerned for his friend, first of all wondering if he had survived (he did), and if so what sort of treatment he might receive, having landed so close to the battery of enemy gunners. "Later we discovered that the gunners had beaten him severely," Olmsted wrote. "He was one of the finest pilots in the squadron, a marvellous shot, and always keen to engage the enemy, regardless of the danger or the odds."

Several days later, on November 7th, Flying Officer Curtis was killed during a dive-bombing operation—yet another blow to 442 Squadron and its leader, Bill Olmsted. He noted that Young, Costello, Millar and Curtis had been close friends, having joined the RCAF at the same time. They had been with the squadron from its inception. Now only Olmsted and Flight Lieutenant Stan McLarty remained from 442's original roll.

Of course, bad luck did not belong exclusively to the pilots of 442 "Caribou" Squadron. Following a period of four days that saw little activity due to bad weather, the Rams and Bears (401 and 411) took off on the afternoon of November 16th. Poor visibility limited ground attacks by 401 at Geldern and Wesel, but 411 found its target area near Venlo. A second section led by Flight Lieutenant Mercer attacked a rail flyover at Winterswijk, with inconclusive results, before moving on to the area of Borken. There, accurate light flak hit Mercer's aircraft and he was forced to bail out over enemy territory. By day's end he was still listed as "not yet returned."

Heavy rain prevented sustained operations for the next two days. To everyone's astonishment, the morning of November 19th dawned sunny and clear for a change (a miracle that was attributed, in typical Canadian fashion, to the arrival overnight of a chinook). "The first hard day of work in over a week was good for morale all round," the Summary of Operations noted, adding that the loss of four pilots from 412 Squadron had put a "serious damper" on the programme. Flying Officer Bellingham was lost during an attack on the rail lines at Geldern. The other casualties were from another section led by Flight Lieutenant Phil Charron. It had just finished bombing a railway bridge near Veen and was forming up to start an armed recce when Pilot Officer H W Cowan spotted forty-plus FW 190s. Intrepid as ever, Charron was heard to call on the R/T, "Let's get into the bastards!" Cowan was hit early in the dogfight but returned to Volkel. Charron and the others, Flying Officer Johnston and Warrant Officer Comeau, were much less fortunate. They were missing after the action.

"Charron was a fine fellow and as keen as anyone," Monty said afterwards. "His career had been meteoric in the past two months, likely too much so because he threw caution to the wind, and you can't afford to do that in any game."

Tragedy found ways to claim men on the ground, too. On November 20th, a Spitfire from another wing, its engine having quit after take-off, tried to land at Volkel but was thrown off course by a gust of wind. The aircraft slammed into one of 401's Spitfires waiting to take off on a weather recce, injuring its pilot and killing LAC Joe Butler, a mechanic who was standing nearby. Butler, who was one of the wing's "old timers," had recently learned he was being repatriated after three years overseas with the RCAF. He was buried at Volkel instead.

Fair weather greeted the pilots and groundcrew on the morning of November 21st, although the southern portion of the wing's target areas were obscured by cloud. Targets farther north were found, and a full programme of rail interdiction was planned. Late in the day, a new tactic was adopted, as squadrons started operating in formations of eight. "One foursome bombs while the other covers, and then the fours reverse for the second target," Monty explained. The purpose of this was to provide "additional security against the large gaggles of Huns" that were appearing more often over the battlefront in Holland, and in Germany itself.

Enemy aircraft were certainly present in the skies that morning. This was unusual—which explained November's score of only two destroyed—as well as fateful. For Monty especially, the day would provide more headaches than he could imagine, as he was called upon to determine which pilot had achieved the distinction of shooting down the two hundredth Hun since the wing's formation.

A section of 411 Squadron started the day's operations, with Pilot Officer Kerr leading four aircraft to dive-bomb an ammunition dump in a wooded area near Rheinburg. A direct hit on a building in the woods erupted into flames billowing clouds of red and white smoke. The section continued on a weather recce in the Wesel-Kempen-Erkelenz area, and reported good conditions particularly in the northern area. Armed with this information, in addition to the usual complement of bombs strapped to their Spitfires, a second section led by Flight Lieutenant Crawford left Volkel at 0910 to attack a rail junction at Xanten. Instead, they intercepted a formation of FW 190s, which they promptly engaged.

Later, in an attempt to settle the dispute concerning which pilot rightfully claimed the two hundredth enemy aircraft, Monty procured the morning's R/T log from Group Control. But even with the transcript, it was impossible to determine who had shot down the 200th Hun (it was difficult enough deciding the order in which pilots had spoken). The spotlight fell on Monty, who was charged with making the call.

"The R/T log, and a good thrash between the pilots concerned, only proved that the times of combat were closer than anyone had thought likely," said Monty, "with 401 attacking the last of the twenty-plus FW 190s from behind just about the same time as Flight Lieutenant Crawford of 411 made a head-on attack on the first of the same bunch." The section belonging to 401 Squadron was led by Flying Officer D F Husband. Accompanied by Flight Lieutenant W C ("Bud") Connell, Flying Officer K Gallinger and Flight Lieutenant F R Sheehy, they had set out to dive-bomb a railway near Rheydt. The target was obscured and so the section made for Wesel. En route, they came upon as many as twenty-four FW 190s and attacked—incredibly, at the same time that 411 was engaging the same gaggle of enemy aircraft from a different angle. "Worse," said Monty, "F/L Sheehy and F/L Connell of 401 were chagrined to find that the FW 190 they each 'shot down in flames' was one and the same. Fortunately these situations arise only rarely—but it would be the 200th Hun!"

No decision! By day's end all that was certain was that the pilots had destroyed two FW 190s (and damaged two more).

"The CO, Group Captain McGregor, to keep peace in the family, generously offered a duplicate trophy to the one put up by INT/OPS so that each squadron's history-making score would be rewarded," Monty finally allowed. "We wiggled out of that pretty craftily, I must admit."

Still, the battle over the honour had "waxed pretty hot and heavy" while it was on. "And I bet the pilots in each squadron would still be ready to argue it even now at the drop of a hat," Monty concluded.

Unrelated to the controversy concerning the 200th Hun was another R/T transcript that Monty preserved in his personal files. Its value was the clarity with which it illustrated that almost every mission was crammed with some measure of excitement, suspense and danger. Those on the ground could experience, however vicariously, the wing's progress in the clouds by listening to the far-off chatter of pilots on their open-channel R/T, as well as admire the coolness they exercised in the midst of life-and-death situations.

"A good leader with a clear and steady voice never sounds excited even if he's in the middle of shooting *three* Huns down," Monty explained. "Of course, he's not likely to be saying anything at all during an actual combat. He's too busy with other things. But if he knows the form and has a slow, calm, steady voice, he can be a great influence in steadying his whole formation. That can make a big difference in the results of a combat." Monty said that Bill Klersy and Don Laubman were among the pilots he remembered best for their poise on the R/T. "Bill's low, slow drawl was often comical and always confident—regardless of the situation, regardless of the odds. Soft-spoken Freddie Murray of 412 Squadron and later a flight commander of 401, was a completely different person in the air. He had a strong, firm, precise voice and made a superb leader, but he was always very unassuming on the ground. Winco Dal Russel had pretty much the same calm, quiet tone in the air as on the ground and was likely the most easily recognised when heard on the R/T."

To conceal identities, units operated with callsigns. In the transcript Monty saved, 401 is referred to as "Blackout," Flying Control is "Pinkface," while Group Control is "Kenway." The mission begins at 1536 hours, when Blackout Leader (Red 1) asks and receives permission from Pinkface to scramble. In a matter of seconds the squadron is airborne and vanishing towards the horizon.

At 1539 Blackout Leader informs Kenway that the squadron is on course. Kenway acknowledges, "Roger." For ten minutes the pilots are silent as they head for their target. Then at 1549 Blackout Leader breaks in with a sharp warning to beware of flak. They are approaching a heavily defended area. "Forty-five degrees to port," he instructs his squadron mates.

Barely a minute passes when Red 3 calls his leader. "Aircraft four o'clock below."

"Yes, I see them," Blackout Leader responds. "They're only Typhoons." Moments later Yellow 3 calls with a report of six aircraft at nine o'clock below. Again, Blackout Leader informs everyone they are friendly.

For several minutes more the R/T crackles with numerous reports of Typhoons, Spitfires, Mustangs and Thunderbolts, all cruising around over enemy-held territory. Then, at precisely 1600 hours, comes the first spot of real excitement.

Blackout Yellow 3: "Hello Red 1. There's some transport down there on that little road."

Red 1: "I don't see it. Where?"

Yellow 3: "On that small road at 9 o'clock running west to east."

Red 1: "Oh, yes, I get you. There's about six trucks going from west to east."

Yellow 3: "Yep, that's it."

Red 1: "Hello Yellow 1, do you see those trucks?"

Yellow 1: "Yes, Boss."

Red 1: "Okay, take your section down and get them. Red and Blue sections stay up as cover. Watch the flak."

There is a moment of radio silence, during which the Spitfires dive on their targets. Those at the airfield can only imagine the scene while they await word of its outcome.

Red 1: "Nice going, Yellow Section. There's three trucks smoking beautifully. Like to have a go at the others, Blue Section?"

Blue 1: "Sure thing!"

Red 1: "Okay, down you go. Yellow Section, reform and give cover."

More silence. Far away the Spitfires of Blue Section are attacking. Four pilots are lining up ground targets in their sights, and firing through a barrage of enemy flak. It is over in seconds.

Red 1: "Okay, Blue Section. Form up."

Red 4: "There's one bastard still not hit. Can I have a go?"

Red 1: "No, he's not worth the trouble. Let's form up and get going."

Red 3: "There are two more trucks down there on that other road, Boss. How about it?"

Red 1: "Yes, I see them. Go down and have a go. Take Red 4 with you."

This time the silence is interrupted by an urgent call.

Red 3: "Hold your fire, Red 4. They're ambulances."

Red 4: "Roger."

Red 1: "Okay, Red 3, rejoin formation and let's get going. Blackout Squadron, ninety degrees port." Then Blackout Leader calls Group Control for information concerning any bogies that might be showing on radar.

Red 1: "Hello, Kenway, have you got anything for me?"

Kenway: "No, Blackout, nothing definite at the moment. I'll call you later."

Red 1: "Roger, out."

Blue 1: "Hello, Blackout Leader. There's five or six enemy vehicles drawn up under those trees at seven o'clock below."

Red 1: "I don't see them."

Blue 1: "They look like ammo trucks. Can I have a go?"

Red 1: "Go ahead, Blue Section. Red and Yellow give cover. Watch out for flak."

The four Spitfires of Blue Section dive on the wooded area, which soon erupts in a brilliant explosion.

Red 1: "Nice going Blue Leader. You got two of them."

Blue 4: "What a hell of a bang!"

Blue 3: "Yes, I felt the force of it as I was pulling out."

Blue 4: "It sure went up!"

Red 1: "Stop nattering, Blue Section. Red Section, follow me down on the others. Blue and Yellow, give cover. Watch the flak, Red Section."

Blackout Leader is about to attack when he is called by Group Control, reporting a dozen or more enemy aircraft in the area.

Red 1: "Where are they, Kenway? And what height?"

Kenway: "I haven't much gen. I suggest that you vector 075 for three minutes at Angel 15."

Red 1: "Roger, Kenway. Get together, Blackout. Vector 075, Ang 15."

For three minutes there is silence while the Spitfires go off in pursuit. Listening to the R/T, an erk remarks the Canadian pilots are like "hounds after a fox."

Kenway: "Hello, Blackout. Huns are now reported SSW of you at Angels 20. Suggest you climb and steer 200. The Huns are in some strength."

Red 1: "Thank you, Kenway. 200, Blackout. Climb to 20,000. Keep your eyes skinned."

Blue 1: "Aircraft nine o'clock same level."

Red 1: "I think they're Mustangs but watch them."

Kenway: "Hello, Blackout. The Huns are only a mile or two away from you now. They are in considerable strength, so keep your eyes open."

Red 1: "Thanks, Kenway. Are they still at Angels 20?"

Kenway: "Yes, about that. They should be approaching you from the starboard."

Red 1: "Thank you, Kenway. Okay Blackout, level out at 20,000 and keep a sharp look-out."

Yellow 3: "There are some kites coming out of that cloud at two o'clock a thousand feet below."

Red 1: "Yes, they're Huns! Get into the bastards!"

Blue 1: "There's about thirty of them! FW 190s and Me 109s!"

Red 1: "Yep, get into 'em!"

Kenway: "Hello Blackout, some friends are on their way to assist."

There is no reply. For most of four minutes, the R/T is silent. Then at 1622 the suspense is broken by a yell from one pilot to another: "Watch out, Bill, there's a bastard on your tail!" The enemy aircraft is shaken. A sudden resumption of chatter among the pilots indicates the dogfight has ended.

Red 1: "Okay, Blackout, reform below this layer of cloud. The Hun seems to have beaten it."

Blue 3: "Hello Blue 1, I am flying alongside you."

Blue 1: "Okay, let's get down through this stuff."

Blue 2: "How did you do, Blue 1?"

Blue 1: "I got two FWs. How did *you* do?"

Blue 2: "I got one 109."

Red 1: "Shut up, Blackout. Reform below cloud."

Yellow 4: "Hello Yellow 1. Where are you?"

Yellow 1: "Below cloud, waiting for you."

Yellow 4: "Okay, coming down. I got one of the bastards."

Red 1: "Stop nattering, Blackout! This isn't the *Daily Bulletin.* Join up below cloud. Hello Blue Leader, are you okay?"

Blue 1: "I can't find Blue 4."

Blue 4: "I'm here, Boss. In Yellow Section."

Blue 1: "Roger."

Red 1: "Are you okay, Yellow Leader?"

Yellow 1: "Yellow 2 went down, Boss."

Red 1: "Did you see him?"

Yellow 1: "Yes, he went down in flames."

Red 1: "Did he bail out?"

Yellow 1: "No, Boss."

There is a pause while this information is painfully absorbed. Those listening at the airfield now know as well that one of the wing's pilots will not be coming back.

Red 1: "Okay, form up and let's get out of here. Anybody with less than twenty gallons left?"

Yellow 4: "I've got just twenty."

Red 1: "That's enough. I guess we had better get a homing. Hello Pinkface, can you give me a vector?"

Pinkface: "Hello Blackout Leader, steer 255."

Red 1: "Roger."

There is a bit more excitement on the return leg, when one of the squadron's pilots reports his engine has cut and he might have to "hit the silk." Blackout Leader persuades the pilot to coax whatever he can out of his aircraft so he can land at another airfield nearby. The pilot makes it down safely. The rest of Ram Squadron returns home, now reduced to ten from the dozen that started the patrol.*

Heavy rain and cloud grounded the wing with its scoreboard still showing 200 enemy aircraft destroyed. There was plenty of opportunity to revive the dispute during the day. Meanwhile, another significant milestone was observed. "Today the 500th job was turned out by R&I since the wing landed in France," Monty recorded in the daily Summary of Operations for November 22nd. "The total is made up of 30 engine changes, 328 inspections, and 142 minor repairs. The event was celebrated a little ahead of time by a party—*sans femmes*—where the men let their hair down and told each and every one what they thought."

Two more days of duff weather followed. On the 25th, only six sorties were mounted by 401 and 411. Each claimed a locomotive destroyed at Venlo and Winterswijk respectively. In the latter action, Flying Officer L G D (Ping) Pow was killed while crash landing after his aircraft was hit by ground fire from a flak car. Then, on the 26th, sunshine and clear skies gave the "ground-weary pilots a chance to get up into the blue" in earnest again. The wing's squadrons—including 442, which had just returned from a gunnery course at Warmwell— logged a full day of operations. Rail cuts amounted to seven certain and three probable, in addition to several more locomotives, vehicles

---

*The action cited above likely occurred sometime in the autumn of 1944.

and a number of barges that were claimed as destroyed. Following the
last show of the day by 412 Squadron, Flying Officer Murray spotted
several FW 190s which he had initially mistaken for American aircraft. Their markings included a roundel but, on closer inspection,
also a black cross instead of the familiar white star. Murray singled
out one of the enemy fighters and attacked. His victim was last seen
going down in smoke and flames, and was subsequently credited as
destroyed—only the fifth for the wing in November, alongside two
on the scoreboard listed as damaged. But this was as nothing compared to the devastation wrought on the ground. Sixty-two rail cuts.
Six locomotives destroyed, twenty-seven damaged. More than a hundred vehicles left as flamers or smokers. An unknown number of
troops, killed. Incredibly, too, the wing's Spitfires had mounted sorties virtually every day of the month, in spite of the appalling weather
and the washed-out conditions at B80. Millions of rounds of ammunition were spent, at least two thousand bombs were dropped.

On December 1st, the wing's diarist again lamented the foul climate
that plagued operations at Volkel. Only one mission was carried out
that day—a weather recce by four aircraft of 412 Squadron. It reported the obvious, which was subsequently described in the Summary of Operations as "entirely unsuitable for air operations." In the
usual postscript where daily results were listed, the diarist laconically
stated: "no hits, no runs, no errors."

Come to think of it, the weather was too lousy even for baseball.

The next day offered more of the same. "An early mission by six
aircraft of 411 squadron showed that the weather over enemy territory was not only bad, but dangerous." The pilots had to unload their
bombs south of Goch, without any observed results, and return to
Volkel at low altitude: ice began forming on the wings of their aircraft at only three thousand feet. En route, they dodged accurate
light flak from the enemy. "The section was so incensed by the flak
that it strafed positions east of the Maas River near Boxmeer," noted
Monty. Successful operations were finally logged on the 3rd. The
wing's total for the day—in just a morning of operations—was two

good railway cuts, one on the line near Viersen, which was scored by 412 Squadron, and another by 442's pilots south of a junction near Coesfeld. Five locomotives were damaged and a barge destroyed. To add to the day's total, Squadron Leader E G Lapp and Flight Lieutenant E T Gardner of 411 Squadron together shot down a FW 190 over Venlo. However, any exhilaration the men might have felt was shortlived. High winds accompanied by rain and hail swept across the battlefront. The next day, too, the wing "fought the weather valiantly … and succeeded just sufficiently to justify the effort," noted the ORB. For many of the groundcrew, their work consisted of putting up tents that had blown down during the previous night's icy gale. Talk of comfortable billets elsewhere provided a release from the dreariness of living at Volkel.

For several weeks rumours had suggested the wing would be moving soon to an airfield that was being constructed at another Dutch village. On December 2nd, an advance party had moved to the new site, known as B88. It was far from completion yet, and as muddy as Volkel after the recent storms. But the promise of permanent quarters, if nothing else, was welcomed rapturously by the wing's personnel.

Eight more railway cuts were accomplished on the 4th, mainly in the Bocholt-Borken area. In addition, one locomotive was destroyed. Several other ground targets were strafed to complete the wing's outing. An early start the next morning paid handsome dividends. Twenty-seven rail cuts, two locomotives destroyed and one damaged, as well as numerous vehicles. Flight Lieutenant Banks shot down two Me 109s, while Flying Officer Murray scored two destroyed and one probable. In this same operation, Pilot Officer C W H Glithero crash landed—evidently without injury. He reported on the R/T after he had landed, in Allied territory, but by day's end his whereabouts remained unknown.

In the Summary of Operations, it was reported that Wing Commander Russel had landed at the new airfield and subsequently declared it fit for operations. "Living accommodations are far from what they should be," the wing's diarist complained, "considering the time that has been available for preparation." He added: "All ranks are heaving great sighs of relief to know that at last they are moving into buildings and can shrug off that bent-over posture acquired from working and living in tents."

Throughout the day, aircraft left Volkel for B88. There, the pilots competed with groundcrew and other personnel eagerly setting up their new digs, while scrounging—as usual—for whatever they lacked. No one seemed to mind that the weather had turned nasty again: a "duff day" was just what most wanted. "Ground crews were perking up a bit with a real roof over their heads and a proper floor underfoot. Conditions were better than many had expected. And how that wind howled last night to remind us."

Harking back to their proud days in Normandy after D-Day, when their unofficial motto at Beny-sur-mer was *"B4 is Never B-hind,"* the wing's personnel grudgingly adopted the slogan, *"Better late at B88 (than Volkel at all!)."*

7

DECEMBER

I N THE AUTUMN of 1989, while excavating for the construction of an industrial park in the Dutch village of Nistelrode,
near Kleinwijk, local contractors unexpectedly came upon a
large cache of ammunition and explosives. These were obviously of
Second World War vintage. It was even likely the site had been part
of the advanced Allied airfield at Nistelrode that was occupied, in
the winter of 1944/45, by hundreds of Canadian pilots and their
groundcrews. The area was known for various artifacts cropping up
occasionally, attesting to their presence. It was still possible, while
cycling along the shady lanes surrounding Nistelrode, to find a gate
or dunghill embellished with a strip of PSP, the material used to
construct wartime runways. In exceptional cases, a goat or calf
might be seen tethered to a curled peg that had once cramped the
steel plating in the ground.

But finding explosives was unusual. The discovery led to further
research by members of a historical society active in the community,
and, based on the many hitherto unknown details that were uncovered, an exhibition was planned to honour the Canadians who
served at the airfield they called B88. It would coincide with celebrations marking the village's seventh centenary in 1991. On behalf of
the local population, Nistelrode's municipal council named a new

road, located on part of the old landing strip, *Canadabaan*—
"Canada Way"—as a further tribute. In doing so, the people of this
Dutch village also corrected a misunderstanding concerning the location of the airfield. It had always been referred to as Heesch, which
was the name of another village nearby. An unfamiliarity with the
area's ragged municipal borders may have been responsible for the
confusion. "It is also possible that Heesch was chosen because it can
be pronounced more easily in English," ventured Harrie van
Grinsven, a researcher with the Dutch historical association that
sponsored the 1991 exhibition in Nistelrode. He's probably right.

Plans to build a number of forward airfields in Holland were hastily
adjusted following the Allied debacle at Arnhem in September,
1944. Instead of moving north of the river Maas and part of the
Waal, two sites were selected to the south. The new airfields would
be B86, at Helmond, and B88. Each would accommodate one wing.

By the end of September, a stores park was established at the
Heesch/Nistelrode location. The following month, as many as 2,000
refugees from fighting around Nijmegen moved into barracks that
had previously belonged to conscripted Dutch labourers. They were
relocated when the British 16 Airfield Construction Group moved in
and started work on the airfield on October 18th. The site was levelled and (so they thought) properly drained. Six to nine inches of
sand were brought in to form a base for the 30,000 sheets of PSP required to lay a runway 36 metres wide by 1,000 long. A crash strip
adjacent to the runway was graded. Dispersals were covered with
more PSP and protected by unfused bombs. Paved connecting roads,
workshops for repairs, and other buildings—including a small hospital, a cinema, fire station, post office, and military police post—were
eventually added. Existing buildings were repaired, Nissen huts were
erected, and new barracks were built. Searchlights were used at night
so that engineers and local contractors could continue their work.

By the end of November, the airfield was virtually ready for occu-
pancy. In the final stages of construction, only the sails of an old
windmill situated at the south of the runway needed to be removed

so as to clear a flight path. Military officials at Nistelrode were chagrined after their order to remove the sails from "Johnker's windmill" was interpreted more widely than expected. The local millers were all closely related: many, in fact, had the same surname. As a result, more sails in the district were dismantled than was intended.

The arrival of almost eleven hundred Canadians with 126 Wing in the first week of December completed the transformation of Nistelrode.

They were greeted by a steady rain. On December 7th, Wing Commander Russel logged the only flight of the day—"a short spin of local flying," the Summary of Operations noted. As it was St Nicholas Day, the wing's personnel hosted a Christmas Party that night. Five hundred children attended. Black Peter escorted St Nicholas on his rounds. St Nick announced that the party was made possible by his brother Santa in Canada, who had sent five special transport aircraft filled with presents. "Every man who contributed gifts was well satisfied that the kindness helped to warm many hearts," Monty recalled. The festivities became part of Nistelrode's folklore. Attending the village's 700th anniversary celebrations in 1991, Monty was astonished to hear the event vividly described to him by the couple he was staying with during his visit. Even more remarkable was that the wife had been one of the children at the Christmas party in 1944.

The occasion lasted several hours. "I remember there was a lot of singing," said Monty, "and a choir of forty children that rendered 'O Canada' in perfect English as a fitting climax."

There was also a sense among the Canadians that they had landed in relative luxury, in spite of the weather. "We had been drowned in mud at de Rips and flooded by rains and wind at Volkel, so to be housed in buildings, with a real roof and real floor, was a great treat," Monty recalled. But not everyone enjoyed such comforts, yet. Tenting continued for a brief period after the wing's arrival. Nor were all the huts heated, including one that housed 411's airmen. In the middle of dinner one evening, a party of chilled pilots marched into the busy mess hall, disassembled a stove near the doorway and brazenly carried it away to their barracks.

Even so, the Canadians were in better condition than many of the local villagers. "They didn't have very much," Monty remembered, "but they welcomed us warmly and tried to be helpful. The egg-bartering market was quite something. Both the wing's military police and the local constabulary made an occasional round-up in an effort to curb it. The most serious action I saw was one night when a dozen villagers were found all through the camp and were hustled into the Guard Room. It was against the rules to be on the camp after dark, without a good reason, for we were in easy striking distance of saboteurs. Well, as I was the Senior Intelligence Officer, I had to threaten the lot that they might be shot without warning if they were found on the camp after dark again. The intruders were turned over to the civilian police, who were delighted because they found one fellow who had always said he didn't have any surplus eggs to give to the poor people in the community, yet they found him with no less than five dozen that he was ready to barter away for cigarettes or chocolate or soap."

According to Monty, the value of eggs soon settled down to between one for five cigarettes or three for twenty, or one or two for a bar of chocolate. No Dutchman would take money in payment. At the beginning, it was an egg for a cigarette, and a half-dozen for a chocolate bar. "I knew of a fellow who was trading regularly eighteen eggs for one cake of soap. He wasn't doing too well."

As the weeks wore on another feature of the wing's new location impressed itself on Monty. "Our airfield seemed to be in the direct path between V1 launching sites and targets in the Antwerp area," he said. "They were buzzing over constantly, day and night, often very low, and often in formations up to six at a time. The red exhaust flames streaking low across the sky were an eerie—and unforgettable—sight."

But that was later. On December 8th, the wing logged its first full day of operations from B88. Squadron after squadron "bounded into the blue to harass and punish the tired enemy," Don Stewart noted in the Summary of Operations. An impressive total of sixteen rail cuts was achieved. The first section of six aircraft from 401 Squadron, under Flying Officer Husband, left the airfield at 0904. Their target was a flyover northwest of Coesfeld, but it was obscured by cloud. The pilots bombed a bridge west of Hengelo instead. Two of the section's Spitfires landed at Venlo with bomb hang-ups, while a third, flown by Flying Officer Dack, went off the end of the runway after returning to B88 and overturned. Dack was slightly rattled by the incident, but uninjured. His aircraft was more seriously damaged. It must have torn up part of the landing strip as well, since, afterwards, pilots were diverted to Volkel.

The wing was grounded most of the next day due to rain and cloud. A few pilots left by car for nearby Oss, where warm showers were located. The duff weather at least gave personnel time to settle in at B88. Word was received that additional huttage was on its way to relieve the overcrowding.

"Whoever is i/c Dutch weather seems to make it a practice to alternate each duff day with a flying day," Gord Panchuk noted in the Summary of Ops on December 9th. "And so following yesterday's nil activity the wing was again able to squeeze in a fair number of sorties, even though it got off to a late start."

Eight rail cuts were logged and a railway bridge across the Twente Canal was completely destroyed. Six enemy transports and various other ground targets were damaged. That morning, a section led by Flight Lieutenant Sinclair spotted two gaggles of enemy aircraft: four Me 109s on the deck and eight FW 190s at about 5,000 feet. Flying Officer D F Church charged into the lot below and destroyed one, while Flying Officer Cameron damaged two of the 190s above. A number of erks were singled out for special mention that day, too. They did a complete wheel change on Flying Officer Harrison's Spitfire, which had blown a tire on landing, and got the aircraft underway again in eight minutes. Aircraft still in the circuit—some low on fuel—were able to land safely as a result of this outstanding effort.

Over the next few days, weather conditions were such that only a minimal number of sorties left the airfield. On the 12th, although conditions hardly warranted it, each squadron logged one mission each. Bombing was virtually impossible. A single rail cut was scored and four trucks were damaged—and that was it. However: "Sufficient glimpses were had below cloud to show that the Huns were taking full advantage of the duff weather on the ground," noted the Ops Summary. Something was going on. Unfortunately, though, "no sorties were possible after noon to disturb them," Monty added.

The morning of the 14th dawned typically enough with heavy fog. Many at the airfield assumed it would be another duff day for flying. As though to confirm their expectations, Wing Commander Russel logged a weather recce at noon and reported conditions were unfavourable. However, early in the afternoon it was decided to send a section of 412 Squadron out on a divebombing mission. This proved to be eventful enough and, as the weather began to improve late in the day, was the start of a few rather busy hours for all four squadrons.

Flight Lieutenant Fox of 412 led the first Spitfires off the ground at 1349. Unfortunately, he had to return early, leaving his section under the command of Flight Lieutenant Earle. They attacked a train heading southwest from Bocholt, and later divebombed a factory. In the latter action, Squadron Leader Newell silenced a three-gun flak position that had been firing at the Canadians. Newell came at the battery from as little as fifty feet, scoring devastating direct hits.

South of Coesfeld, the Falcons encountered twenty-plus bandits. Newell destroyed a Me 109 while Flight Lieutenant Richards "scalped" a FW 190. Flight Lieutenant Earle also damaged one of the enemy aircraft. The others got away.

Flight Lieutenant Everard led the first section of 401 Squadron out at 1445, despite uncertain weather, to divebomb a rail junction northwest of Rheine. Aircraft providing top cover spotted four Me 109s at 15,000 feet. Flight Lieutenant L W Woods and Flying Officer Church each damaged one.

The first show by 442 was led by Squadron Leader Olmsted. After one section dropped its bombs on a marshalling yard at Bocholt, the covering section unloaded over Stadtlohn. Then Olmsted regrouped the Spitfires and went in search of ground targets for strafing. He spotted a train hurtling towards Enschede.

His instincts told him it might be more rewarding a target than it appeared. Olmsted ordered his section to follow as he dived on the engine and watched "as streams of Wehrmacht soldiers jumped from the cars, seeking protection in the railroad ditches and low scrub," he said. "We then strafed the ditches, flying parallel with the tracks while our targets, fully armed, bravely returned our fire."

Then Kenway interrupted. "Caribou leader, we have some bogies southwest of your position. Are you interested?"

Olmsted requested details.

"Opening the throttle wide, I pulled the aircraft up from the last dive and headed due west, climbing as fast as the Spitfire could go. I took a quick glance to the left to see how the rest of the planes were doing, and then a quick glance to the right for a final assessment of the damage done to the train. As I swung my head, I just happened to glance at the radiator temperature gauge located on the lower right side of the instrument panel. The needle flicked from a normal 90 to 140 and back to 90 again in the flash of an eye, at exactly the instant I looked at it."

Olmsted, like many experienced pilots, seldom actually looked at his engine instruments. "The feel of the aircraft—the sound of the engine or the touch of the controls—was almost all I required to know that my machine was functioning properly," he said. Instead, he swung his head from side to side, searching for prowling enemy aircraft, in deference to the fundamental advice his instructors had drilled into him, "It's the Hun you don't see who will get you."

Having by mere chance noticed the gauge, Olmsted realised instantly his aircraft was in trouble. He radioed Kenway.

"Caribou leader here. Mayday, Mayday. Aircraft hit and in trouble. Give me vector for our closest front line. Mayday, mayday. Caribou leader out."

Squadron Leader Edison, the senior controller, responded immediately. "Steer 200. Nijmegen is your closest landfall. Good luck." Olmsted said that the conversation was conducted in a quiet, unexcited manner, and that Edison's steady voice "had a calming effect."

Soon after his conversation with Kenway, Olmsted's Spitfire began to shake violently. He was about to switch off the engine to prevent it from bursting into flames when the connecting rods broke through the engine block, severing oil and glycol lines.

"Caribou Leader, I am unhooking my straps, jettisoning my hood, and getting ready to bail out if a fire starts," Olmsted radioed to his fellow pilots. He then proceeded to glide the last twenty miles over territory he said was "crawling with Hitler Youth troops" that reportedly "took no prisoners." He thought of the telegram he had sent his mother a week before, in which he told her he was finished with operations. Mrs Olmsted had "no need to worry anymore." In fact, Wing Commander Russel had told Olmsted shortly after they moved to B88 that he was finished with operational flying. Olmsted had persuaded Russel to give him an extension, ostensibly to permit him to finish grooming Milt Jowsey as his replacement. Russel agreed to let Olmsted fly ten more hours—fewer if he was hit by flak.

Unable to see through the hot oil covering his Spitfire's canopy, Olmsted now depended on his section mates to guide him by radio while descending. "The courage of the [other] pilots, exposing themselves at this low altitude and at slow speeds to heavy enemy fire, was incredible," he said in his memoirs.

Eventually the Rhine slipped beneath Olmsted's wings, at which point he was again faced with the dilemma of whether to crash-land or bail out. He decided that attempting to touch down at the airfield was too risky. The alternative did not cheer him much. "The Irving Parachute Company did not guarantee a parachute opening safely under eight hundred feet, whereas I would have only five hundred feet of height and probably less."

Olmsted hit the silk not far from Grave. He watched his battered Spitfire dive into the ground and explode while he floated, albeit briefly, to a safe landing. Canadian soldiers in the area drove him back to B88. "I actually arrived in time to put the finishing touches on the operational summary of our sortie, gleefully mingling with the pilots as we rehashed the successes for our spy." His debriefing with Monty concluded, Olmsted went to Russel's caravan for a drink and was summarily informed he was finished with operational flying. "I'll drink to that," he said to Russel, smiling—and, he confessed, "in a rare and carefree mood."

As expected, Milton Jowsey took over from Olmsted as CO of 442 Squadron. There were other changes that month. On December 17th, Flight Lieutenant Newell—an Irishman from Warren Point who was working in New York City when the war began (he enlisted in Montreal)—replaced Squadron Leader Lapp, whose second tour of duty had ended. Lapp's departure was the fifth in the past week, and effected a complete turnover of pilots since D-Day. On days when operational flying was either minimal or impossible, they spent their time getting "genned up" or, following orders from above, with small arms and rifle practice. There was some urgency even in these pursuits. On the 16th, the enemy had launched a major counter-offensive in the Ardennes. The operation was timed to take advantage of poor weather conditions, which, it was expected, would negate Allied air superiority long enough to split their armies and drive on to Antwerp. There, the enemy hoped to cut off a main terminus for Allied supplies. Twenty-four German divisions, many of them armoured, spearheaded this bold initiative that came dangerously close to succeeding.

"All Hitler wants me to do," complained Sepp Dietrich, commander of the Sixth SS Panzer Army—and ordinarily one of the Fuhrer's most loyal supporters—"is to cross a river, capture Brussels, and then go on and take Antwerp. And all this in the worst time of the year through the Ardennes when the snow is waist deep and there isn't room to deploy four tanks abreast let alone armoured divisions. When it doesn't get light until eight and it's dark again at four and we re-formed divisions made up chiefly of kids and sick old men—and at Christmas!"

Dietrich's analysis was insightful, but also futile. Nothing would dislodge Hitler from his conviction that the *blitzkrieg* tactics he had used so successfully in the Ardennes in 1940 would again achieve a brilliant victory. Then, his Panzers had swept through the region's seemingly impenetrable dark forests and narrow valleys with little concern that they would be discovered, for the French were convinced the Ardennes provided a natural barrier to attack and had left it undefended, until it was too late. In a stunning repetition of the strategic error made four years earlier, Supreme Allied Headquarters had decided in the autumn of 1944 that the Ardennes were a secondary front. Consequently, the bulk of the Allied forces were concentrated to the north and south. Hitler could barely contain his excitement when he studied his situation maps, and realised that his adversaries had left themselves vulnerable. Never mind that in 1940 he had launched his invasion during the balmy days of early May, and that it was now winter. The operation, codenamed "Autumn Mist," was ordered to proceed.

The same low cloud and heavy snow that had hampered Canadian operations at B88 in mid-December effectively concealed the gathering offensive in the Ardennes. Then, on the morning of December 16th, eight Panzer divisions fell upon the US VIII Corps with complete surprise to start the six-week struggle. The Allies failed initially to appreciate the magnitude of the offensive. But when their forward positions were quickly overrun and reports of casualties began to rise, they reacted. Eisenhower committed his reserves to bolster the collapsing front. The US 101st Airborne, still resting after its part in "Market-Garden," was sent at breakneck speed to the outskirts of Bastogne, in an attempt to blunt the attack. Though not equipped to defend against tanks, the 101st put up a determined fight and prevented the enemy's Panzers from entering. Later it was reported that at one point General McAuliffe, who was commanding the Americans, had contemptuously rejected a demand that they surrender. He replied, simply: "Nuts."

The day "Autumn Mist" began, the pilots of 126 Wing were staring gloomily at duff weather that all but prevented flying. Only one mission was carried out, and it was uneventful. The next morning, scattered showers and varying visibility prevented a full programme from getting underway. Two sections of 401 Squadron were up, briefed and ready to take off by 0930. No sooner had they left at 1042 when five to eight Me 109s flew "balls out" over the airfield. "One intrepid type actually took time out to bank steeply from side to side, possibly endeavouring to identify the joint. Some crust," noted the wing's diarist. "All in all today has been rather hectic for the nerves of all concerned."

The next morning, two Me 262s buzzed the airfield at five hundred feet. "Our ack-ack guns were right on the job and gave them a very warm reception. However, no damage either to the Hun or ourselves was sustained." Four aircraft of 401 Squadron took off in pursuit, but the jet-jobs disappeared too quickly. That day, too, the wing began supporting the Americans in the area of Aachen, where the weather was better. No contacts with enemy aircraft were made, although the Canadian pilots must have provided some reassurance to the American forces. Several days later they sent word through 83 Group HQ, expressing their gratitude for the effort particularly in view of the difficult conditions the Canadians had met.

Fighter sweeps were carried out in the Dusseldorf and Paderborn areas on the 19th, despite a persistent ground haze at B88. Later in the day Wing Commander Russel led a sweep by 412 and 442 to the Rheine-Osnabruck area, "but no joy resulted." Squadron Leader Jowsey led a section of 442 to the area of Malmedy, which was closer to part of the actual "bulge" that was developing in Allied territory, and returned just as empty-handed. Tantalised by continuing reports of enemy air activity, the wing's squadrons persevered. On the 23rd, Flight Lieutenant Boyle of 411 Squadron damaged a jet-job east of Eindhoven—the only claim for the day. But on the 24th, the Luftwaffe was again up in strength. The Spitfires of 412 Squadron ran into forty-five plus FW 190s while sweeping between Neuss and Duren. As the Spitfires had the advantage of height, they bounced the enemy "to the tune of 2-1-2." Jet-propelled aircraft were also active, although none was engaged. An intelligence summary by 83 Group HQ noted: "In spite of some ground haze, a clear, sunlit day gave the Group the chance for which it has waited for nearly a week. A hard day's work was done in the face of a number of hazards, of which flak was perhaps the worst." Of the more than six hundred sorties flown, more than half were contributed by fighter patrols and sweeps over the battlefront. The squadrons of 126 Wing flew the most—125—without any casualties.

With operations looming for Christmas Day itself, Wing Commander Russel warned all squadrons to "soft-pedal" the festivities.

The atmosphere at B88 was further dampened by an order that personnel were to carry sidearms, both on and off duty. A signal to all wings from 83 Group HQ partly explained the reasoning behind such measures. "Paramount importance all unit commanders take precautions ensure unit security against enemy agents disguised Allied uniforms and civilian clothes," the flash read. "Checking of identity of visitors to RAF sites must be carefully carried out irrespective of rank service or nationality and purpose of visit. If suspects are found probable that their identity papers will appear satisfactory but should be asked produce identity disc." Monty said the order was expected and even welcomed by a large number of personnel with the wing who felt that events in the Ardennes proved "once again that the 'it-can't-happen-here' attitude" was dangerously false.

As predicted, Christmas Day was hectic. Indeed, for all the significance the wing's personnel might have liked to give the occasion, it was quickly evident that the day was in fact not so different from most others. Flight Lieutenant MacKay of 411 shot down a Me 109, while another was shared by Flight Lieutenant W C Connell and Flight Sergeant Woodhill. In the same action, Squadron Leader Everard was hit by debris from one of the 109s and had to bail out south of Venlo. His precise whereabouts were not immediately known.

The most thrilling moment of the day occurred during the midday Christmas meal at B88, when Flight Lieutenant Jack Boyle of 411 Squadron returned to the airfield and encountered a Me 262. Boyle describes how the incident came about:

> Our entire wing received orders to provide maximum air support in the American sector to the south, where the German army had broken through our lines in what came to be known as the Battle of the Bulge.* Our excitement was running high as we were briefed on the extensive German fighter activity around Bastogne, and that our entire Wing ... would be taking off within

---

* It is referred to as "The Battle of the Ardennes" in British historical texts.

the hour. 411 was the last to go and it wasn't too long before we could hear the R/T chatter of those ahead reporting enemy sightings. Our sense of anticipation grew by leaps and bounds. In the midst of this, I couldn't believe my ears when I heard my new Number 2 calling to report a ropy engine that was running so rough he thought he shouldn't go on. Since a lame aircraft was never permitted to go home alone, this meant I would have to escort him back to base and miss out on all the activity going on just ahead of us. I decided that we couldn't risk going on and reported to the CO that we were heading for home. I was sorely disappointed by this turn of events and grumbled to myself all the way home.

As we neared Heesch, we were far too high; and in an irritable mood, to get rid of excess height, I stuck the nose almost straight down in a screaming spiral dive. As my speed shot well past the maximum permissable, out of nowhere appeared a German Me 262 jet. It took only a second to see to my gunsight and gun's safety catch and then I was right behind him. My first burst of cannon fire hit his port engine pod and it began streaming dense smoke. He immediately dove for the deck as an evasive tactic, but with only one engine he couldn't outrun me. I scored several more hits before he clipped some tall treetops and then hit the ground at an almost flat angle. His aircraft disintegrated in stages from nose to tail, ripping up the turf as it cartwheeled in a trail of smoke and flame. As I circled, Dutch farmers emerged from the barns and waved up to me.

Monty said the airmen lined up for their turkey dinner fell like a row of dominoes when Boyle first blasted the enemy jet-job over the airfield, and later watched with mounting excitement as the stricken aircraft crashed nearby. Boyle himself experienced a delayed reaction to the episode. "In the few minutes it took to return to base, I thought about how fast the whole thing happened, and realised that I was more excited than during the actual attack." After landing and taxiing to his usual spot in the dispersal area, Boyle was immediately surrounded by his mechanics, who were ecstatic. An armourer came up and said he had always wondered, while reloading the guns on Boyle's Spitfire, about the circumstances in which they were fired. "What a thrill it was for him to actually see 'his' guns shooting down an enemy aircraft," Boyle said. "Later, everyone said what a thrilling spectacle it had been for them. For me too!"

Beer, cigarettes and cigars were abundantly available for the Christmas festivities that night. The wing's ORB declared the day had been "very successful." Boyle was crowned "jet-job king" for his dramatic action over the airfield.

In fact, the wing led 2nd TAF in destroying or damaging the enemy jets. On the 26th, a section of 411 Squadron led by Squadron Leader Newell encountered a Me 262 over Geilenkirchen. Flight Lieutenant Ireland was credited with damaging the aircraft. On the 27th, during a sweep over Aachen, Flying Officer M A Perkins of 442 Squadron damaged another at 19,000 feet. It was an eventful day for most of the wing. Four Me 109s were cleanly destroyed and a number of ground scores were made for the first time in many days. There were several other incidents. Flight Lieutenant Banks of 412 Squadron returned after a particularly narrow escape. His section, led by Flight Lieutenant Fox, was on a sweep of the Münster-Rheine area when it was bounced from above by three Me 109s over the Rheine airfield. Wriggling out of a potentially nasty situation, the section went on the offensive and shot down one of the enemy aircraft. The other two were chased to almost deck level, with Banks in hot pursuit. But bad luck prevented his scoring. In the shooting frenzy that followed, a 20mm shell sheared away a blade of his propeller. Banks skilfully coaxed his Spitfire back to B88 and landed safely, evidently to the surprise of his squadron mates. He had been given up as lost. Fortunately, too, his Spitfire was salvageable, although the wing's maintenance erks were already working flat-out. That day the Summary of Operations gave particular credit to Corporal Harper and four men of the R&I Unit, who had worked non-stop outside for more than twelve hours in the bitter cold to effect a complete engine change on a Spitfire.

No less noteworthy for the day was the arrival of 402 Squadron as a permanent addition to the wing's strength. The squadron had been based at B64 at Diest, in Belgium, as part of the RAF's 125 Wing. Known as the "City of Winnipeg," or "Winnipeg Bears" squadron, unit code AE, it was formed originally as No 112 (Army Cooperation) Squadron (Auxiliary) at Winnipeg in October 1932. Arriving in England in 1940, it became No 2 (Fighter) Squadron at Digby, Lincolnshire. Later it was redesignated in the 400-block as 402 (Fighter) Squadron. From October 1941 to March 1942 it was the only RCAF unit with the fighter-bomber version of the Hurricane. Subsequently converted to flying Spitfires, the squadron began offensive and defensive operations and had played an active role in operations in Europe since D-Day.

The Winnipeg Bears were led by Squadron Leader J B Lawrence of Edmonton, who seems to have been determined to make his presence felt early. Many of the squadron's Spitfires were still at Diest, despite much petitioning (weather conditions to the south were responsible for the delay), yet almost continuous two-man patrols were carried out on the 28th. Of six patrols conducted on the 29th, the one from 1430 to 1544 was easily the most extraordinary. Kenway had vectored Lawrence and Flying Officer Lalonde towards *thirty-plus* FW 190s south of Enschede. Notwithstanding the incredible odds against them, each pilot scored one enemy aircraft damaged. "402 thus gained its baptism of fire with the wing and will be a potent threat from now on," Monty noted in the Summary of Operations.

In fact, the 29th was hectic almost from the outset. By day's end Group Captain McGregor was moved to heartily commend everyone for the high number of sorties flown—157—and the results obtained. Flying Officer Gallinger of 401 Squadron earned McGregor's special congratulations for returning safely despite having lost a part of one wing during a scrap and being hit by flak during his return flight. The squadron had surprised twenty-plus FW 190s and Me 109s east of Enschede, but had the tables turned on it when six more enemy fighters bounced the Canadians in return. Flight Lieutenant Sheehy's aircraft was shot down in flames almost immediately. A parachute was seen in the area, but Sheehy was thought to have been killed. To avenge the loss, Flying Officer Murray and Flying Officer

Cameron each destroyed a FW 190, while Pilot Officer Horsburgh and Flying Officer MacKay damaged two more. That same day, a sweep of the Münster-Rheine area by 412 Squadron had resulted in one Ju 88 damaged by Flight Lieutenant Fox. The aircraft was seen to crash land, wheels up, at the German-held Rheine aerodrome, where as many as three Me 262s were sighted but not engaged. A sweep by twelve aircraft of 411 Squadron was even more productive. The Grizzlies had started their day by shooting up several trains north of Osnabruck and in the Rheine area. "One locomotive blew up so completely that it set a nearby building on fire. Some of the trains were attacked as they passed each other, causing much confusion on the ground." South of Borken, Flight Lieutenant Boyle and Flying Officer Gilberstad encountered a gaggle of FW 190s. They selected two for destruction. Gilberstad had only damaged one when he found himself out of ammunition and being chased by several of the 190s. He evaded one of the enemy fighters so adroitly that at 1,000 feet it stalled, flicked over and "spun off into the deck for its pains," Monty noted. Gilberstad was credited with one FW 190 destroyed.

Flight Lieutenant Ireland led the squadron's Spitfires during a second mission later in the day, from 1256 to 1417. They left B88 and turned eastwards. Kenway reported enemy aircraft in the Rheine area. Taking off in pursuit, the pilots had no inkling they were soon to be involved in one of the wing's most historic outings of the war. Eight enemy aircraft were destroyed—one by "Irish" Ireland, another by Flight Lieutenant R M "Cookie" Cook, and a third by Flying Officer McCracken. Incredibly, the others were accounted for by a single pilot, Flight Lieutenant R J (Dick) Audet, until then just another 22-year-old from Lethbridge, Alberta. His record-setting feat of destroying five enemy aircraft in a single operation was exhaustively documented by Monty, for it seemed as incredible then as it does today.

In many respects, Richard Joseph Audet was an enigma even to his fellow pilots. He could hardly be described as one of the "Brylcreem

Boys." For one thing he was too quiet, too unassuming. He seemed more like film actor Gary Cooper.

"Yet," said Monty, "looking at Dick, you could see something of the fighter in him. Tall and lean, dark-skinned with black curly hair, deep-set sky-blue eyes. But you had to look. I saw him come into the bull-pen after his five-in-one outing and you wouldn't have known anything had happened to look at him, or even to hear him talk. He was as polite and thoughtful as always, to the point of wondering where to put the ash from his cigarette."

Audet had learned his humility while growing up in western Canada, the youngest of six children of French-Canadian parents. Raised on a ranch in the foothills of the Rocky Mountains, he became an athletic young man. He enlisted with the RCAF at Calgary in 1941. The recruiting officer who interviewed him said he was a "clean cut lad, keen to be a pilot." Posted to a manning depot at Brandon, Manitoba, Audet underwent the usual rudimentary drill instruction while he waited for a vacancy in the aircrew training program. By all accounts, he was an exemplary student from the moment he began flight instruction in February 1942. He received his wings in October; and six weeks later, he was in Britain for advanced training prior to being posted. His first assignment, in July 1943, was to 421 Squadron, part of 127 "Airfield" at Kenley, Surrey. There he flew only four operational sorties, and never fired his Spitfire's guns. But it was at Kenley that Audet came under the almost mystical spell of "Buzz" Beurling. Later, the "handsome youth with dark features," as historian Hugh Halliday described Audet, was transferred to Bournemouth. For a while he was assigned to such ignoble tasks as pulling target drogues back and forth for the benefit of anti-aircraft gunners practising their aim. In July 1944, he married an English girl, Iris Gibbons. The following month he was posted to the continent, and in September he joined 411 Squadron while it was stationed at Evere.

But there, too, aerial combat eluded Audet. The Luftwaffe went virtually into hiding after the Allied victories in France and the Low Countries. In October, when the wing's squadrons began their "train busting" operations in earnest, Audet began to show some of his skills. Earlier on that fateful day in December, his section had destroyed four locomotives, damaged five and shot up as many as thirty-nine trucks. "Audet's remarkable eyesight was responsible for finding much of this and he led his section right into it to score a large part himself," Monty said.

But in every other respect prior to December 29th, Audet seemed fairly average. He had chalked up only fifty-two sorties, and three dogfights. Then, almost inexplicably, he vaulted into the ranks of Canada's fighter aces in a single bold stroke.

As the wing's Senior Intelligence Officer, Monty was saddled with the job of "establishing that those five Huns were destroyed—with no mistake," he said afterwards. "There was talk of knocking it down to four and the AOC at Group wanted it crystal clear that five were destroyed. Fortunately, the cine films corroborated it all several days later, but an initial decision had to be made at once so the press and radio could take the story without fear of it bouncing."

So, Monty grilled Audet for almost two hours. He felt awful for most of it. "It was as though he was in a police cell and I was trying to break down a criminal's alibi. Audet himself almost got fed up and said he didn't care what was decided."

The debriefing continued the next day, when duff weather grounded most operations and there was more time to review what had happened. Numerous handwritten drafts of Audet's combat report surviving in Monty's personal archives attest to how much accuracy was sought.

In the end, this is how it happened.

Date:	29th December, 1944
Squadron:	411
Type & Mark of Aircraft:	Spitfire IX E
Time Up & Down:	1300 – 1415
Place of Attack:	10 mi N.W. Osnabruck
Height of E/A On First Sighting:	10,000'
Own Height on First Sighting:	10,500'
Our Casualties:	Nil.
Enemy Casualties:	3 FW 190s – 2 Me 109s Destroyed

General Report:

"I was leading Yellow section of 411 Squadron in the RHEINE/ OSNABRUCK area when Control reported Huns at RHEINE and the Squadron turned in that direction. An Me 262 was sighted and just at that time I spotted 12 e/a on our starboard side at 2 o'clock. These turned out to be a mixture of approximately 4 Me 109s and 8 FW 190s.

1st Combat

I attacked an Me 109 which was the last a/c in the formation of about 12 all flying line astern. At approximately 200 yards and 30° to starboard at 10,000 feet I opened fire and saw strikes all over the fuselage and wing roots. The 109 burst into flames on the starboard side of the fuselage only, and trailed intense black smoke. I then broke off my attack."

"Flying Yellow 2 I witnessed the above combat and saw this Me 109 go down in flames."

(signed)
(D F Campbell), Flying Officer

"I, too, Yellow 3 saw this aircraft attacked by Yellow 1 and I saw it burst into flames and go down, crashing into the deck about 6 miles NW of the OSNABRUCK [aerodrome]."

(signed)
(J M McCauley), Flying Officer

2nd Combat

"After the first attack I went around in a defensive circle at about 8500 feet until I spotted an FW 190 which I immediately attacked from 250 yards down to 100 yards and from 30° to line astern I saw strikes over cockpit and to the rear of the fuselage, it burst into flames from the engine back and as I passed very close over top of it I saw the pilot slumped over in his cockpit, which was also in flames."

"I witnessed the above combat and saw the a/c go down, flaming around the cockpit."

(signed)
(D F Campbell), Flying Officer

3rd Combat

"My third attack followed immediately on the 2nd. I followed what I believe was an Me 109 in a slight dive. He then climbed sharply and his coupe top flew off about 3 to 4,000 feet. I then gave a very short burst from about 300 yards and line astern and his aircraft whipped downwards in a dive. The pilot attempted or did bail out. I saw a black object on the edge of the cockpit but his chute ripped to shreds. I then took cine shots of his a/c going to the ground and the bits of parachute floating around. I saw this aircraft hit and smash into many flaming pieces on the ground. I do not remember any strikes on this aircraft. The Browning button only may have been pressed.*

4th Combat

I spotted an FW 190 being pursued at about 5,000' by a Spitfire which was in turn pursued by an FW 190. I called this Yellow section pilot to break and attacked the 190 up his rear. The fight went downward in a steep dive. When I was about 250 yards and line astern of this 190 I opened fire, there were many strikes on the

---

* Audet was referring to that part of the three-way switch on the control column that fired his Spitfire's Browning machine guns (when pressed in the middle, both cannons and machine guns fired, while each could be selected independently by pressing the top or bottom part of the button). Firing activated the cine gun camera automatically. It could be controlled on its own as well, using another button on the control column, which explains Audet's earlier remark about taking cine shots of the third aircraft going down.

length of the fuselage and it immediately burst into flames. I saw this FW 190 go straight into the ground and burn.

5th Combat

Several minutes later while attempting to form my section up again I spotted an FW 190 from 4,000', he was about 2,000'. I dived down on him and he turned in to me from the right. Then he flipped around in a left hand turn and attempted a head-on attack. I slowed down to wait for the 190 to fly past in range. At about 200 yards and 20° I gave a very short burst, but couldn't see any strikes. This a/c flicked violently, and continued to do so until he crashed into the ground. The remainder of my section saw this encounter, and Yellow 4 (F/O McCracken) saw it crash in flames."

"I watched Yellow 1 (F/L Audet) attack the FW 190. It flicked over on its back and flicked several times as it dove straight in and burst into flames."

(signed)
(R C McCracken), Flying Officer

"Gyro Gun sight was used for all combats as well as Cine camera gun.
  I claim 3 FW 190s DESTROYED and 2 ME 109s DE-STROYED.

(signed)
(R J Audet), Flight Lieutenant

(signed)
*(Monty Berger), Flight Lieutenant, Senior Intelligence Officer,
No 126 (RCAF) Wing HQ*

In his first combat, Dick Audet had become an "ace"—a seemingly impossible accomplishment. He was recommended for an immediate decoration, and subsequently received the Distinguished Flying Cross. Yet, as Monty had observed, the modest young pilot seemed almost unwilling to believe it himself and had to be persuaded by hard evidence that he had destroyed five, and not just four, of the enemy fighters.

Fortunately, the evidence was at hand, although Monty in the role of wing "spy" (actually, he seemed more like a city detective in the circumstances) had to work some overtime to put it all together for the record. There was also one Me 109 claimed by Flying Officer R C (Bob) McCracken, flying Yellow 4, which had to be confirmed. It, too, stood up to scrutiny and was allowed.

There was a boisterous celebration in the mess that night. It may have had as much to do with the approaching New Year as Audet's victories. In any event, Audet wasn't a part of it. According to Monty, "He didn't drink and, actually, as a rule he went to bed very, very early."

Two days later, on December 31st, six more enemy aircraft were added to the wing's scoreboard. Flight Lieutenant Boyle destroyed a Ju 88, while fellow 411 pilot Flying Officer Graham shot down a FW 190. The other four, all Me 109s, belonged to pilots of 442 Squadron—one each by Flying Officer M F Doyle, Flying Officer G H Watkin, Flight Lieutenant R C Smith, and one shared by Flying Officer M A Perkins and Flight Lieutenant D M Pieri. Warrant Officer M Thomas of 401 Squadron provided some additional fireworks when he shot down a V1. His section was returning from an uneventful armed recce and was in the circuit when the buzz bomb zoomed across the airfield at Nistelrode. "He scored a nice hit on it and it nosed over and plunged into an open field and exploded," Monty recalled. "Everyone in INT/OPS was pretty damned worried about it, too. We had just asked Group if we were allowed to shoot down V1s because the pilots were quite keen to knock them down if they could. Just as 401 came into the circuit the reply came that our ack-ack was not allowed to open up and that our aircraft could only shoot them down over enemy territory. The ruling made good sense, because it was dangerous shooting them down in an area heavily inhabited by troops. We hadn't had time to inform the pilots. However, nothing ever came of it—and we didn't mind using the extra chalk on the wing's scoreboard."

By New Year's Eve, the scoreboard showed a total of 32 enemy aircraft destroyed (with 3 probables and 17 damaged) for the month, and 236 since the wing's formation. This put the wing well over the 200 mark since D-Day. "We had modestly hoped to reach that figure by the New Year," Monty allowed. "In building up that total the wing had worked and fought hard to overtake many wings ahead of it." He added that to conclude the year as the top-scoring wing in the 2nd TAF was as much a tribute to the erks, "for it meant they had kept the aircraft serviceable and ready to fly at a moment's notice."

There was also cause to reflect on the sacrifices of many good pilots over the past six months. That afternoon, Flight Lieutenant R M (Bob) Earle was killed when his aircraft spun into the ground for some unknown reason while attacking a ground target in the Rheine-Münster area.

So ended 1944—with memories of tragedy, as well as victory.

8

CLOSE
SUPPORT

Twenty-three-year-old Leading Aircraftsman Jack Ivamy of Burnaby, British Columbia, had just finished breakfast after working his usual night shift in the signals van. Stepping out of the airmen's mess, he drew a breath of the fresh morning air and admired the brilliant sunshine that welcomed New Year's Day, 1945. Now all he wanted was a few good hours of sleep. He had set out on foot for his billet, and was almost there when all hell broke loose over the airfield. Forty-plus Me 109s and FW 190s swept across shortly after 0900, catching everyone at B88 completely by surprise.

"The Jerries came over—*brrp, brrp, brrp*—and I jumped over a low brick wall alongside the road," Ivamy recalled. "Then the buggers came back, and so I had to jump over the wall on the other side!"

Leading Aircraftsman Garry Whitmore, who had joined the wing only days before as an airframe mechanic, remembers he was standing around a barrel with a fire in it, keeping warm with several of his new mates, when the enemy aircraft appeared over the trees at the end of the runway. "I thought they were American Thunderbolts at first," he said. "But almost immediately they were right in front of us, and we could see the big, black crosses. Boy, I headed for the bushes!"

Monty never did see the enemy fighters. "I was in the mess at breakfast. We took cover for the short span of the roar of the aircraft over the airfield, then rushed to INT/OPS where we took stock of the situation."

Ironically, for one of the most forward Allied airfields in Europe, B88 was spared the brunt of the enemy's series of heavy attacks that day. "It's strange that we weren't a target, you know," Monty reflected, "because we were the most vulnerable to a quick dart in and out by the enemy." The Luftwaffe had more ambitious plans. It had scraped together virtually every available machine—as many as 800 aircraft—many of which were piloted by raw recruits who had so little training they had to fly in special formations with more seasoned pilots. Then it swept southward to raid Allied airfields in Holland, Belgium and northern France. The boldness, even recklessness of the enterprise reflected the desperate land situation in the Ardennes, where the enemy's December *blitzkrieg* had stalled and the so-called "bulge" was collapsing under the weight of determined counterattacks. Allied air superiority had again played a part in preventing Hitler from obtaining the victory he envisaged.

There is also the possibility that an absurd mix-up saved Nistelrode from the destruction wrought elsewhere. Information obtained after the raids indicated they had been planned originally to coincide with the start of the Ardennes offensive. "However, the weather was pretty bad at the time for several days, eliminating the Hun air support—and most of ours, incidentally," Monty explained. "The Hun air staff, instead of cancelling the operation, apparently merely postponed it to the point of preserving all the maps and plans. Although 126 moved, and we presumed the Huns knew about that, the plans were never changed. Volkel showed as a target on the programme. The forty or more enemy aircraft that zoomed over Nistelrode on New Year's Day were there only because their course was set southward."

The wing was lucky in another respect. "Few pilots had overstepped the mark in the celebrations the night before," Monty noted, "mainly because the Winco had again warned everyone to be on their toes the next day." In fact, three of the wing's squadrons were in the air already on patrols or armed recces. "The luckiest break of all was that, just as the Huns flew over, 401 Squadron was forming up at the end of the runway, waiting for the OK from Flying Control to take off. The enemy swooped right over their heads. In a few seconds, of course, the whole squadron was airborne and chasing after the Hun. And what a morning it turned out to be!"

Twenty minutes later, Flying Officer Cameron returned with empty ammo belts and claiming three Me 109s destroyed. He had knocked them off in short order, he said, and all within a few kilometres of the airfield. Meanwhile, one of the squadron's sections had raced off to the Reichswald Forest area. Flight Lieutenant Johnny MacKay used up most of his ammunition to destroy one Me 109, and emptied the balance into a second shortly after, but apparently without result. He chased the enemy aircraft anyway, until it ran out of room to manoeuvre and crashed. MacKay then closed on a FW 190 at low level, and repeated the daring stunt. Three down. Flight Lieutenant J W Foster damaged a FW 190 in the same action. Later in the day, while chasing a jet-job, the squadron's pilots came upon a dozen or more 109s and 190s in the circuit at the Rheine aerodrome. They opted for the larger gaggle. Each pilot emptied his ammunition in the combat that followed, with the result that Flight Lieutenant "Jake" Lee and Flying Officer Don Church both claimed one destroyed and one probable, while Pilot Officer Doug Horsburgh shot down one more for no losses to the section. Flight Lieutenant MacKay and Flight Sergeant Woodhill also shared a claim for a damaged Me 262. They had caught up with the jet-job south of Rheine.

Flying Officer Len Wilson of 442 Squadron, in Spitfire Y2-F, was with a section led by Flight Lieutenant Norm Keene, DFC, when the raid began. He describes what happened.

We were at about 10,000 feet in the vicinity of Venlo doing an armed reconnaissance patrol, when a call came out from Heesch to return immediately as the base was being attacked. We had just completed our turn toward base when I spotted a few aircraft on the deck flying roughly at right angles to us. I reported them to the section leader and stated I was going down on them.

My number two, Flight Lieutenant "Tex" Pieri and I peeled off and came down behind them, gathering speed all the way down. To my astonishment, there were not just a few aircraft, but at least twenty. I was in an ideal position as I drew up behind my selected victim, but I hesitated a second too long to clearly identify the aircraft before firing, so that as the opening burst got off I immediately had to push the nose down to avoid a collision and wound up directly in front of my target.

What to do. To climb would put me in the sights of the entire *Staffel*. I was too low to dive out of the predicament. All my training made me instinctively break around to port in order to get around behind him for another pass.

A Spitfire can out-turn a FW 190. Unfortunately, this is only true given relatively similar air speeds. Having dived from 10,000 feet and gathered speed on the way down, I must have had 150-180 miles an hour increase in speed over the e/a and therefore could not out-turn him in this circumstance. Half-way around the turn I felt an explosion behind me, the aircraft flicked-rolled further to port, I hastily gained control and continued in my turns to get on his tail. I looked over my head to the left and saw an FW 190, telltale flashes of wing guns firing making it evident he was intent on finishing me off. At the same time he was firing, he was being fired on by a Spitfire flown by my Number 2, Flight Lieutenant "Tex" Pieri. The FW fell away, later claimed by Tex as destroyed. In a flash the sky was empty of aircraft.

Straightening out to look for any targets, I found that the aircraft was extremely difficult to manoeuvre. It could only be flown straight by putting on full right rudder combined with left aileron, resulting in the aircraft slicing through the air with the wings at about a thirty degree left slant. It was virtually impossible to do a turn to the right. I immediately did a left climbing turn to about 5,000 feet, and proceeded to fly in a northerly direction toward base.

Because of the extreme fatigue in my right leg from having to apply full right rudder, it was necessary every now and then to break into a left turning circle to rest my leg. Hence I made my way slowly back to base, flying straight, then resting in a turn, flying straight, then resting, all the while looking about for enemy aircraft and hoping I would not encounter any in my crippled condition. Luck was with me. Though alone, I was able to hear some of the chatter from the rest of the squadron. In particular I remember my very good friend Flying Officer Don Brigden, calling in his low-key laid-back style for help, "I've got about four Huns cornered here over Nijmegen, can anybody give me a hand?" Alas, he was overwhelmed and we buried him in Nistelrode cemetery a couple of days later.

As Wilson came into sight of B88, he was faced with another dilemma:

How was I going to land with the aircraft damage requiring such aberrant behaviour on the controls? Would it affect the stalling speed, or cause me to flick to the left on landing? Nothing to do but go in and trust to luck. Fortunately, as I reduced speed on the approach for landing, the twisting effect on the damaged tail was reduced, and as I pulled off power at the roundout, most of the slipstream torque disappeared and I made a normal landing. Eagerly I awaited Tex Pieri's return to thank him for saving my life. I also wanted to ask him if he had seen what had happened to the aircraft I was firing at, whether it had crashed or not. He said that, no, he had not seen that aircraft crash. This news made me reluctant to claim even a damaged. This was a pity in retrospect, because even had I not laid so much as one shell on the FW 190, the camera gun would surely have revealed one of the greatest close-ups of a FW 190 nearly about to bite the dust.

Years later, at a fighter pilots' reunion in Comox, British Columbia, Wilson was exchanging recollections with one of his former wingmates. "He told me that it was not really my turn to be put on the flying roster for the early morning trip, but because I did not drink at the time, I was put on to let one of the drinking pilots on the squadron celebrate the New Year with abandonment." So much for the virtue of sobriety, Wilson concluded.

He had another close call when, after his Spitfire was repaired, he took it out on a test flight. "I almost veered off the runway on take-off, and when finally airborne, had some of the same difficulty maintaining straight flight," he recalled. Later he discovered that the wires to the rudder trim were crossed, so that full right rudder required on take-off to counteract the aircraft's tendency to swing to the left under full power became full left trim. It was a rare example of a mechanic's error during a repair job. Wilson nearly crashed.

As it was, Wilson was already in better shape than some of his fellow pilots. Flight Lieutenant D C "Chunky" Gordon of Vancouver, who also flew with 442, was hospitalised with numerous shrapnel wounds in his back. He had developed engine trouble shortly after the squadron left the airfield on New Year's Day, and was returning when he spotted a gaggle of Huns on its way towards Eindhoven. "He got into them and destroyed two," Monty explained. "But in doing so, he was somehow wounded by a flak-burst and his kite was so badly shot up he was forced to crash-land south of the airfield." Stepping gingerly out of the cockpit and lowering his huge frame carefully to the ground, Gordon was greeted by an overzealous Dutch woman who ran up to him and shouted: "Happy New Year" and clapped him heartily on the back! He was recuperating at Eindhoven.

Flight Lieutenant R C (Jack) Smith also returned early, with a gimpy jet-tank, and heard of the scrap going on near Eindhoven. Like Gordon, he decided to go after a piece of the action. "He thereupon found himself to be the lone Allied aircraft amongst two score or more enemy aircraft," Monty reported. "Undaunted, he attacked no less than ten without waiting to see any results. Then he returned to base, running out of petrol at 7,000 feet partway back. He made a perfect dead-stick landing on the runway."

The pilots of 412 Squadron were still in their dispersals when the attack began. They got off the ground at once and chased after the enemy aircraft, finally intercepting thirty-plus FW 190s west of Venlo. Together, Squadron Leader Dover and Flying Officer Kelly destroyed one, while Flight Lieutenant J B (Joe) Doak, Flight Lieutenant (Moe) MacPherson and Flying Officer Smith claimed one each. Dover led a second go that day, which resulted in a Ju 88 shot down by Flight Lieutenant Banks thirteen kilometres south of Hamm. Two stray 109s were sighted southeast of Osnabruck during a third outing. Dover destroyed one. The second was brought down by Flight Lieutenant "Jock" Swan. In the midst of this combat another Me 109 appeared seemingly out of nowhere to catch Doak. His aircraft crashed in flames not far from where the 109s went down. Doak was the wing's second loss that day.

In return, the wing's squadrons had scored twenty-four enemy aircraft destroyed—a new record for a single day of air combat. The tally sheet attached to the daily Summary of Operations filled an entire page. The only squadron that had not claimed any victories was 402, which was still carrying out two-man patrols owing to a continuing scarcity of its serviceable aircraft at Nistelrode. It had sent out the first such patrol at 0819, well before the enemy's attack began, and had eagerly chased after various sightings, but without success. For its part, 411 Squadron was out on an armed recce at 0850, led by Flight Lieutenant Ireland. Near Twente, two FW 190s were sighted. They were quickly despatched by the wing's newest ace, Flight Lieutenant Audet. The remaining pilots complained afterwards of having missed "all the fun" over the airfield.

Monty, too, and his staff working in the intelligence vans had almost more work than they could handle throughout the day. In the morning the AOC ordered the wing to demonstrate with as much vigour as possible that the enemy offensive had not restricted its effectiveness. Special arrangements were once again laid on to allow a quick turnaround in re-arming and refuelling aircraft, as well as feeding, briefing, and debriefing pilots. There were literally dozens of combat reports to verify and numerous inquiries from Group HQ to be answered. The crash sites of enemy aircraft yielded a bountiful supply of German maps and other "indiscretions carried in pockets," all of which had to be assessed. In the middle of the day, wing personnel attended to the crew of a British Lancaster that crashed several kilometres from the airfield. Sick quarters received badly burned crewmen, who were treated and sent along to a field hospital. Some time after it was learned that one of the patients, RAF Flight Sergeant G Thompson, a wireless operator, was posthumously awarded the Victoria Cross for his heroism in rescuing two gunners from a fire aboard the bomber before it came down.

Hard work they could take. Losses, especially their own, were always difficult. Most of all, though, everyone realised the New Year's Day raids were a disaster for the Luftwaffe, even if it had undoubtedly inflicted damage on a number of their targets. Three wings based at Eindhoven, in particular, were badly hit. Heavy attacks developed outside of Brussels and at other Allied airfields in Belgium, resulting in a loss of perhaps as many as 300 front-line fighter aircraft. But the losses could be replaced almost immediately. Not so for the Luftwaffe. It would be hardpressed to compensate for its own losses that day, which were almost as great—an estimated 200 aircraft destroyed, most if not all with their pilots.

Worse, the Luftwaffe had failed in its bid to deliver a knock-out blow. The raids were a desperate act, the last throw of a gambler's dice. All that they had achieved, like the December offensive in the Ardennes, was to briefly delay the Allies' preparations to break into Germany, while drawing men and equipment from the eastern front where they might have stemmed the Red Army's advance into southern Poland. Hitler gloated that he had inflicted almost 20,000 fatal casualties on the US 12th Army Group alone, and taken 15,000 prisoners while spreading general alarm throughout Belgium. The fact remained Germany's military resources were badly depleted. There was little left, it seemed, to stop the enemy in either the east or the west.

Except, perhaps, the weather. The onset of winter snowstorms virtually closed down B88 for most of January. Pilots had some success finding ground targets to shoot up—mostly locomotives—but only four days in the entire month saw engagements with enemy aircraft.

The first such occasion followed shortly after the New Year's Day raids, on January 4th. First light had given every indication the weather would be "clampers again," but by midday it had lifted enough that it was decided to set out a few armed recces. Flight Lieutenant "Hubbie" Husband led 401 Squadron to the Lingen-Osnabruck area, which was uneventful. Next off was 412 led by Flight Lieutenant Dave Boyd. For their efforts, the pilots reported only a fair amount of flak in the area of Burgstienfurt. More productive was an outing by 411 Squadron early in the afternoon. Seven-plus FW 190s were sighted in the area of Hengelo. Flying Officer Graham scored two destroyed. Dick Audet and Flight Lieutenant Boyle each added one more and shared a third, while Flight Lieutenant Carr claimed one as well—the squadron's sixth for the mission, which prompted the wing's diarist to note officially, "another nice effort, lads." The last mission of the day was carried out by 442 Squadron, which accounted for one probable and a damaged after it ran into fifteen-plus 109s and 190s, again at Hengelo.

Four days of contemptible weather followed. On the 8th, the wing's diarist reported that snowstorms prevented even a weather recce. "Late afternoon saw some fifty-odd pilots getting some real exercise for a change, wielding a shovel, endeavouring to clear runway, perimeters, and dispersal, mainly in the hopes of getting a few hours flying in on the morrow. So ended another quiet, boring day." Low cloud and intermittent flurries grounded the wing the next day, too. Pilots were out again with shovels, clearing the runway and spreading sand. A photograph of the airfield that appeared in the *London Illustrated News* was accompanied by the caption, "snow-swept expanse of an RAF airfield on the continent." It was as depressing a sight as one could imagine, relieved only by the sight of local Dutch kids who begged, borrowed or stole empty Jerry cans from the airfield and used them as makeshift toboggans.

By the 13th, the weather cleared enough to send out an armed recce, the first operational sortie in six days. Even then conditions were deplorable. Poor visibility and a low ceiling restricted the range of one mission by pilots of 412 Squadron. Nevertheless, two damaged enemy transports were scored near Stadtkill. Fair weather the next morning allowed 402 Squadron to get away for its scheduled date at an armament practice camp in England. The rest of the day saw a considerable number of sorties flown by the wing's remaining squadrons—and more combat with the Luftwaffe.

To start with, 401 Squadron caught a dozen FW 190s with jet tanks in the circuit over the aerodrome at Twente. They attacked at once. Flight Lieutenant MacKay shot down three of the enemy fighters, while Flight Lieutenant Murray and Flying Officer D B Dack each claimed one. Flight Lieutenant R J Land was forced to bail out when his Spitfire was hit by flak. In the middle of this fulminating action, 442 Squadron came along and provided excellent top cover as well claiming a few good scores of their own. Flight Lieutenant G E Reade, Flight Lieutenant J N Dick and Flying Officer A J Urquhart each destroyed one 190. But Urquhart, too, was forced to abandon his aircraft. He bailed out over enemy territory and, like Land, was subsequently listed as missing.

Fifteen minutes after the action started, 411 Squadron caught more 190s taking off from the Twente airfield. Audet, Boyle and Flying Officer J A Doran each claimed one destroyed. The day's total for the wing was eleven, for the loss of two of its own pilots. They hadn't met the enemy often in January, but the wing's pilots had certainly inflicted a heavy toll on each occasion.

The weather closed in again with a vengeance the following morning, leaving the airmen to return to whatever they did to keep themselves occupied. Weather recces were carried out when conditions seemed the least bit promising, but the results generally confirmed what had been predicted already by the wing's many armchair meteorologists. Those days when the weather cooperated enough to mount even a modest number of missions were especially nerve-wracking for the cautious staff of Flying Control. The area surrounding Nistelrode was known to be mercurial: one minute the airfield would be marginally acceptable for flying, and in the next, visibility might be nil as a thick ground fog came rolling in with an astonishing suddenness or a snow squall developed. It was Flying Control's job to ensure pilots got back before conditions deteriorated. The staff huddled inside its van filled with all sorts of black boxes and six telephones, which seemed to ring incessantly, while they kept in touch with the pilots aloft. Flying Control always had a close relationship with the four-man signals unit that lived inside "another queer vehicle" parked nearby. This was the direction finding van, more commonly known as "D/F Homer," where LAC Jack Ivamy spent his nights. "Lots of pilots owe their lives to the smartness with which the lads tucked inside old Homer snapped out the right answer," said Monty. "The Homer boys listened to the same frequency as Flying Control, and when any of the wing's aircraft was operating one of them is continually taking bearings on the pilot's transmissions. As soon as the pilot says he is in trouble, or he wants a check-bearing, the D/F operator passes the bearing to the Flying Control Officer who in a matter of seconds has passed it on to the pilot. Scores of aircraft have been homed quickly and safely, through bad weather and cloud, when otherwise they might have had a very sticky time of it." Monty, with his seemingly unending supply of statistics, noted that in the course of eleven months some 800 homings were passed, requiring some 3,000 vectors to 2,500 aircraft.

As good as both Homer and Flying Control were, something went wrong on the 20th. Snow squalls and leaden skies greeted the pilots early in the morning, but by 0900 they had cleared enough to permit operations. First off was 411 Squadron to attempt an armed recce in the Emmerich-Münster-Osnabruck-Lingen area. The mission was aborted due to 10/10 cloud conditions and "generally duff weather," which must have been an understatement given that Flying Officer Ellement vanished. He was last seen in formation with the squadron south of Zutphen, "and nobody can really say what happened to him," the wing's diarist noted. Squadron Leader Newell reported that he had been unable to contact Ellement by radio earlier in the mission. It was the start of a run of bad luck for the wing that day. Shortly after 412 Squadron left on an armed recce to the same area, the four pilots of Blue Section disappeared after one of them, Flight Lieutenant Richards, called on the R/T to say his engine had cut and he was about to attempt a forced-landing in a field somewhere near Nijmegen. The squadron later sent two aircraft on a search recce, but no trace of the missing pilots was found. By the end of the day, Richards along with the rest of Blue Section—Flight

Lieutenant McPherson, Pilot Officer McPhee, and Pilot Officer Walkom—were unhappily listed as NYR.*

An incredible fifty-four sorties were flown that day, resulting in the loss of five pilots. There were no claims, which was a rarity for the wing even in such conditions.

The weather hardly improved overnight. Perhaps chastened by the previous day's experience, fewer sorties were attempted. Poor visibility and heavy flak in the area of Deventer, where 411 Squadron was sent on one armed recce, limited the Grizzly Bears' claim to only a single enemy vehicle damaged.

Two days later, though—it was the 23rd—early morning snow gave way to crisp, clear skies. Flight Lieutenant Ireland led 411 Squadron on the first armed recce, leaving at 0917 for the Lingen-Münster area. The enemy seemed to be more active on the ground. Almost every mission during the day reported considerable road and rail traffic, particularly during deeper penetrations of enemy-held territory late in the day. These afforded "steady pickings," Monty noted, and missions that were "interesting for the number of Hun 'bods' that met a gory end." Monty's account of an armed recce by 442 Squadron was typical. The squadron, led by Flight Lieutenant Jackson, left at 1000 and returned in an hour and a half with numerous claims for ground casualties in the Lingen-Osnabruck-Münster area. Monty noted in the Summary of Operations that 442's pilots had left the scene after "damaging a truck and trailer and clobbering at least fifteen troops as they attempted to escape. One other transport was destroyed and three damaged. A horse-drawn transport was literally blown to pieces and one horse is claimed destroyed, the other probably, plus one driver very badly startled." Later in the day, too, the squadron shot up ground targets until it ran out of ammunition. Flying Officer Red Francis also damaged a FW 190 north of Rheine—the wing's second that day. Earlier,

---

* According to Monty, all four pilots were captured after making forced landings in different parts of northern Holland. "They were all released and got home all right after VE-Day, which was a happy ending. We never knew, though, until after the war, what had happened to them. It seemed as though they had simply vanished."

during 411's first mission, a 190 was destroyed by Flight Lieutenant Cook. The pilot bailed out, but his parachute got tangled on his aircraft—a surprisingly easy thing to do—and both went into the ground.

Shortly after 411 left, Squadron Leader Klersy led 401 out on its first recce of the day. The Rams surprised as many as fifteen jet-jobs "in varying stages of going and coming at Bramsche aerodrome," north of Osnabruck. There is some confusion concerning the combat that followed. Both the ORB and Summary of Operations indicate that three Me 262s were destroyed (Flying Officer Church and Flying Officer Hardy claimed one each, while Flight Lieutenant Connell and Pilot Officer W Thomas shared one), and six were damaged (one claim was subsequently accepted as a "probable" by Group HQ). But afterwards, the pilots reconsidered the matter and decided the aircraft they had claimed were in fact Arado 234s, the Luftwaffe's other jet-propelled "blitz bombers." There should not have been as much doubt. The Arado was smaller, not so fast and more lightly armed in comparison with the Me 262. Its slouching Perspex canopy section up front was also distinctive. But it was the first time the pilots had seen the aircraft outside of a recognition test. Monty, as SIO, allowed the claim of 3-1-5 Ar 234s to stand in his list of air victories.

A second mission by 411 late in the day gave Dick Audet an opportunity to raise his own score. All extant records agree that Audet destroyed two Me 262s, one on the ground and one during a combat. He also claimed numerous ground targets. The squadron also bounced two Me 109s east of Osnabruck, but was unable to finish them off. Flying Officer G G Harrison, who was last seen chasing the enemy aircraft, was listed as missing as a result of this action. The next day, Audet added another damaged Me 262. His meteoric rise in the scoring columns over the past few weeks was a great personal triumph, as well as a contributing factor in the wing's surprising tally for January.

In only a handful of good flying days that month, its scoreboard showed an almost incredible 46-3-17 for enemy aircraft destroyed, probably destroyed and damaged.

The impressive numbers were probably announced, with some light-hearted commentary, during one of the regular evening broadcasts by B88's own radio station, WTAF, more popularly billed as "The Voice of 126 Wing." Monty claims the idea for a broadcasting unit was promoted by Flight Sergeant Les Taylor, who began working on it while the wing was at Evere, near Brussels. "There were three long months of hard work in the meantime," Monty recalled. "Using every minute of his spare time, often far into the night, Les devoted himself to the advancement of his plan. First he built a receiver using any material he could scrounge and, if none was available, he made his own components to suit his purpose. Next, he constructed the transmitter. Many tests and alterations were required before he was satisfied. Even after its official opening at B88, improvements and modifications were needed until WTAF became one of the greatest 'little' broadcasting stations we had. It brightened a lot of dull days."

WTAF operated from 0900 to midnight, rebroadcasting AEF programmes as well as those originating from its own "studios," which were in fact a tent. The station's regular programming included a popular request hour, known as "Strictly on the Beam," from 2300 until sign-off. On Sunday evening, religious programming was provided. Another favourite of the airmen was the show, "Roy Logan and his Alberta Ranch Boys," which featured old-time music and songs. Few would argue that the programmes were a vast improvement over the old system of announcing information over the Tannoy. "Nobody seemed to know how to speak into it, and there never seemed to be the same person using it twice running," Monty said. Stan Helleur was so irritated by the device and its users that he wrote a newspaper piece on the subject.

HOLLAND—A Tannoy public address system is a great thing to have around a camp such as this RCAF base commanded by G/C G R McGregor, OBE, DFC, Montreal, but there should be a book of directions on how to use it.

For example, one evening the camp heard this announcement: "There will be a bomb detonated within the next half-hour."

But the voice didn't say where and reactions were hair-trigger for the next hour, people taking cover whenever an ankle cracked. That was about two weeks ago, and they're still waiting for the bang.

Recently a cultured voice announced: "It is reported there will be a slight frost tonight. The usual precautions will be taken." Unfortunately, the voice failed to prescribe the "usual precautions."

The testing business is sure to crop up a couple of times a day. It goes something like this: "(Loud blow) Testing. One, two, three, four, five (another loud blow). Five, four..." and so on, resulting in half the camp being on the verge of hands-on-hips, knee-bending in accompaniment.

But the most radical opposition comes from those unfortunates located between two loud-speakers, so that you get the old double-talk like this: "This-this is-is London-London calling-calling through-through the-the overseas-overseas service-service of-of the-the bee-bee-bee-bee cee-cee."

Another item that surely elicited comment from WTAF's broadcasters was the arrival on January 26th of Wing Commander G W (Geoffrey) Northcott, DSO, DFC, to replace Dal Russel as the wing's CO. Russel had known for weeks that he was on his way home after a third tour of operations.

"Winco Northcott felt right at home in short order," Monty recalled. "He was always most cheerful and easy to get along with, and he knew the score inside out." Northcott, originally from Minnedosa, Manitoba, had served in the Middle East before finishing a second tour in England as CO of 402 Squadron. His score was a modest 7½-0-5 (citations credit him with nine destroyed), yet he was highly regarded for his leadership qualities and skill as a pilot. The latter point surfaced oddly enough during a gathering at the officers' mess one night, when Group Captain McGregor related an anecdote from his early days with 401 Squadron. Monty recalled the story:

The Groupie, who was then 401's commander, was returning with the squadron from a quiet sweep over northwestern France.

Coming out over Boulogne, he saw a Spitfire losing height and smoking. So he called over the R/T, "Green 2, escort that aircraft across the Channel and when he bails out pin-point the spot for Controller and stay with him as long as you can." The Groupie then carried on and didn't get a chance to see what had happened for some minutes. When he looked next, he saw this aircraft smoking even more and a lot lower, and still all alone, apparently trying to glide as far as possible. He didn't think the kite would get to the coast. He called angrily on the R/T, "Green 2, get down there and look after that smoking kite!" Nothing happened.

Later, when the squadron had landed and the pilots congregated to review the operation, the Groupie scowled at the lot and demanded, "Who's Green 2?" There was a hushed silence. "Don't tell me we're missing two kites," the Groupie exclaimed. He counted heads. There were eleven. Only one missing, after all. And then he discovered that there had been a shuffle in the wing's formation. No one else had noticed it either. It was Green 2 who had been in trouble, and he'd been shouting at him to escort himself all the way home.

Now, Winco Northcott, who was listening to the Groupie's story, suddenly piped up, "Do you know who Green 2 was, Sir?" "I don't," answered the Groupie, "but he was some sprog sergeant pilot who had just joined the squadron. He did a good job, though, managing to glide just far enough over the English coast to crash-land safely."

"Well, Sir," said Winco Northcott, "that sprog was me. My R/T had gone u/s when I was hit over Boulogne and I couldn't tell you. But I can tell you now that I nursed that kite for every ounce. I didn't want to come down in the Channel 'cos I can hardly swim!"

Monty said it was immediately obvious to all that McGregor and Wing Commander Northcott would have no trouble working together as a team.

It was just as well, too, for the wing was about to play an important role in fighting for the western Rhineland. Allied planning for the operation had gathered momentum following the enemy's collapse in the Ardennes. "The enemy is in a bad way," Montgomery declared on the eve of the offensive, "he has had a tremendous battering and has lost heavily in men and equipment. On no account can we relax, or have a 'stand still,' in the winter months; it is vital that we keep going."

It would not be easy. The plan was to deliver a series of heavy blows along the entire length of the western front. Montgomery expected "difficulties caused by mud, cold, lack of air support during periods of bad weather, and so on." Throughout January the ground had at least stayed frozen, which helped the movement of vehicles. But a sudden thaw during the first week of February left many roads reduced to a sticky gumbo. Nor were the difficulties experienced only by soldiers. The high-flying pilots of 126 Wing were often grounded for days by bouts of "Dutch weather." Aircraft wallowed in the muck as they taxied to and from the runway; some even sank almost to the tops of their wheels and had to be prised out. For a while, life at B88 was drearily reminiscent of Volkel.

Yet operations continued. In retrospect, the month saw fewer claims for enemy aircraft, but substantially more damage was wrought on the ground—although on the first day of the Allied offensive, February 8th, the wing got off to an auspicious start in both categories. More than a hundred sorties were flown by all five of the wing's squadrons (402 had returned from its gunnery course at Warmwell: "post-graduate honours" went to Flight Lieutenant Sleep, who destroyed a Ju 88 north of Coesfeld during the squadron's first mission that day). Southeast of Wesel, 442 Squadron mixed it up with five Ju 87s—better known as Stukas—which were not often seen in their area let alone engaged. Flight Lieutenant "Chunky" Gordon, sufficiently recovered from his earlier injuries, downed two of the enemy divebombers and shared another with Flight Lieutenant Boyle, who was also credited with one of his own. The last was claimed by Flight Lieutenant Barker, for a total of five down. On the same mission the squadron damaged three locomotives and shot up some vehicles. It was a good day, albeit short due to the weather. And Dick Audet had a narrow escape. His aircraft was badly damaged by flak. Unable to land, he bailed out near Heesch. He landed safely and found his way back to the airfield in time to be debriefed.

Duff weather, "patchy weather"—the wing's diarists had difficulty sometimes finding new ways to describe the stuff. On the 11th, during one of the few missions that left the airfield, Flight Lieutenant Hodges of 402 Squadron lost formation in dense cloud and was killed when his Spitfire crashed near Volkel. For the first time since the wing's arrival on the continent, casualties to both men and aircraft were beginning to mount. The same day Hodges was killed, Flying Officer Arnold Gibb of 412 Squadron had a close call when he was forced to bail out over the Reichswald Forest due to engine failure. His Spitfire was a write-off, but Gibb was lucky. He landed in an area that had been captured by Allied troops only hours earlier. An unidentified pilot from 402 Squadron barely survived an incident on the 12th. Flight Lieutenant Ken Sleep led a section into the area around Enschede. One eager young train buster, while diving on a locomotive, suddenly came upon a high tension wire that stretched across the railway. In the instant he had to manoeuvre or fly into the obstacle, he decided to pass *beneath* the wire. He made it, but in doing so completely severed twelve inches off the tail of his Spitfire and a large piece of a propeller blade. The pilot returned to the airfield and faced the erks responsible for mending such damage.

The wing's best day in weeks followed shortly after, on the 14th. Despite a gusting crosswind that made taking off and landing risky enterprises, pilots logged 237 sorties—their largest number since landing on the continent. Monty noted that sightings of road and rail transport were not plentiful but enough pickings were found to keep pilots interested. Three squadrons on divebombing missions made fourteen good rail cuts on "priority lines" as well as shooting up a substantial number of ground targets. "Enemy aircraft—chiefly jet-jobs—were elusive all day, likely trying to draw red herrings across the paths of our ground attack missions," the Ops Summary reported. "A goodly number of enemy aircraft were seen on the 'dromes as well and 411 Squadron couldn't resist the sight of 30-plus glistening twin-engine aircraft lined up in full view on Münster-Handorf a/d. And so a quick dart was made by F/L Jack Boyle and

F/S Watt, resulting in two He 177s going up in flames and three more damaged."

The arrival of some vital pieces of equipment to permit the carrying of 500-pound bombs under 402 Squadron's new Spitfire XIVs promised greater effectiveness. There had been concern that the squadron was not inflicting as much damage as it could in support of efforts on the ground, and the squadron itself had loudly protested the delay in receiving the equipment it needed. The matter had become somewhat rancorous. Expectations of the wing's role in the ground offensive ran high, while the pace of activity at B88 spawned a short tolerance among the Canadians for any criticism of their efforts. "It is a great pity that all those calamities should occur for the want of a few small gadgets that probably exist in profusion in some not-so-far-away depot," Monty added.

Losses suffered by the wing merely added to the level of stress. On the 21st, 402 Squadron went out on its last armed recces before converting the next day to divebombing. Several ground targets were attacked, resulting in five trains destroyed or damaged, and twenty-three railway trucks shot up. But during this mission, Flight Lieutenant "Lem" Barnes was hit by flak and had to bail out over Haltern. His fate was unknown. Prior to the beginning of operations that day, pilots had been specially briefed on the subject of interrogation methods in the event they were captured. Squadron Leader Keene, now with 83 Group HQ, had given the talk, which was interrupted at one point by a Me 262 that zoomed noisily over the airfield after dropping a bomb a kilometre to the east. If Barnes was taken prisoner, it was hoped the morning talk had some impact. The fate of Flying Officer J C McAllister, his Number Two that day, left little doubt. He crashed while landing at B88 and was killed. "McAllister had just joined the squadron but was very well liked," Monty recalled.

More tragedy followed. The next day, during an armed recce by 401 Squadron, Flight Lieutenant Freddie Murray's Spitfire was hit by flak and he was forced to crash-land in enemy territory north of Hengelo. Squadron Leader Jowsey of 442 had to bail out over Germany as well when his aircraft was disabled by its own bullets ricocheting off ground targets during a low-level attack. He was seen to land safely, but it was not known if he had escaped or was captured. "His loss will be keenly felt by the whole wing, and particularly his own squadron," Monty observed in the Summary of Operations. Flying Officer Bill Cowan of 412 was killed when he bailed out east of Nijmegen. He had developed engine trouble on the return trip from a divebombing mission along the Emmerich-Borken-Bochalt rail line, and reported over the R/T that he was bailing out. The cause of Cowan's death was unknown, although it seems likely he was killed in his jump. Every pilot recognised the inherent risks of parachuting. Even when planned, it was fraught with the potential of getting knocked about or even caught on a part of the aircraft (as had happened recently to one Luftwaffe pilot who attempted to escape after his Me 109 was shot to pieces by one of the Canadians). Bailing out, as a matter of last-resort, often left little choice in the terrain over which the desperate act was committed. Aside from the question of whether or not it was friendly, parachutists ran the risk of coming down too hard or even landing amidst such obstacles as woods or bomb-damaged buildings.

The loss of Cowan and the others would be keenly felt, despite the arrival of a number of new pilots and success in the wing's operations for most of the day (402 had made a good start on its divebombing, claiming seven rail cuts, one locomotive destroyed and a number of railway coaches destroyed). A grim resolve began to characterise operations. Treacherous weather conditions that grounded the wing for a day lifted enough on the 24th to permit sorties, but even then the losses continued. Flight Lieutenant Boyle and Flying Officer Cousineau went chasing after several enemy aircraft they had sighted during an armed recce by 442 in the Rhine area, promptly lost their squadron mates in the clouds and vanished themselves shortly after. "Beyond some R/T chatter nothing further is known about either pilot," Monty recorded. "They seem to have run into a mixture of flak and Jerry a/c that was too much for them."

Favourable conditions on the 25th gave the wing a long-awaited opportunity to seek revenge. In addition to a number of rail targets that were successfully blasted, several buildings and a flak installation were destroyed by 401 and 402. The latter had also mixed it up with a number of enemy aircraft, resulting in a claim for one Me 262 that was damaged by Flight Lieutenant Sleep and Flight Lieutenant Innes. The Luftwaffe was out in strength that day, adding to the determined resistance the Allies were facing in their march over the Rhineland. Early in the morning 412 Squadron encountered some Me 109s while flying constant patrols over the area of Enschede. Flying Officer MacLeod destroyed one and damaged another. Later, 442 ran into forty-plus 109s west of Rheine. For a change, too, "the Hun wanted to play," said Monty. In the end seven 109s were destroyed, two each by Flight Lieutenant R K (Ken) Trumley, Pilot Officer Baker, and Flying Lieutenant Barker (who also claimed one damaged). "Chunky" Gordon was also credited with one destroyed. "This combat was carried out with no losses to the squadron," Monty noted happily, "although a couple of our kites were holed." But other squadrons had not escaped casualties. Flight Lieutenant Harvey of 402 last reported he was bailing out near Enschede after his Spitfire was hit by flak, while 411 had lost Pilot Officer Watson. His Spitfire was engulfed in flames when he parachuted to an unknown fate somewhere in enemy territory.

Except for a combination of extraordinary piloting skills and possibly even a measure of Providence, Flight Lieutenant Reid of 411 Squadron might have been another of the wing's casualties on that last day of action in February. His aircraft was so badly shot up it seems a miracle he was able to return to the airfield. Monty recorded the extent of the damage in the wing's Summary of Operations. It is hard not to share his incredulity at both Reid's survival and the durability of the Spitfire. Looking over the aircraft, Monty found: "three feet of one blade of the prop sheared off; the engine had sprung several oil leaks; the oil tank had vibrated off its moorings and was hanging by one clamp; the air intake scoop was just hanging, that's all; the front engine bearer bolts were sheared; and the fuselage was distorted." The vibrations Reid experienced as a result of the damage had literally knocked his helmet off. "And yet," Monty added, "the kite landed safely."

It was more than could be said for an alarming number of the wing's Spitfires—and, for that matter, pilots as well. The matter came up in a report by Wing Commander Northcott. Ten pilots were missing or killed; twelve had been lost in the previous month. "No generalised reason for the losses can readily be found, other than straight bad luck," Northcott reported. Flak was a constant worry, but it was not known to have accounted for more than two, possibly three of the losses. Enemy air activity may have caused two more. The balance was attributed to either accidents or incidents "not known to be due to enemy action." Most worrisome were the losses of formation leaders, which Northcott said were disproportionately high. One squadron commander and three flight commanders had been recorded as NYR. Northcott added that the enemy apparently had been given a "shot in the arm" and was showing an inclination to stay and fight more frequently. For its part, the wing's tactics remained much the same with modifications in light of changing conditions and more experience. "It is considered that dive-bombing efforts are best undertaken in flight strength, with the flights alternating as top cover," observed Northcott. "Nearly all air-to-air engagements demonstrated the … absolute necessity of a careful watch for a bounce from above prior to and during the engagement of any enemy formation."

Surprisingly, Northcott's report did not mention the state of morale among the wing's personnel. Notwithstanding the loss of so many good young pilots recently and the generally gloomy weather, life for the most part was good at B88. Improvements had been made to the barracks and briefing rooms. For entertainment there were movies, WTAF's nightly broadcasts and regular performances by the wing's own orchestra, which had been revived that month under the direction of "part-time intelligence officer" Donald Stewart.

There was a sense, too, that the war was entering its final stages. Such a notion was bound to raise flagging spirits, even if it meant leaving the comforts of B88 sometime soon for whatever lay ahead—most likely in Hitler's Reich.

9

VICTORY

THE TELEGRAPH was brief. "Regret to advise that Flight Lieutenant Harry Peter Mackenzie Furniss C One Nought Eight One is reported missing after air operations overseas March First. RCAF Casualties Officer."

In fact, Furniss—a muscular twenty-five-year-old who bore a striking resemblance to Laurence Olivier—was alive and well, except for a badly twisted ankle, and arguably safe despite having been captured. Shot down by a FW 190 during an armed recce, the 401 Squadron pilot had bailed out over Wesel and landed in the backyard of a farmhouse that was occupied by enemy flak gunners. He was stripped of his possessions and marched eight kilometres under guard to see the local Kommandant. Later he was locked in a cellar for the night and given some black bread and thin potato soup. The next morning Furniss was allowed outside, but only briefly. "Come and breathe some good German air," the guard said. Then it was back to the cellar, where undoubtedly he reflected on the bizarre circumstances that had led to his predicament.

Only a few weeks before, Harry Furniss was lingering over drinks in a West End club in London, enjoying a brief respite with his vivacious young English wife, Enid. Furniss had spent a year and a half flying Spitfires with the RCAF's 400 (City of Toronto) Squadron, a photo reconnaissance unit, and was on his way back to active duty. "I should have gone home to Canada when we reached Eindhoven in December 1944," he explained afterwards, "but I talked my way into flying fighters with 401 at Heesch—with disastrous results!"

Both 401 and 412 had left early on March 1st to search for enemy aircraft reported in the area of Dorsten. After flying for some time without any sightings, the Canadians were suddenly bounced by forty-plus Me 109s and FW 190s. Monty later reported that "412 couldn't quite work into the tussle; 401, however, was well and truly involved. Squadron Leader Klersy had a busy few minutes, scoring three destroyed—two 109s and one 190." Flight Lieutenant Johnny MacKay, leading "A" Flight, shot down one 109 and damaged one more as well as a 190, while Flying Officer Sawyer added a 109 as a probable. But the squadron had its hands full on this outing. Flight Lieutenant "Dusty" Thorpe wound up a lengthy tour of operations in a spectacular fashion. "He had just positioned himself for a couple of quick kills, with visions of what a nice way it was to spend his last sortie, when suddenly his aileron controls were shot away and he found himself at 3,000 feet from 15,000 in no time at all. He just managed to regain control, with both hands on the stick, and limped back to Volkel where he landed wheels-up beside the runway—at 195 mph! It took a substantial shot of rum from the MO to restore him to speech."

Monty's only information concerning Furniss was that he was "apparently hit in combat and said on the R/T he thought he could make it home." He didn't. Later, Furniss said his Spitfire with its distinctive call letters YO-Y had been shot so full of holes that he had no choice but to bail out. Another casualty.

Furniss spent several weeks in enemy hands, mostly on a forced march along with other PoWs. There was barely enough food to eat and on numerous occasions he was beaten and nearly shot by angry German officers or lynched by "bomb-happy" civilians. Near Frankfurt, which was "a shambles" after Allied raids, he was locked in a cell. He spent the entire next day in a box car in a lumber yard before moving to a damp cellar for the night, throughout which was an almost constant aerial bombardment. Travelling at one point on a

PoW train, he had an opportunity to see first hand the effects of his wing's continuing rail interdiction operations. He spent hours waiting because the lines ahead had been cut, and then while underway the train itself was strafed.

Eventually Furniss arrived at Dulag, where he was interned at a PoW camp. Doctors taped his ankle, the first treatment he had received for his injury since being captured. There was a noticeable difference in the attitude of his captors. Many openly declared the war was all but finished; others had deserted already. Those who remained were perhaps seeking the favour of a good recommendation by the PoWs in the event the camp was overrun by the Allies.

Towards the end of March, the camp's *Kommandant* was able to find enough men left to send out a patrol in an attempt to find out what was happening in the sector. The men were promptly rounded up by a platoon of GIs. A short while later, Furniss recalled, "some Yanks arrived in a jeep. Terrific welcome. We took over the radios, set guards on the camp to keep out stray Jerries, and listened to the BBC. Oh boy!"

Furniss and the others were sent back through Allied lines, where they received proper medical attention. Soon after, another Canadian Pacific telegraph was sent to Mr and Mrs G M Furniss of 900 Sherbrooke Street West in Montreal. "Pleased to advise your son Flight Lieutenant Harry Peter Mackenzie Furniss has arrived safely United Kingdom. RCAF Casualties Officer." And later: "Safe and well in England. Harry Furniss."

No better news was ever conveyed to his parents. For Harry Furniss, the war was over by early April.

It was almost finished, too, for those still fighting in Europe. The day Harry Furniss was shot down, the Allies had advanced along a wide front to within striking distance of the Rhine. Germany was crumbling under relentless pressure.

But not easily. As Canadian military historian Charles Stacey cautioned, "Let no one misconceive the severity of the fighting during these final months. In this ... the defenders of the Reich displayed the recklessness of fanaticism and the courage of despair. In the contests west of the Rhine, in particular, they fought with special ferocity and resolution, rendering the battles in the Reichswald and Hochwald forests grimly memorable in the annals of this war." Stacey was speaking of the ground war, of course, in which Canadian soldiers were very much involved, but it could have also been applied to the the air war, too. The Luftwaffe, when it could be found, seemed possessed by an equal measure of "ferocity and resolution," as the men of 126 Wing knew only too well. Pilots who spent their days flak-dodging were no less inclined to suggest there was still plenty of fight left in the enemy. The element of risk remained extremely high. And, sadly, it was just as indiscriminate.

March 3rd. Sorties began before sunrise in an attempt to catch the enemy by surprise, but no ground movement was sighted. A sweep by 411 Squadron over the area of Coesfeld late in the day finally located some activity. Two locomotives and a number of other ground targets were attacked. As usual, there was heavy flak. Flight Lieutenant Dick Audet's aircraft was hit while diving at one of the locomotives, and started pouring glycol. It burst into flames almost immediately, plunged into the ground from 500 feet and exploded.

For months afterwards, Monty said, rumours circulated that Audet had been seen in a military hospital, and even in England. Neither was possible. Audet was killed instantly. He was just ten days short of his twenty-third birthday.

"It was a great loss to the wing," Monty remembers, "and a greater loss to his young wife in England, with whom he had just spent some leave. In fact, he had returned to active duty only the day before that fateful mission. He was blessed with much skill and equal humility, and was an outstanding example for all the pilots. He was also a swell guy."

Audet's record stood at 11½-0-1. He had logged 108:45 operational hours in 83 sorties. His good work with 126 Wing had recently earned him a Bar to his DFC. An official announcement of the award was made in the *London Gazette*, but it came too late for

Richard Joseph Audet to see it. He had already paid what Monty said was "the price of the wing's great achievements."

Twelve days passed before the wing attacked any more ground targets. In the meantime, during a two-man patrol over Wesel on March 12th, 401's Flight Lieutenant L H Watt destroyed a Me 262 that he had spotted zooming along under the cover of clouds at 2,500 feet. Watt gave the jet-job a short burst, and watched it go down in smoke before he had to break off due to "very accurate fire" from Allied guns also trying to bring down the enemy fighter. The next day, Flying Control vectored 402 Squadron to intercept another jet-job near Gladbach. It was shot down in short order by Flying Officer Nicholson. Several others were reported in the area of Goch, but they eluded the Spitfires sent after them. The wing's road and rail interdiction resumed on the 15th, resulting in fifteen good cuts as well as a petrol dump destroyed. Intermittent weather conditions hampered operations for days after this, although scores were made on the ground and in the air (the latter were all claimed by pilots of 412 Squadron, who shot down two FW 190s on the 17th and three Me 109s on the 25th).

Much of the wing's attention seemed to be focused on the fortunes of its hockey team, which was on its way to a championship match with 52 Mobile Field Hospital after thrashing 39 Wing at a playoff game held in Antwerp. There was also some growing enthusiasm for the resumption of baseball tournaments—weather and other demands permitting—on a diamond to be established at B88.

Sadly, though, the games would be without 442 Squadron. It was returning to England to be re-equipped with Mustang IIIs based at Hunsdon, Herts, as part of Fighter Command. A farewell party was held for the "Caribou" pilots on March 20th. Donald Stewart noted that "a bountiful dinner headlined by steak and eggs and topped off with champagne" was laid on for the departing airmen. There was also some genuine emotion shown during the occasion on behalf of the men who had contributed so much to the wing's success in a relatively short period. The next day in the Summary of Operations,

Gord Panchuk listed "Fond Memories" in the column previously occupied by 442. In the report's narrative he added, with obvious regret: "The Caribous ain't here anymore."

That first day of Spring found the Allied armies poised on the
west bank of the Rhine, ready to plunge into the heart of Germany.
Field Marshal Montgomery's 21st Army Group (which included the
British 2nd and the Ninth US) would lead the assault, which was set
to commence on the evening of March 23rd. Operation "Plunder"
began with one of the greatest artillery bombardments of the Second
World War—greater, even, than that which had preceded the Normandy Invasion. More than 1,300 British guns pounded the
enemy's positions on the far side of the Rhine where the attacks were
to be launched, while a smokescreen eighty kilometres long concealed Allied moments until the last moment. Amphibious crossings
of the river began at 2100; a second wave followed an hour later.
There was hardly an opposition—at first.

The next morning, Operation "Varsity" was launched. It, too,
was staggering in scale: an aerial armada of more than 3,000 aircraft
and gliders vaulted across the Rhine to spearhead an airborne
assault. It was, as one Canadian unit declared, a "tremendous spectacle." Nine hundred Allied movements, including the Spitfires of
126 Wing, provided a protective umbrella throughout the landings.
Three of 126's squadrons—401, 411 and 412—left at first light to
provide standing patrols at 12,000 feet in Area "C" between
Zutphen and Winterswijk—the deepest penetration of 2nd TAF
fighters that day (127 Wing covered the dog's leg from Winterswijk
to Dorsten)—while 402 joined 125 Wing freelancing closer to the
battlefront. Weather conditions were ideal. "All hands were out
expecting the Hun to put up at least a reasonable fight on this
second D-Day," Gord Panchuk noted. "Everybody was due for a letdown, though. The Hun just wouldn't play. For 219 sorties flown,
nary a Hun was seen." Not surprisingly, the day's only claims were
by 402 Squadron, which had shot up a number of ground targets.
For this the wing had nevertheless worked flat out. The pilots of 411
were first off at 0550; 412's pancaked at 1835. In the Ops Summary,
Panchuk made sure credit was given to groundcrews for their part in

this almost superhuman test of endurance. "We are all inclined to regard it as commonplace for four or five squadrons to take off and land and generally keep flying to 'cover' a certain area or perform a certain mission," he wrote, "but it is not often fully realised the large number of ground personnel involved in order to keep the aircraft flying." Panchuk added that Group Captain McGregor wished especially to "congratulate and thank all the ground crew personnel for their excellent and unstinted effort throughout the day."*

They were just as busy the next day, which, like D+1 in June 1944, proved more productive for the wing flying over the battle zone. Patrolling between Zutphen and Winterswijk, twelve-plus Me 109s and a single FW 190 were bounced by 412 Squadron, led by Wing Commander Northcott. After the smoke cleared it was determined that Squadron Leader Boyd, Flight Lieutenant Pieri and Flying Officer Smith each destroyed one 109, with no casualties to 412. A respectable number of ground targets were shot up as well by all four squadrons. The lion's share went to 402, but it had also suffered a severe blow. Squadron Leader "Les" Moore, while leading a section during one low-level attack, was hit by either flak or his own ricocheting machine gun fire. His Spitfire dove straight in and crashed. "Squadron Leader Moore was CO of 402 for only a short time, but he had become a very popular leader," the Ops Summary observed. "He will be greatly missed by pilots and groundcrew alike."

The last days of March saw the wing continuing its punishing ground attacks, as well as more luck against the Luftwaffe. On the 28th, 30th, and 31st pilots from 401 and 402 combined to bring down six enemy aircraft. But heavy flak encountered while strafing or divebombing had also claimed several pilots. Flying Officer

---

* The Summary also provided the following important news flash: "The final game of the 2nd TAF Hockey League was played at Antwerp on Thursday, March 22nd, between 52 MFH and 126 Wing. The score was 8-2 in favour of 126 Wing. The score was never in doubt from midway in the first period when 126 Wing swept into a two-goal lead." Panchuk added: "It was a fast, well played game but a little rough at times." Following the match, the wing's team left by Dakota for Scotland and playoffs with "the Bomber pros." The war in Europe paled in comparison with such hockey updates.

McCracken of 411 and 412's Flight Lieutenant Burchill were both seen to land safely after bailing out over enemy territory. Flight Lieutenant Anderson of 412 was not so lucky. He was killed on the 30th when his Spitfire was hit in the drop tank and he went straight down in flames northeast of Emmerich. In the same mission Flight Lieutenant James bailed out, although he was able to coax his flak-battered aircraft to friendly territory before he hit the silk.

At the same time, several pilots previously listed as missing were beginning to turn up. The latest was Flight Lieutenant Bill Harvey of 402 Squadron, who had bailed out over Germany in February. He had spent some time in a PoW camp, escaped and was hiding with "friends" when, like Harry Furniss, he was found by American troops. Flying Officer Ellement of 411 Squadron had returned, as well. He was followed several days later, on April 3rd, by 442 ace Milt Jowsey. There would be others. In fact, twenty-one of seventy-nine pilots lost since D-Day eventually returned to the wing. Monty calculated that one pilot went missing for every 251 sorties, based on the wing's total of 20,000 sorties in the period following June 6th. For the month of March, the averages had improved to one pilot lost for every 400 sorties flown (Monty noted also that since landing at Normandy the wing had gone through no less than 325 Spitfires, of which 153 were returned to service, 102 were completely written off and 79 were missing). Each pilot that returned was cause for a celebration, even before they had been debriefed by the intelligence staff. Monty and his cohorts were particularly interested in any useful observations concerning the welcome the wing might anticipate from civilians in Germany. It seemed only a matter of time, now—and not much of that—before they expected to hear officially that the wing was leaving for a new airfield.

An advance party left on April 8th for Goch, Germany, just west of the Rhine, where B100 was located. Two days later, however, they crossed the river at Wesel and turned northeast, travelling 150 kilometres to B108 at Rheine, where it was expected the wing was to be formally established. On the 13th a "B" party of the wing arrived and discovered that Group Captain McGregor had flown to another airfield, B116, at Wunstorf, and had firmed up arrangements to settle there instead. The first convoys set out that day. Traffic was bumper to bumper on difficult roads clogged with refugees and PoWs, and littered with the waste and debris of armies that had swept through recently. There were a few accidents, including one that left one of Monty's staff, Flight Lieutenant John Barrowman, in rough shape with a fractured skull and possible chest injuries. Another mishap that occurred seemed to fall into that category known by military personnel as a "snafu." Due to a lack of space in the first convoys, the wing's dance orchestra had to leave behind its piano, a set of drums, music stands and a case containing music sheets. When personnel returned to Goch later in the day to retrieve the articles, they were nowhere to be found. "Frantic signals are burning up the ether to the other wings stationed at Goch in the hope that they unintentionally took the aforementioned music accessories thinking they had been abandoned," Donald Stewart noted in the day's Ops Summary. "Needless to say, this is a severe loss to our orchestra and will write 'finished' to their efforts to provide much-needed entertainment for the wing."

More worrisome was the fate of 402's CO and the wing's leading ace, Squadron Leader Don Laubman. He bailed out in the area of Celle, an old Ducal town on the Aller (in fact it was first settled in 990 and had preserved its princely character, so far emerging unscathed during the current conflict). Laubman's Spitfire was shot up during a low-level attack on some vehicles. It was believed he landed in friendly territory, but his condition was not known.

In the days that followed, more convoys arrived after harrowing journeys along the crowded, and mostly unmarked roads leading to Wunstorf. Numerous sections were lost for brief periods after taking wrong turns. Don Stewart knew from personal experience how easy it was for a convoy to be misdirected. He had somehow ended up in Hanover during his trek to B116. The large industrial city was mostly flattened rubble and eerily silent—"not a person, not a bird, no service police, nothing stirring," he recalled. But eventually everyone

found the airfield. Most agreed their hard travelling was amply rewarded. Until recently, B116 had been a busy Luftwaffe station used
primarily by bomber crews, who obviously left in such a hurry that
they had little opportunity to demolish buildings or remove equipment—including many of their aircraft. "There were rows and rows
of them," remembers airframe mechanic Garry Whitmore, "fully
armed and ready to go. But every gas tank was empty." Among the
captured aircraft was one that mystified some of the wing's personnel. Possibly it was a Dornier *Pfeil,* which had two engines driving
"push-pull" airscrews. It was just one of many unconventional exper-
imental aircraft built but never used by the Luftwaffe (although it
seems to fit the description given by Whitmore), and clearly a prize
for Allied aviation experts. But one night, while a petrol bowser
parked nearby was being loaded, a spark set it on fire. "We scrambled
to get all the jerry cans out of the area before they went up, too,"
Whitmore added.

Better than captured Jerry kites, according to a few erks, were rumours that a cache of beer and champagne was hidden in a cave not
far away. "They took a truck and picked up quite a number of kegs of
beer and a large box, probably about five feet square, filled with
champagne," Whitmore recalled. "They were about to take another
one when the military police came along and stopped them, but we
were well supplied with beer for a long time. There was a keg with a
spigot on it outside most of the tents, and all you had to do was go
and get a mug-full any time you wanted it."

Carl Reinke, the former Canadian Press newspaperman who was
touring the continent on behalf of the RCAF's Historical Section in
London, recorded his own impressions of the airfield when he visited
shortly after the arrival of 126 Wing. "It was a very complete, permanent training station, with luxurious billets and messes, tremendous
hangars, beautifully fitted canteens and recreation buildings," he
wrote. The officers' mess was "a large two-storey red brick building
with a steep-pitched roof ... ultra-modern in design and decor." Inside was a lounge, a bar, and two large music rooms "in addition to a
palatial dining room, beautifully wood-panelled ten feet up [to] a
ceiling about twenty-five feet high." Reinke added:

The fixtures, specially made, blend perfectly in all rooms with the natural wood trim and panelling. The water colours and etchings throughout are in excellent taste. There are as many bathrooms as in a small, posh hotel; and the (cold) water and electricity still run. Down in the basement are two bowling alleys of unique design (a concave alley about fifteen inches wide).

Reinke and a companion bowled a few games, acting as pin boys for each other. Then they continued their sightseeing tour of the building:

> There is a big billiard room with three medium-sized tables… The outside of the mess building was covered with screening like bamboo curtains, but done with fine wire and some special kind of long coarse straw. I don't know whether this was for camouflage or to keep the sun off.

The tops of the well-built hangars were unquestionably camouflaged, Reinke observed, with odd conical shapes resembling treetops. These blended with the general appearance of the airfield, which reminded George Killen, with the wing's medical section, of "a small model town in a pine forest." There was a good grass landing strip, as well as dispersals and paved connecting roads. "Sick Quarters was a large T-shaped two-storey building, equipped with x-ray and all the conveniences of a small hospital. The staff spread itself over the whole building, and lived in complete luxury. All the conveniences were intact and soon operating. Besides good quarters, the airfield provided a good cinema, a fine gymnasium, an outdoor pool, and a playing field."

For all the amenities, the sense that everyone could relax at Wunstorf was illusory. There were still risks, including some that were new to the wing's personnel. Said Killen: "Some of the fitters or riggers, having nothing to do (the kites hadn't yet arrived), decided to explore a bit and went off to a PoW compound we had seen shortly after moving into Germany. First thing we knew one of them was beating on our tent flaps complaining that something was biting him. It sure was. He was covered with fleas and they were hungry. We rushed him out in a nearby field, stripped him down, washed him with airplane gas and burned his clothes, probably averting an epidemic with the possibility of typhus." Killen added that a number of refugees wandering freely about the field, carrying with them "any number of potentially infective epidemic diseases," were rounded up and sent off for treatment.

There was also the war itself. Armed recces by the wing's squadrons continued throughout the transition to Wunstorf. On April 15th, 401, 402 and 412 started their day at B108 (Rheine); most finished at Wunstorf after a number of ground targets were destroyed and damaged. Some aircraft were held back due to deteriorating weather. By noon the next day, servicing echelons began to encounter difficulties supplying the wing's Spitfires. Petrol and particularly ammunition were virtually unavailable. An emergency airlift produced 20,000 rounds of 20 mm ammunition and some essential lubricants, but even this was insufficient. That evening, all available transport was rounded up and formed into a convoy to leave at dawn on the 17th for an armament park. "The present superfluity of targets will not lack of attention if it can possibly be helped," promised the wing's diarist.

The shortages were accounted for mainly by the wing's continuing road and rail interdiction operations. Following the success of "Plunder" and "Varsity" in late-March, the Allies had pressed full speed deep into the heart of Germany. The enemy's last plan of defence rested mainly on holding the lower Rhine, and when it failed, there was virtually nothing left to prevent the Allies from racing on towards Berlin. Aircraft of 2nd TAF did their part in delivering the final, punishing blows. The pilots of 126 Wing found plenty of ground targets during armed recces into the enemy's last area of retreat. Numerous trains, buildings and even barges were "clobbered." Squadrons returned to refuel and rearm and were promptly out again in search of anything that moved. They also put numbers on the scoreboard of enemy aircraft. On April 16th, Flying Officer Wilson and Flight Lieutenant Gordon both destroyed a Ju 88, while Flying Officer Bazett claimed one FW 190. The scores were all the more impressive given that 411 Squadron was functioning with minimal groundcrews. Flight Lieutenant Johnny MacKay of 401 also damaged three Arado 234s on the ground. The wing's own losses amounted to one Spitfire IX damaged (it was listed as Category "B", meaning damaged to such an extent that it was not repairable at its unit), and Flight Lieutenant "Jake" Maurice, who failed to return from one of 402's armed recces. It was hoped he had bailed out safely over friendly territory.

More bad news followed on the 17th. Flying Officer Dunn, who had just rejoined the wing with 401 Squadron on his second tour, was lost while attacking a railway between Lubeck and Kyritz. He was listed as NYR, but it seemed likely he was killed when his aircraft was caught in the blast from a petrol train he was strafing. The rest of the squadron's pilots, too, had inflicted heavy damage on the ground throughout the day. The only claim for enemy aircraft was by Flying Officer "Red" Francis, who shot down one Me 109 over Neuenburg. However, "411 Squadron hit an all-time high in heartbreaks this morning when they sighted 15 Me 109s after they had expended all their ammunition on ground targets," the Ops Summary noted in sympathy.

The continuing ammunition shortage was relieved somewhat by the arrival of 20,000 more rounds sent by a RAF wing, but petrol remained scarce. Urgent pleas by radio in the morning resulted in a promise of thirteen Dakotas to airlift fuel for the wing. These were to be despatched from Goch with orders to make a quick turnaround so they could reload for a second delivery. Late in the afternoon one aircraft arrived, followed by only eight more. Further insult was delivered by the Winco in charge of the Dakotas when he stated he had a commitment to evacuate casualties elsewhere and, as he had no authority to disregard such an order, he would not be returning. The wing would have to get by somehow on its own for the time being. For this miserly treatment, personnel at Wunstorf grumbled that the grass strip had suffered additional abuse for little reward. In fact, it had begun to disintegrate under the combined punishment of the wing's own Spitfires and the fuel-carrying Daks. INT/OPS expressed the widely held hope that a new metal-tracked

runway under construction at B116 would be finished within
twenty-four hours, as estimated. If not, said the wing's diarist, a period of "aerodrome unserviceability" was predicted. In the meantime,
Wunstorf was too far forward to be left unvisited by a number of dignitaries, who flew in to the further detriment of the existing airstrip,
while heavy concentrations of enemy ground targets meant that operations were pushed as much as possible. On the 18th, several of the
wing's missions were cancelled due to the almost non-stop arrival of
transport aircraft. "Fortunately, as once happened at Evere, the AOC
was present to witness the effect on Spitfire activity," Gord Panchuk
noted. "It is sincerely hoped that something may be done to divert
the Transport traffic from this aerodrome while operational targets
continue in their present quantity." Notwithstanding such interference, standing patrols over bridges between Celle and Renthem were
maintained by at least one squadron, leaving the others to carry out
armed recces. The latter, said Panchuk, were so productive they
"brought back memories of the Falaise Gap days." Only the mad-
deningly limited reserves of ammunition at Wunstorf prevented the
Canadians from inflicting more damage during their low-level
ground attacks.

The new metal landing strip at B116 was completed on the 19th.
It was reserved almost exclusively for the wing's Spitfires, while the
old grass strip was left to transport aircraft. The result, observed Don
Stewart, was "a full day's ops and everyone happy" (though ironically,
RAF Stirlings, which had caused the most damage to the grass landing strip, were diverted to B118 early in the afternoon). Four-man
patrols over the Elbe by 401 Squadron were largely unprofitable,
while armed recces in the area of an enemy-held aerodrome at
Hagenow, eighty kilometres east of Hamburg, saw considerably
more action. Six-plus FW 190s were found "milling about" and were
quickly engaged by 412 Squadron. Flight Lieutenant "Tex" Pieri destroyed one and shared another with Flight Lieutenant Stewart.
Flight Lieutenant D J Dewan and Flying Officer G M Horter
claimed one each in the same combat. Four down. Then 402's pilots
came along, destroying one more and damaging three (Flying Officer H C Dutton of Niagara Falls, Ontario, was credited with one in

each category). Later in the day they returned and found fresh targets over the enemy's aerodrome at Parchim. Flying Officer MacConnel shot down one Ju 88. But relentless flak from the airfield also took its toll on the Canadians. Flight Lieutenant "Hank" Cowan—"always intrepid and very keen"—got too close. His Spitfire was hit by flak, and he crashed.* Undaunted, pilots continued to harass the enemy's airfields. Squadron Leader Klersy, leading a patrol by 402, destroyed one FW 190 in the same area that afternoon. His score might have been higher, too, except that on the last patrol of the day, Klersy's cannons jammed with an Ar 234 in his sights! Still, it was a good show for all—seven enemy aircraft destroyed and three damaged, in addition to ground targets (the score of vehicles alone, destroyed and damaged, was 10 and 43)—even if the loss of Cowan gave it a sombre aspect. "Every sortie was made to count, and only a lack of aircraft prohibited higher scores being piled up," Stewart noted. There seemed to be no greater satisfaction among the wing's pilots than adding their share of pressure to the enemy's increasingly desperate situation.

Their determination paid off richly on the 20th. Twice, large numbers of enemy aircraft were caught taking off from airfields inside Germany. The largest share of claims went to 401 Squadron, which had started its day by shooting up as many as 27 vehicles (out of 34 claimed by the wing). In the first combat, the Ram pilots attacked some Me 109s taking off from a grass airstrip southwest of Schwerin. It was so easy some feared it might be a trap. Sure enough, the Canadians were led to another gaggle of twenty-plus flying topcover at 10,000 feet. "But, trap or no trap," said Monty, "the score was eleven Me 109s destroyed and three damaged." That evening, more enemy aircraft were surprised at Hagenow Aerodrome. Several others were flying eastward at almost tree-top level—so low that a couple of them hit the trees and went in, trying to evade their pursuers. Squadron Leader Klersy shot down two long-nosed FW 190s, both of which exploded and crashed. His wing-leading score for the

---

* Cowan was listed as NYR even though it was assumed he had been killed.

day was 3½, which brought his personal tally to 14½ victories. "Scoring honours for the balance were well distributed," Monty recorded. The list seemed incredible: Flying Officer J P W Francis of Battleford, Saskatchewan, scored one Me 109 destroyed, one damaged, and the same count in FW 190s; Flight Lieutenant W R Tew of Toronto and Flying Officer J A Ballantine of Oshawa, Ontario, each claimed two Me 109s; Flight Lieutenant R H Cull of Sebabeach, Alberta, shot down one Me 109 and one FW 190; Flight Lieutenant L W Woods of Belleville, Ontario, shared with Squadron Leader Klersy one Me 109 destroyed and claimed another completely for himself; Flying Officer G D Cameron of Toronto took credit for one FW 190 destroyed, one damaged, as did Flight Lieutenant L H Watt of Scudder, Ontario; Flight Lieutenant Johnny Mackay of Calgary and Flight Lieutenant J H Ashton of Virden, Manitoba, both claimed one Me 109 destroyed, while Flying Officer D B Dack of Taber, Alberta, got one FW 190. Flying Officer R C Gudgeon of Shawinigan Falls, Quebec, and Pilot Officer D W Davis of Vancouver each filed for one Me 109 damaged. And that was just 401's tally! Two pilots of 402 Squadron prevented the Rams from making a clean sweep of the totals: Flight Lieutenant R J Taggart of Toronto and Flying Officer T B Lee, who hailed from Pachuca Hilalgo, Mexico. Both shot down one FW 190.

"Twenty on the twentieth," Monty observed. The victories were all the more astonishing given that the wing had operated understrength most of the day. Except for 401 Squadron only seven or eight serviceable Spitfires were available to carry out missions. Losses (including 401's R W "Andy" Anderson, whose plane was seen crashing in flames that morning, and 402's Warrant Officer VE Barber of Wellwood, Manitoba, who bailed out after his Spitfire was hit by debris), and accidents were mainly responsible for the wing's increasingly impoverished state. Supply difficulties also contributed to the shortage of aircraft, as maintenance and repair work relied on the timely acquisition of parts. "Groundcrews deserved a special pat on the back for their part in the wing's success that day," Monty recalled. "They did a terrific job of keeping the few kites we had in the air so that our pilots could run up such fantastic scores." Monty

Open-air servicing in Normandy in August 1944. Mechanics are doing an engine job on a 442 "Caribou" Squadron Spitfire.   DND PL31363

H W "Bud" Bowker of 411 Squadron, with captured helmet and motorcycle after the wing moved to the continent   DND PL30259

Flying Officer Aleck Whiting (right) of Toronto was richer by a fistful of francs, the prize for bagging the 100th enemy aircraft since the wing's formation.   DND PL30911

Washing up after a meal at B80 in Volkel, Holland, November 1944. "Mud, mud, mud!" Living in tents in the cold rain and wind of gale-like proportions ... "the latest competition is to determine whose tent has the most leaks."   KEN PIGEON

F/L R J (Dick) Audet, DFC and Bar, of 411 Squadron became an instant
"ace" on December 29th, 1944, when he shot down five enemy aircraft in one
operation. He is seen here at B88, Heesch, Holland in February 1945,
just days before his tragic death.   DND PL41716

An unusual view of 126 Wing at B152, Fassberg, Germany, soon after VE-Day
in May 1945. The INT/OPS vans known as the "Siamese Twins"
are at the lower left of the photograph.

Monty and INT/OPS staff after the wing moved to the continent.

MONTY BERGER

The flight line at B84, de Rips (Holland) in October 1944. KEN PIGEON

When Air Marshal R Leckie, CB, DSO, DSC, DFC, Chief of the Air Staff, Ottawa, visited the top-scoring 126 Spitfire wing in 2nd TAF, the wing's own dance band entertained with music at the lunch for the distinguished visitor and his party. Wielding the baton in such sprightly fashion is F/L Don Stewart of Paris, Ontario, whose normal duties were as an intelligence officer. The INT/OPS section operated 24 hours a day, seven days a week. DND PL42119

Monty (back row, second from left) with several cohorts.

Pilot Officer Gord Panchuk is standing, right. MONTY BERGER

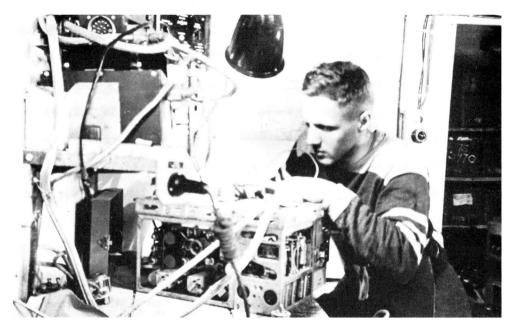

Ken Pigeon, who captained the wing's hockey team during its championship season in 1945, wearing his favourite colours while servicing Spitfire radios in his workshop.
KEN PIGEON

Wing Commander Geoffrey Wilson Northcott, DSO, DFC and Bar, in his office tender. The twenty-four-year-old ace from Minnedosa, Manitoba, was appointed 126's Winco Flying in January 1945, and continued until the Wing was dissolved in April 1946. MONTY BERGER noted that the victories lifted the wing past the 300-mark to a total of 317 enemy aircraft destroyed since D-Day, and a grand total of 346-17-151 since its formation in 1943—"a figure that no one reckoned would be reached in this war." His operational summary, which ran a full three pages (usually a single page or a page-and-a-half sufficed) reflected the historic nature of the event-filled day. He noted as well that two pilots had walked away—"more or less"—with only slight injuries from wrecked and flaming aircraft at B116. Actually, it was a miracle either man survived. Flying Officer F R (Fred) Dennison of 411—a Grizzly Bear from Buffalo, New York—crashed while taking off and broke his back. Later in the day, Flight Lieutenant E B Mossing of 401, who also had his engine cut during take-off, scraped his Spitfire's belly tank over an obstacle and came down so hard the impact ripped its wings off, broke the fuselage at the instrument panel and left what remained of the aircraft a mass of flames—yet Mossing "extricated himself with one bone broken in his leg," Monty recalled. The incidents followed a number of engine problems that were attributed to the introduction of 150-grade fuel in early February. Pilots mistrusted it, and were no doubt relieved when the air force brass decided to revert to 130-grade. "The vast majority of pilots, I'm sure, were beginning to wonder if the additional seven pounds of boost they got from 150-grade were worth the price being paid." The matter was being discussed at Wunstorf when, incredibly, a spark at the petrol dump ignited and two petrol bowsers containing almost two thousand gallons of the much-despised fuel burst into flames. "A good deal of hard work on the part of all groundcrew within range confined the fire to the bowsers and saved the dump," Monty recalled.

So ended one of the wing's most extraordinary days on the continent, with fireworks that lit up the night sky around the airfield at Wunstorf. The next day London newspapers carried obituaries for the Luftwaffe, which added amusement to the high scores and prompted the pilots of 126 Wing to "inject some semblance of credence" to the reports while carrying out its missions. But only a few enemy aircraft were sighted. Flight Lieutenant E R Burrows of 402, while leading a four-man patrol in the area of Hitzaker, shot one Me

109 in a gaggle of nine-plus they encountered. His Number Two and Number Three, Flying Officer Dutton and Flight Lieutenant W O Young, each claimed one damaged in the same combat, although evidence supported raising Dutton's to a destroyed (a parachute was seen in the vicinity). North of Putlitz, Flight Lieutenant McLarty was just finishing off a locomotive when he spotted a lone Me 109 flying at 300 feet. He chased it down and fired a burst that sent the enemy aircraft crashing in flames on a railway flyover. McLarty, in one stroke, was credited with one 109 destroyed and a rail cut.

In every other respect, though, the day constituted only "a routine effort" by the wing. Only forty-eight sorties were flown by all four squadrons. The chronic shortage of airworthy Spitfires was again largely responsible for the low number of missions flown. A few replacement Spit IXs and XIVs were arriving, although more were needed. Low cloud and occasional showers over the next several days further hampered the wing's operations. On the 22nd, just seven front-line patrols from Lauenburg to Lenzen were carried out by 411 Squadron, and a single armed recce by 401. The latter was uneventful except for 10/10 cloud almost to the deck. The Ram pilots returned early and were barely even debriefed for their effort. The day's only excitement occurred during one of 411's patrols, when Flying Officer M F (Michael) Doyle and Flight Lieutenant E T (Ted) Gardner spotted a lone FW 190 at 4,000 feet west of the Elbe. They shot it down, and shared the claim. On the 26th, conditions improved enough that all four squadrons were able to carry out patrols or armed recces. Road and rail movement was hard to find, but 402 Squadron found unusual targets in a number of He 115s. The Luftwaffe's impressive twin-engine seaplanes, capable of mine-laying and even torpedo-strike sorties, were moored at Putnitz. Flight Lieutenant B E Innes and Flight Lieutenant R H Roberts respectively claimed one destroyed and one damaged. More were discovered on the 27th near Ribnitz by 402 Squadron. There they were, virtually undefended; for the Canadian pilots it was like shooting fish in a barrel. Squadron Leader Gordon and Flying Officer A G Ratcliffe each destroyed one in the water, while Flying Officer H R Robertson left another damaged. Fog and continuing low cloud prevented the

Canadians from finishing off the remaining Heinkels at either installation on the 28th. Only fifty-six sorties were mounted, resulting in a
couple of locomotives and several vehicles damaged, all within relatively short striking distance of B116. If the weather wasn't bad
enough, during one of 412's patrols Flight Lieutenant Stewart had to
bail out when his engine cut. He landed safely and returned to Wunstorf later in the day. Of course, his Spitfire was another write-off.
Flying Officer Horter encountered similar engine problems and attempted a forced landing. His aircraft caught fire and exploded. An
army unit that watched him crash thought it likely he was killed. In
any event, as Horter came down in an area where only recently the
unit had lost a lieutenant and a sergeant to enemy mortar fire, they
did not seem overly keen to investigate. It was a tragedy whenever
any young pilot was lost: more so now that the war seemed to be
reaching its end. Incredibly, though, Horter survived. Squadron
Leader Boyd pinpointed the downed pilot's position well enough
that a medical officer found him two days later, badly injured and
still strapped in the cockpit of his Spitfire, which had completely broken up on impact. Horter had dangled perilously over a deep ditch
filled with murky water, drifting in and out of consciousness until he
was rescued. "He was faintly irrational but may live," noted Carl
Reinke. The ubiquitous RCAF historian was around on the 29th,
too, when for a change several erks of 6411 Servicing Echelon made
it into the record books. Early that morning a Ju 52 came in with its
navigation lights on, circled the field slowly and landed. The erks
who eventually took the Luftwaffe crew into custody said the aircraft
had taxied so nonchalantly to a spot near the wing's dispersals they
thought it was a Dakota! Monty later reported that one of the captured airmen had remarked laconically that Germany was "*kaput.*" It
was hard to argue the point. The enemy seemed to be flying "with no
apparent mission beyond offering target practice," as Gord Panchuk
observed. That day a 412 patrol ran into a gaggle of ten-plus FW
190s flying south on the deck over Winsen. Flight Lieutenant R L
Hazel, Flying Officer Arn Gibb and Flying Officer J H MacLean
each destroyed one. Ten minutes later, the section sighted two more
190s at cloud level northwest of Luneburg, and gave chase. Gibb

caught up with one and added it to his personal score. Later, a section of 411 ran into another small formation of FW 190s that had just finished dropping its bombs in the Elbe. The Canadians attacked at once, emerging unscathed with one enemy fighter damaged by Flying Officer Denny Wilson.

The all-out massacre of the Luftwaffe continued on Monday, April 30th, when conditions permitted a full day of sorties. The first aircraft took off at Wunstorf before dawn, the last pancaked under the fading rays of twilight. By then, the wing's scoreboard had increased by 15-0-8. Starting off with an armed recce in the Hagenow-Schwerin-Wizmar area, 402's pilots claimed eight destroyed and four damaged "for no trouble at all," according to Gord Panchuk. They must have been efficient in their business, for they had enough ammunition left over to shoot up a few ground targets, including a locomotive. A second outing produced even more results. The next show was spectacular. Flight Lieutenant S M (Stan) Knight of Calgary, who earlier in the morning had shared in the destruction of a Ju 88 east of Lubeck, caught another one wandering about alone and shot it down. Five minutes later his section encountered a gaggle of five or so FW 190s flying at 500 feet in the Schwerin Lake district. Knight destroyed one, as did Flight Lieutenant Bud Young and Flight Lieutenant F E ("Hank") Hanton, DFC, of Kenora, Ontario. Hanton, who had only recently joined 402, damaged another. One got away. Ten minutes later, after Kenway had reported more enemy fighters in the area, Flight Lieutenant D R (Doug) Drummond of Montreal "tussled briefly" with a 190 before sending it down in flames. All this before lunch-hour. Pilots returned to Wunstorf to refuel and rearm, and were out again for more action. Groundcrews kept the Spitfires going, while Monty's staff kept track of the scores. Gord Panchuk reported the Ops Summary was "going to press," expecting 412 to land momentarily with "nothing to report," when Flight Lieutenant "Tex" Pieri returned and claimed one FW 190 destroyed. Then Squadron Leader Boyd rang from another airfield to add four Me 109s shot down, and two damaged. The Summary was dutifully revised to reflect the new totals, but noticeably without the usual crowing after so many victories. Their adversary could offer only meagre resistance, having exhausted its resources and, it seemed, its will to fight.

And so ended April. For the record, it was the wing's best month yet, its scoreboard of enemy aircraft alone showing an additional 58-1-31. The number of sorties flown was equally impressive considering the supply difficulties, bad fuel and shortage of airworthy Spitfires. There was satisfaction also in having done so much in support of the Allies' race for Berlin, which in the latter half of the month had rolled up vast stretches of territory on all sides of the capital. Faced with the imminent collapse of his beloved Third Reich, Hitler was hiding in his underground bunker with his mistress, Eva Braun. His ardently loyal *Reichsfuhrer* and chief of the notorious Waffen SS, Heinrich Himmler, took charge. Himmler's clandestine offer to surrender to the British and Americans, but not to the Soviets, was firmly rejected with a reminder of previously established demands for unconditional surrender. The encirclement of Berlin continued. By the 28th, the Soviet Red Army was within a kilometre and a half of Hitler's bunker and pounding what remained of the city's Nazi monuments into more rubble. On the 29th, Hitler married his mistress and drew up his Political Testament, in which he blamed the German people for failing him in the fight against Bolshevism. He appointed Gross Admiral Dönitz as his successor. The next day, the Fuhrer and his faithful wife committed suicide. Their bodies were carted outside, doused with petrol and burned. Berlin itself presented an appropriately apocalyptic scene: artillery boomed, the air was hellish with smoke and the stench of death; it was chaotic and malevolent, which was Hitler's legacy as well.

"Everyone knew the end must be only a matter of days now," Monty remembered, "but nobody took time off to think about it too much. There was lots of flying still. The pilots and fitters and riggers were busy keeping their kites in the air. Armourers, electricians and photographic men all had their jobs to do. Equipment erks were rushed off their feet trying to keep pace with the drain on petrol and ammunition. Flying Control coped with the wing's operations while beating off vast numbers of Dakotas and Lancasters ferrying supplies, taking away released prisoners of war and displaced persons eager to return to Belgium and France. Intelligence was working flat out preparing for one mission while collecting claims and information gained from another, interrogating Luftwaffe aircrews that had surrendered, vetting alleged PoWs, digesting the enormous amount of maps found at the aerodrome—and so on."

On May 1st, low cloud prevented all-out activity over the wing's assigned tactical area. Most patrols were uneventful, although Wing Commander Northcott and Squadron Leader Klersy both claimed damaged Me 109s for their efforts. Pilot Officer P B (Burt) Young disappeared during one of 411's armed recces north of Hagenow, while 401's Greg Cameron was badly hit by flak over Schwerin Aerodrome and he had to bail out. Klersy followed Cameron down to 4,000 feet, enough to determine he landed safely—albeit in enemy-held territory.* The paltry scores were hardly worth such casualties.

That same day, Hamburg radio announced that Hitler was dead. It seemed almost too fantastic. But to Monty Berger, the news was hardly comforting. In his last craven act, the Fuhrer had escaped retribution for all the evil he had unleashed. Monty had spent the day investigating for himself evidence of some of the worst atrocities committed to millions of people in the name of National Socialism. His excursion to the recently liberated concentration camp at Bergen-Belsen, not far from Hanover, was strictly unofficial, even somewhat clandestine—ostensibly a short trip on a day when duff weather all but prohibited operations from Wunstorf. But for Monty, it was also an urgent necessity. If nothing else, his faith impelled him to visit a place where as many as 115,000 people—mostly Jews—had perished.

The camp had become a disturbing symbol since its discovery by the British in mid-April. Said author Martin Gilbert in his authoritative history of the Holocaust: "Photographs, films and articles about Belsen circulated widely in Britain by the end of April, making so

---

* Cameron was brought back the next day by a German doctor, who gave himself up.

great an impact that the word 'Belsen' was to become synonymous with 'inhumanity'." Violette Fintz, one of the camp's survivors, told Gilbert: "Many people talk about Auschwitz, it was a horrible camp; but Belsen, no words can describe it. There was no need to work as we were just put there with no food, no water, no anything, eaten by the lice."

Anne Frank died at Belsen—of typhus—only weeks before the camp was liberated. Her diary, written while hiding with her family in the attic of a tiny rowhouse not far from the Royal Palace in Amsterdam, was found after the war by her father, who survived the horrors of Auschwitz. Published in 1947, the diary was a moving testament to the durability of the human spirit. "In spite of everything I still believe that people are really good at heart," she had written hopefully.

That was before her family was discovered by the Gestapo in August 1944 and she was sent to a succession of concentration camps, ending with Belsen.

Thousands of slave labourers used to build defences or repair bomb-damaged railways and bridges were moved to the camp in the last months of the war. They, too, suffered unspeakable cruelties. In early April, inmates watched in mounting dread as their German SS guards prepared to flee. Many feared they might be slaughtered. Then on the 13th, advance British troops arrived. For two days the camp was nominally under their command, although a number of Hungarian SS guards still maintained iron-fisted control. Seventy-two Jews and eleven others were shot for such minor offenses as taking potato peels from the kitchen.

British troops entered Belsen in force on the 15th, and were horrified by the sight of 10,000 unburied bodies. Most had died of starvation. "There had been no food nor water for five days preceding the British entry," an army review reported. "Evidence of cannibalism was found. The inmates had lost all self-respect, and were degraded morally to the level of beasts. Their clothes were in rags, teeming with lice, and both inside and outside the huts was an almost continuous carpet of dead bodies, human excreta, rags and filth." Added one high-ranking officer who was obviously moved by the tragedy inside the camp, "The dead and dying could not be distinguished."

British army doctors marked a red cross on the foreheads of those they thought had a chance of surviving. One of those was Fania Fenelon, deported from Paris in January 1944 to the concentration camp at Birkenau, where she was chosen to play in a small orchestra for the officers' amusement at Belsen. In her memoirs, she recalled the first days after their liberation:

> A new life breathed in the camp. Jeeps, command cars, and half-tracks drove around among the barracks. Khaki uniforms abounded, the marvellously substantial material of their battle-dress mingling with the rags of the deportees. Our liberators were well fed and bursting with health, and they moved among our skeletal, tenuous silhouettes like a surge of life. We felt an absurd desire to finger them, to let our hands trail in the eddies as in the Fountain of Youth. They called to one another, whistled cheerfully, then suddenly fell silent, faced with eyes too large, or too intense a gaze. How alive they were; they walked quickly, they ran, they leapt. All these movements were so easy for them, while a single one of them would have taken away our last breath of life! These men seemed not to know that one could live in slow motion, that energy was something you saved.

Even after massive Allied aid reached Belsen, 300 inmates died each day for the next few weeks. Many could not digest the food rations they were given, or were simply too far beyond medical help. The death rate slowed to sixty per day by the end of April, but conditions at the camp were still appalling. Supplies continued to pour in, including a huge truckload of food and medicine donated by the personnel of 126 at Wunstorf. The wing's Protestant chaplain and several erks from the Equipment Section stayed up most of one night sorting and packing the goods before they were shipped out. "An army padre at Belsen estimated conservatively that at least 500 lives might be saved by the shipment," Monty recalled. Upon hearing this, he redoubled his efforts to visit the camp.

His chance came that first day in May. Gord Panchuk and

another of the wing's intelligence officers, Bob Francis, wanted to accompany him, and when Carl Reinke heard of their plan he asked if he could go along also. They set out at noon under grey skies, driving north in a borrowed Opal. Reinke, who made copious notes in his personal diary, remembered the roads were crowded with refugees, ex-PoWs and all sorts of other human traffic. "There were the usual groups on bicycles," he said, "and some driving a horse and cart or just dragging a four-wheeled cart. We saw Poles going west and Poles going east, which seemed to sum up the current confusion."

A half-hour or so later they reached the outskirts of Belsen, where they were directed to the gates of the camp itself. Their first discovery was shocking enough. Said Reinke indignantly: "The Hungarian guards who had helped confine those pitiful creatures for the Nazis are still doing the same thing—for us!" He added: "Not very surprisingly, they are meticulous about saluting visiting officers." Reinke attributed their presence to a manpower shortage in the British army unit responsible for Belsen.

Inside the camp, a Jewish-Canadian padre led Monty's small party to a "dusting room" set up in the headquarters building, where each man was treated. "This involved having DDT (anti-bug powder) squirted down your neck, fore and aft, over your hair, in your cap and up your sleeves," Reinke said. "We looked like millers." Then the padre escorted the men outside—and into hell itself.

They moved somewhat hurriedly, aware that their visit lacked official approval. They passed rows of nondescript grey huts, which by their outward appearance might have been on any military establishment. Then they came upon a group of elderly civilians with shovels, looking dejected. The padre said they were a burying party. The camp's SS guards, who previously carried out such work, couldn't "take it" any longer. German PoWs refused on legal grounds. "So German civilians had been ordered to continue the ghoulish job of loading the stinking corpses on carts, unloading them into great pits and burying them," said Reinke.

Inmates lingered around the barbed-wire fences. They were heavily clad, most in winter coats and other eclectic rags to keep warm, even though it was a mild spring day. Each had a lifeless, glassy stare, as though scarcely conscious of their surroundings, and pallid complexions over their sunken cheeks.

Between two of the huts were a dozen corpses on the ground. They were like skeletons. The padre said they had died that morning, and were carried outside by their fellow inmates.

Inside one of the huts they found men and women crowding three levels of bunks. Others, wrapped in overcoats, were lying on the floor. Few seemed to be aware they were being watched. The hut was filled with a sickly, fetid stench that was overwhelming.

The padre said that a hundred of the camp's victims were buried that morning, only two of whom were identified.

On their way back to the headquarters building before leaving, they passed a stack of signs ready to be posted. "Grave 5, approx 800," one read. "Grave 8, approx 5000."

Mostly Russians and Poles, the padre explained sadly.

In *Song of the Murdered Jewish People*, Yitzhak Katznelson wrote:

"I had a dream,/A dream so terrible:/My people were no more,/No more!"/"I wake up with a cry./What I dreamed was true:/It had happened indeed,/It had happened to me."

No civilised man or woman, regardless of their faith, could have gone to Belsen as Monty did in the spring of 1945 and be unmoved by the human catastrophe inside its barbed wire fence. Gord Panchuk, Bob Francis and Carl Reinke were profoundly affected by the sight of so many skeletal corpses being loaded into trucks for burial, and the huge open pits filled with bodies piled high, one on top of another. The living dead were just as painful to witness. But for Monty, such scenes were more than pathetic.

"I was sick to my stomach, overcome with revulsion," he said. "Those images stay fresh in my mind. I am outraged and recall them vividly when I hear someone claim the Holocaust never happened."

Monty's brief visit to the camp also confirmed something that had occupied his thoughts long before he even landed in France as part of 126 Wing. Looking back over almost half a century, he tried to put it into words.

"Our day-to-day operations kept us busy," he allowed. "We worked long and hard hours and were totally absorbed in our responsibilities. But not far below the surface was acute consciousness of why we were fighting this war. As the son of a rabbi—indeed, I was the only first-born son in seven generations of the Berger family that did not pursue rabbinical studies—I knew well enough! I had been president of a Young Judea Club in my teens, and later of the Maccabean Circle at McGill. And, not unlike other Jews in Canada, I had heard of cousins and relatives who had disappeared, or were killed in the nightmarish world that descended upon Europe's Jewish population in the late-1930s. My observance of the dietary laws and regular attendance at synagogue services had slipped away during my university years, but my identity as a Jew ran deep. I felt fully the sense of frustration seeing Hitler and the Nazis go unchecked. Why couldn't we do something? So, when war was declared I was ready to enlist, as were all my friends. We didn't think in terms of bravery: we wanted to do our part to stop a monstrous injustice and end the barbarity that was overtaking Europe—even threatening the world.

"Nothing must *ever* diminish the horror in our past," he added, "that millions were slaughtered."

Far from home, young Monty Berger made the same vow as he returned to Wunstorf.

On May 2nd, the AOC-in-C of 2nd TAF, Air Marshal Sir Arthur Coningham, landed by Dakota at B116. He was presented a captured Mercedes, which he acknowledged before leaving almost at once on some top-secret matter. Standing patrols were maintained that day despite duff weather. Most were uneventful, although between Ahrensburg and Zarrentin 411's Denny Wilson claimed one Me 109 destroyed and Flying Officer C N Smith damaged a Me 262. The next day produced even higher scores, although almost all were for aircraft found undefended on the ground. In the afternoon, after performing a flypast over Hamburg to mark the city's capitulation to the British, Squadron Leader Klersy's Ram pilots found a grass airstrip edging gently to the sea at Schonberg, east of Kiel. There, in dispersals only barely camouflaged, were parked twenty-five or more enemy aircraft. They were mostly Ju 52s, the Luftwaffe's ubiquitous tri-motor transport, along with a number of He 111s, an early bomber long considered obsolete but still in use in 1945. The Rams—or at least those who still had ammunition after shooting up some ground targets earlier in their mission—attacked until a dozen 52s, two 111s and one Ju 87 Stuka were completely destroyed. Elsewhere, a section of 402 Squadron led by Squadron Leader Gordon found several Fi 156s on the ground north of Neumunster. Better known as the Fieseler Storch, the Fi 156 was a light single-engine aircraft that looked like every Depression-era kid's homemade model. But it was surprisingly versatile, particularly for its remarkable STOL (short take-off and landing) characteristics. Consequently, it was used in a variety of roles, as a scout plane or battlefield taxi, in virtually every theatre to which the Luftwaffe was sent. More than a few were captured and repainted for use by Allied generals, who seemed to like them just as much as their counterparts in the Wehrmacht. It seemed a shame to destroy them. As it happened, the Fieselers north of Neumunster were well-strafed, but only damaged. Not far away, Gordon's Number Two, Flight Lieutenant W F (Fred) Peck of Toronto, found another one scooting along on the deck. He attacked, but overshot. Gordon took over and promptly shot it down. The day's seemingly effortless sport was not without some hazards, though. Earlier, while attacking the aircraft on the ground, Flight Lieutenant J A O'Brian had to bail out southeast of Hamburg when his Spitfire was hit by its own ricocheting gunfire. He landed safely and was expected to return by nightfall. Flight Lieutenant "Tex" Pieri had developed engine trouble and had hit the silk north of Hamburg, which was believed to be friendly territory by then. He, too, was expected back soon. In the meantime, several other pilots who had gone missing in recent days, including 411's Carl Ellement and 402's Warrant Officer Barber, returned unexpectedly. "It was the second time for each of them this tour," Monty noted. "We trust there will be no need—and no time—for a third."

There was tragedy, too. On its first operation, while attacking some ground targets north of Neumunster, 411's Stan McLarty was wounded by flak. He was being led back to Wunstorf by his Number Two, but apparently lost consciousness. His aircraft went straight in. "Stan was an old-timer in the wing," said Monty, "having done his first tour with 442 Squadron, and was well known to many pilots who met him while instructing at GSU. It was a great loss, especially as it was so close to the end of the war. We all missed Stan and his cheerfulness."

There were no losses on the 4th. A directive from 83 Group stipulated all squadrons were to carry out armed recces, but the weather grew progressively worse. Flight Lieutenant D F ("Sonny") Campbell and Flying Officer T L O'Brien jointly shot down one peripatetic He 111 for the wing's only victory in the air that day. Before the weather closed in completely, 402 went off on a sweep of southern Denmark and shot up some ground targets. "A venturesome Me 262 took objection to this and shot up one of our kites, and then withdrew smartly," noted one of Monty's staff, Flying Officer H H "Red" Skelton, in the Ops Summary. The 402 pilot, Flying Officer J E Rigby of Thorold, Ontario, returned to Wunstorf with only a scratch on his nose and wounded pride to show for his narrow escape. It would be the wing's last hostile encounter with jet-jobs—or, for that matter, any Luftwaffe fighters.

That evening, Skelton, who was the Duty Intelligence Officer, received a message from Group Headquarters. It was the news everyone had been waiting for, but as he could not locate Group Captain McGregor he passed the word along by telephone to Wing Commander Northcott in the officers' mess. Northcott stood on a chair, and called for silence

"From 83 Group Headquarters," he read. "All hostilities on Second Army front will cease at 0800 hours tomorrow, May 5th!"

He never got to deliver the rest of the message (it was insignificant anyway), for a loud and spontaneous cheer erupted instantly.

Monty said every available stock of liquid refreshment on the airfield was raided for the festivities that followed. They were carefree young men again, slapping backs, cavorting recklessly and popping

champagne corks from the second-storey windows of the officers'
mess.

Their celebrations lasted well into the night. Flares, ammunition
and other pyrotechnics substituting for fireworks exploded brilliantly overhead, illuminating the wing's Spitfires parked in their dispersals.

It didn't matter so much anymore if there was barely enough
petrol or ammunition for all of them. The war was over.

EPILOGUE

HURRY UP AND WAIT

TWO UNEVENTFUL PATROLS over Hamburg by Ram pilots early the next morning were all that was required of the wing before VE-Day was marked officially on May 8th. After such a grand crescendo of victories in the air and on the ground prior to the cease-fire, it was good to do a bit of recreational flying for a change. By 0835, when the last Spitfire pancaked at B116, men were already looking forward to some rest, and maybe to a few more parties. Later that day Squadron Leader Don Laubman and Flight Lieutenant Jake Maurice, both shot down in mid-April, walked into the officers' mess at Wunstorf looking fit and ready to celebrate. They had no trouble finding takers.

Even so, the end of the conflict came with a suddenness that left many at the airfield feeling strangely empty. They had lived in a constant state of readiness since moving to the continent, and were accustomed to sudden orders at odd hours. Men conditioned by thousands of kilometres travelled in convoys, sleeping in trucks or under them, on the ground and in slit trenches, putting up tents and pulling down tents, living out of kitbags and on compo rations, in mud and rain and snow, followed incongruously by the comforts of some captured airfield, were still cautious.

Pilots had also shouldered the weight of having been shot at regularly, and of watching friends being killed.

But no more—even if there was still work to do.

On May 12th, the wing moved to B152 at Fassberg in anticipation of its work as part of the British Army of Occupation. Airframe mechanic Garry Whitmore said the airfield had an "eerie feel to it." Its former Luftwaffe occupants had simply stopped what they were doing and walked out. "All their clothes were still hanging on pegs on the walls, with their shoes neatly below." Whitmore explored a metalwork shop, where he found a great many tools that were left behind. The larger machines, however, had been smashed. Yet everyone recognised the atmosphere was deceptive.

"We had to watch out for booby-traps," said Whitmore. "Door knobs could be booby-trapped; or some attractive object, just sitting out, could be a trap. We didn't touch anything or move anything. We just looked until the demolition people had gone through and checked it all over."

Fassberg was further enlivened by Luftwaffe pilots surrendering to escape the Soviets in the east. They flew in with a variety of aircraft—everything from Ju 88s to Stukas, which were soon mixed up amongst the wing's Spitfires on the grassy meadows at B152.

For the next two months, life settled into a relatively monotonous routine. Fresh food and vegetables were in good supply, mostly from Denmark. The accommodations were excellent. Tours expired; men went home. Those who stayed behind might be detailed to a gunnery practice camp in England for a short spell (as were 411's pilots), or assigned to practice flights, cross-country sorties and other exercises over Germany to hone skills and show the flag.

As in any flying, there were risks, even if they paled in comparison to the hurly-burly of wartime combat. Sadly, not even the best pilots were immortal. On May 22nd, while flying with two other Spitfires near Wesel, Squadron Leader William Thomas Klersy, DSO, DFC and Bar, was killed instantly when his aircraft slammed into a hill in thick cloud. Like Dick Audet when he died, Klersy was not yet twenty-three years old. The brilliant young ace from Brantford, Ontario, left behind a record of 16½-0-3½ for his service during the war.

The wing moved again on July 5th to B174 at Utersen, northwest of Hamburg. In a general reorganisation of 2nd TAF, 401 and 402 were disbanded, with their personnel posted or repatriated, and 416, 421 and 443 squadrons were sent from 127 to 126 Wing. 2nd TAF itself ceased to exist shortly thereafter (it was replaced by Air Head-quarters, British Air Forces of Occupation on July 15th), but no one seemed particularly excited by such coming and going. Off-duty recreation preoccupied most men who still had to wait for repatria-tion. If airmen weren't flying or at the Canadian Club at the Phoenix Hotel in Hamburg, a sailing club on the Elbe, or any number of other establishments nearby, they were likely playing baseball on the field at Fassberg.

For his part, Monty suggested to his CO, Group Captain McGregor, that since INT/OPS no longer needed to be staffed twenty-four hours a day, he could be detached from his normal duties to compile the wing's history. The CO agreed. The wealth of detailed informa-tion he had accumulated since D-Day alone was impressive—as were some of the statistics he had compiled along the way. Pilots had flown a total of 22,373 sorties and claimed 361-12-156 in enemy air-craft, making 126 the top-scoring wing in Europe during the Second World War. Leading the way was 401 squadron, with a record of 140½-0-1. And, of 26 pilots in 2nd TAF with more than six enemy aircraft destroyed in the air, nine were from 126 Wing.

They had also left 4,468 enemy vehicles destroyed or damaged, 493 locomotives blown up or disabled, 1,569 rail trucks in flames or holed, and 426 rail lines cut—especially "good hunting," it seemed, during their many "invasions without tears."

The wing's losses were 131 Spitfires and 98 pilots.

Not surprisingly, too, they had consumed vast quantities of equip-ment and supplies in running up their high scores. Monty estimated that from D-Day to VE-Day the wing needed 2,789,804 gallons of aviation fuel and 388,606 gallons of lubricants for its Spitfires. Motor transport oil and petrol supplies amounted to 10,578 and 343,846 gallons respectively. Fuel was issued to the wing in five-gallon jerry cans (which, Monty calculated, meant they had carted 690,658 of them at one point or another). Total aircraft ammunition used was

3,421,527 rounds. This was in addition to the 3,883 250-pound bombs, and 4,426 500-pound bombs issued. Pilots had inhaled 24,219,250 litres of oxygen while flying, expended 2,518 auxiliary drop tanks and used up 2,094 main wheel tires. The logistical effort to ensure such colossal amounts of material reached the wing was Herculean. The wing's personnel had to be fed and kept in uniform, as well. Monty stopped short of counting how many eggs they had consumed, although he noted that approximately 240 tons of clothing and barracks equipment were issued.

No less important were the 5,512 pairs of boots and shoes repaired by the wing's cobblers. After all, they had travelled the continent.

APPENDIX

Ranks

RCAF   *Army Equivalent*

G/C	Group Captain	Colonel
W/C	Wing Commander	Lieutenant-Colonel
S/L	Squadron Leader	Major
F/L	Flight Lieutenant	Captain
F/O	Flying Officer	Lieutenant
P/O	Pilot Officer	Second Lieutenant

Honours

These fall into three categories: Orders, Decorations and Medals. An order confers a special honour or dignity, and entitles its recipient to wear specific insignia. Examples of orders mentioned in the text are Knight Commander of the Most Honourable Order of the Bath (KCB), and Officer of the Most Excellent Order of the British Empire (OBE). A decoration is given in recognition of specific acts of bravery, or meritorious service—the Victoria Cross is a decoration, as is the Distinguished Flying Cross (DFC). Medals, which are usually the first level of award or honour that can be conferred, fall into several distinct groups, including medals for gallantry, war service, commemorative occasions, long service and good conduct. Individuals may receive the same decoration or medal more than once (in which case reference is made to a "Bar" attached to the original award). All such honours emanate from the Sovereign, as the "Fount of all Honour," and are accompanied by letters patent issued under the King's (or, presently, Queen's) signature and seal. Honours must be worn in observance of a specific order of precedence.

126 (Fighter) Wing
Fortitudo vincit
"Courage wins"

Historical Summary

Formed as No 126 Airfield at Redhill, Surrey on 4 July 1943
Redesignated 126 (Fighter) Wing at Tangmere, Sussex
    on 15 May 1944
Transferred to British Air Forces of Occupation (Germany)
    on 6 July 1945
Disbanded at Utersen, Germany on 1 April 1946

Commanders

W/C J E Walker, DFC and 2 Bars	9 Jul 43 - 26 Aug 43
W/C K L B Hodson, DFC and Bar	27 Aug 43 - 19 Jul 44
G/C G R McGregor, OBE, DFC	20 Jul 44 - 27 Sep 45
G/C W E Bennett	28 Sep 45 - 1 Apr 46

Wing Commanders Flying

W/C B D Russel, DFC	9 Jul 43 - 16 Oct 43
W/C R W McNair, DSO, DFC and 2 Bars	17 Oct 43 - 12 Apr 44
W/C G C Keefer, DFC and Bar	17 Apr 44 - 7 Jul 44
W/C B D Russel, DSO, DFC and Bar	8 Jul 44 - 26 Jan 45
W/C G W Northcott, DSO, DFC and Bar	27 Jan 45 - 1 Apr 46

Locations · From / To

Locations	From / To
Redhill, Surrey	5 Jul 43 - 5 Aug 43
Staplehurst, Kent	6 Aug 43 - 12 Oct 43
Biggin Hill, Kent	13 Oct 43 - 14 Apr 44
Tangmere, Sussex	15 Apr 44 - 8 Jun 44
*En route to France**	
Increment to "A" party to Ver-sur-mer	7 Jun
Increment to "A" party to B3, Ste Croix-sur-mer	8 Jun
"A" party to B3, Ste Croix-sur-mer	8 Jun
"A" party to B4, Beny-sur-mer	15 Jun
"B" party to B4, Beny-sur-mer	17 - 18 Jun
B4 Beny-sur-mer, Fr	18 Jun 44 - 7 Aug 44
B18 Cristot, Fr	8 Aug 44 - 27 Aug 44
B28 Evreux, Fr	28 Aug 44 - 2 Sep 44
B44 Poix, Fr	3 Sep 44 - 6 Sep 44

---

* To cross the Channel, personnel of 126 Wing were divided into several parties. The so-called "increment" to the "A" Party, including Monty Berger as Senior Intelligence Officer, consisted of 33 officers and men. It landed on the Normandy beach at first light on June 7th and proceeded the next day to Ste Croix-sur-mer where the airfield known as B3 was being constructed by Royal Engineers. The "A" Party of 18 officers and men, including Wing Commander Keith Hodson, arrived at Ste Croix-sur-mer later on the 8th. By the afternoon of the 9th, aircraft were landing and taking off from B3. On the 15th, the "A" Party moved to Beny-sur-mer to establish B4. The "B" Party of more than 1,000 officers and men was sent to B4 and the wing became fully operational on the continent on June 18th.

B56	Evere, Bel	7 Sep 44 - 20 Sep 44
B68	Le Culot, Bel	21 Sep 44 - 3 Oct 44
B84	de Rips, Neth	4 Oct 44 - 13 Oct 44
B80	Volkel, Neth	14 Oct 44 - 6 Dec 44
B88	Heesch (Nistelrode), Neth	7 Dec 44 - 7 Apr 45
B100	Goch, Ger	8 Apr 45 - 10 Apr 45
B108	Rheine, Ger	11 Apr 45 - 13 Apr 45
B116	Wunstorf, Ger	14 Apr 45 11 May 45
B152	Fassberg, Ger	12 May 45 - 4 Jul 45
B174	Utersen, Ger	5 Jul 45 - 1 Apr 46

401 City of Westmount "Ram" Squadron
Mors celerrima hostibus
"Very swift death for the enemy"
Unit Code YO

Commanders as of July 1943

S/L E L Neal, DFC	22 Jan 43—17 Dec 43
S/L L M Cameron, DFC	18 Dec 43—2 Jul 44
S/L I F Kennedy, DFC and Bar	3 Jul 44—26 Jul 44
S/L H C Trainor, DFC	26 Jul 44—19 Sep 44
S/L R I A Smith, DFC and Bar	28 Sep 44—30 Nov 44
S/L J H Everard, DFC3	Dec 44—25 Dec 44
S/L W T Klersy, DFC and Bar4	Jan 45—22 May 45
S/L E A Kerr, DFC23	May 45—Jul 45

402 "City of Winnipeg"/"Winnipeg Bears" Squadron
"We stand on guard"
Unit Code AE

Commanders as of December 1944

S/L J B Lawrence	29 Oct 44—21 Feb 45
S/L L A Moore, DFC	22 Feb 45—25 Mar 45
S/L D C Laubman, DFC and Bar	6 Apr 45—14 Apr 45
S/L D C Gordon, DFC and Bar	15 Apr 45—10 Jul 45

411 "Grizzly Bear" Squadron
Inimicus inimico
"Hostile to an enemy"
Unit Code DB

Commanders as of July 1943

S/L B D Russel, DFC	16 Apr 43—7 Jul 43
S/L G C Semple	8 Jul 43—25 Sep 43
S/L I C Ormston, DFC	26 Sep 43—20 Dec 43
S/L J D McFarlane	21 Dec 43—9 Apr 44
S/L N R Fowlow, DFC	10 Apr 44—19 May 44

412 "Falcon" Squadron
Promptus ad vindictum
"Swift to avenge"
Unit Code VZ

Commanders as of July 1943

S/ G C Keefer, DFC and Bar	25 Jun 43 - 11 Apr 44
S/L J E Sheppard, DFC	12 Apr 44 - 1 Aug 44
S/L D H Dover, DFC and Bar	2 Aug 44 - 28 Jan 45
S/L M D Boyd	29 Jan 45 - 29 May 45
S/L D J Dewan	30 May 45 - 21 Mar 46

442 "Caribou" Squadron
Un dieu, une reine, un coeur
"One God, one Queen, one heart"*
Unit Code Y2

Commanders as of July 1944

S/L H J Dowding, DFC and Bar	7 Jul 44 - 22 Sep 44
S/L W A Olmsted, DSO, DFC and Bar	23 Sep 44 - 13 Dec 44
S/L M E Jowsey, DFC	14 Dec 44 - 22 Feb 45
S/L M Johnston	22 Feb 45 - 7 Aug 45

*Adopted after the war.

Top "Aces"

The practice of calling a pilot an "ace" has always been unofficial. In the public's imagination, however, the convention is firmly established even if its rules are not well understood. In the First World War, French escadrilles bestowed such an honour on anyone who scored ten or more aerial victories. The Americans arbitrarily set the figure at five, which gained wider acceptance and to this day approaches a standard. It was certainly the benchmark used by Canadians during the Second World War. Thus, Dick Audet became an "instant ace" when he shot down five enemy aircraft in a single day in December, 1944.

To be credited with an official kill, a pilot required an eyewitness. Later, pictures from cine gun cameras were accepted as sufficient evidence. Attempting to list victories with accuracy is a tedious and frustrating business that inevitably leads to argument. For example, it is the practice of some countries to count as kills aircraft that are destroyed on the ground. This explains certain discrepancies, too, in Canadian and British figures for individual pilots during the Second World War.

Table I
The Top Ten Allied Aces of the Second World War

Name	Victories	Nationality	Air Force
S/L M E St John Pattle	41	South African	RAF
Maj R I (Richard) Bong	40	American	USAAF
G/C J E (Johnny) Johnson	38	British	RAF
Maj T B (Thomas) McGuire	38	American	USAAF
G/C C A G Malan	35	South African	RAF
Capt David McCampbell	34	American	USN
S/L Pierre Clostermann	33	French	RAF
W/C B E (Brendan) Finucane	32	Irish	RAF
F/L G F (George) Beurling	31½	Canadian	RAF/RCAF
W/C John Braham	29	British	RAF
W/C Robert Tuck	29	British	RAF

Table II
The Top Ten Canadian Aces of the Second World War

Name and Home Town	Victories	Awards
F/L G F (George) Beurling Verdun, PQ	31⅓	DSO, DFC, DFM and Bar
S/L V C (Vernon) Woodward Victoria, BC	25	DFC and Bar
W/C E F J (Edward) Charles Lashburn, SK	22	DFC, DFC and Bar
S/L H W (Wally) McLeod Regina, SK	20	DSO, DFC and Bar
W/C J F (James) Edwards Nokomis, SK	16½	DFC and Bar, DFM
S/L W T (William) Klersy Brantford, ON	16½	DSO, DFC and Bar
F/O W L (William) McKnight Edmonton, AB	16½	DFC and Bar
S/L J F (John) McElroy Kamloops, BC	16	DFC and Bar
W/C R W (Robert) McNair Battleford, SK	16	DFC and 2 Bars
G/C P S (Stan) Turner Toronto, ON	16	DSO, DFC and Bar

Table III
The Top Aces of Second Tactical Air Force

Name and Nationality	Victories	Formation
FG/C J E (Johnnie) Johnson British	20-0-3½	83 Grp, 127 Wing RAF
S/L D C (Don) Laubman Canadian	15-0-3	83 Grp, 412 Sq RCAF
S/L W T (Bill) Klersy Canadian	14½-0-3	83 Grp, 401 Sq RCAF
S/L D C Fairbanks American	11½-0-2	83 Grp, 274 Sq
F/L J Mackay Canadian	11¹/₅-0-3	83 Grp, 401 Sq RCAF
S/L H Wolmsley Belgian	10¼-	83 Grp, 486 Sq (Belgian A F)
S/L W E Schrader New Zealander	9½	83 Grp, 486 Sq RNZAF
F/L R J Audet Canadian	9½	83 Grp, 411 Sq RCAF
W/C W P Green British	9	85 Grp, 219 Sq RAF
W/C J D R Braham British	9	2 Grp
F/O W J Banks Canadian	9	83 Grp, 412 Sq RCAF
F/O B N Vassiliades Greek	9	83 Grp, 3 Sq

Table IV
The Top Aces of 126 (Fighter) Wing

Name and Home Town	Victories	Squadron	Note
S/L D C (Don) Laubman Provost, AB	15-0-3	412	
S/L W T (Bill) Klersy[1] Brantford, ON	14½-0-3	401	KIFA[2]
F/L J (Johnny) Mackay Cloverdale, BC	11½-0-3	401	
F/L R J (Dick) Audet Lethbridge, AB	9½-0-1	411	KIA[3]
F/O W J (Bill) Banks Hazenmore, SK	9-3-1	412	
S/L H C (Charlie) Trainor Charlottetown, PEI	8½-1-0	401	
F/O D R C Jamieson Toronto, ON	8-0-1	412	
F/L G W (Johnny) Johnson Hamilton, ON	8-0-5	401	
S/L R I A (Rod) Smith Regina, SK	7⅕-0-0	401	

---

[1] According to 83 Group. Other sources indicate 16½-0-3½.
[2] Killed in Flying Accident
[3] Killed in Action

GLOSSARY

ack-ack	anti-aircraft fire
a/c	aircraft
airscrew	propeller
ammo	ammunition
ALO	Army Liaison Officer
AOC	air officer commanding
bandit	enemy aircraft
bind	complaint
bogey	unidentified aircraft
bounce	attack an a/c by surprise from above
bowser	gas refuelling truck
browned off	fed up
bumph	paperwork, information
compo	rations
cinegun	camera synchronised to aircraft guns
circus	bomber support and cover
CO	commanding officer
deck	zero feet (altitude)
ditch	make forced landing on water
dispersal	one of widely separated areas around airfield where aircraft are parked; the crew hut at dispersal

do	any event, from combat to station dance; if unpleasant, a "shaky do"
dogfight	confused air battle
drink	the sea, usually the English Channel
duff	poor or bad
e/a	enemy aircraft
egg	bomb
erk	aircraftsman
FCO	Flying Control Officer
flak	enemy anti-aircraft fire, from German *flugzeugabwehrkanone*
fix	position, or determination of same
flamer	vehicle destroyed in flames
funk-hole	slit trench
gaggle	formation of aircraft
gen	information; pukka (good) or duff (bad)
glycol	engine coolant
gong	medal
increment	additional
INT/OPS	Intelligence Operations
hit the silk	to parachute, or bail out
Jerry	German
kite	aircraft
LCT	Landing Craft (Transport)
lorry	truck
Mae West	life jacket with bulging front
mayday	distress signal
met	meteorological branch
m/g	machine gun
MO	Medical Officer
MT	motor transport
NCO	non-commissioned officer
ops	operations
ORs	other ranks
OTU	operational training unit
pancake	land

pigeon	pilot
penguin	groundcrew; erk
Perspex	windscreen, purportedly shatterproof
petrol	gasoline
prang	crash
PRO	Public Relations Officer
pukka	good, as in "pukka gen"
R/T	radio transmitter
ramrod	short-range bomber raid
ranger	fighter aircraft sweep
recce	reconnaissance
rhubarb	low-level attack on ground targets
rodeo	fighter sweep
SASO	Senior Administrative Staff Officer
SIO	Senior Intelligence Officer
SMO	Senior Medical Officer
smoker	vehicle enveloped in smoke but not seen in flames
snafu	a popular acronym derived from "situation normal: all fucked up"
sortie	operational flight by single aircraft
strafe	machine gun (usu. from the air)
Tannoy	loudspeaker
tender	truck
u/s	unserviceable
Winco	Wing Commander

BIBLIOGRAPHY

Brown, George and Michael Lavigne. *Canadian Wing Commanders of Fighter Command in World War II.* Langley, BC: Battleline Books, 1984.

Deighton, Len. *Fighter: The True Story of the Battle of Britain.* Frogmore, Herts: Triad Panter, 1979.

Gilbert, Martin. *The Holocaust: The Jewish Tragedy.* London: Collins, 1986.

Halliday, Hugh. *The Tumbling Sky.* Stittsville, Ont: Canada's Wings, 1978.

———. *242 Squadron: The Canadian Years.* Stittsville, Ont: Canada's Wings, 1981.

Kaplan, Philip and Andy Saunders. *Little Friends: The Fighter Pilot Experience in World War II England.* Toronto: Random House, 1991.

Kastenuk, Samuel and John Griffin. *RCAF Squadron Histories and Aircraft, 1924-1968.* Toronto: Samuel Stevens Hakkert & Company, 1977.

Keegan, John. *The Second World War.* New York: Viking Penguin, 1990.

McClenaghan, John and Derek Blatchford. *411 City of North York Squadron: 50 Years of History, 1941-1991.* North York, ON: 411 Tactical Aviation Squadron, 1992.

McIntosh, Dave. *High Blue Battle: The War Diary of No 1 (401) Fighter Squadron, RCAF.* Toronto: Stoddart, 1990.

Milberry, Larry and Hugh A Halliday. *The Royal Canadian Air Force at War, 1939-1945.* Toronto: Canav Books, 1990.

Morton, Desmond. *A Military History of Canada.* Edmonton: Hurtig Publishers, 1985.

Natkiel, Richard (et al). *Atlas of World War II.* New York: The Military Press, 1985.

Nolan, Brian. *Hero: The Buzz Beurling Story.* Toronto: Lester and Orpen Dennys, 1981.

Olmsted, Bill. *Blue Skies: The Autobiography of a Canadian Spitfire Pilot in World War II.* Toronto: Stoddart, 1987.

Ritchie, Charles. *The Siren Years: A Canadian Diplomat Abroad, 1937-1945.* Toronto: Macmillan of Canada, 1987.

Ryan, Cornelius. *A Bridge Too Far.* New York: Popular Library, 1977.

Simpson, Allan (ed). *We Few.* Ottawa: Canadian Fighter Pilots Association, 1983.

Shore, C.F. *Second Tactical Air Force.* London: Osprey, 1970.

Stacey, C.P. *The Canadian Army, 1939-1945.* Ottawa: King's Printer, 1948.

Terraine, John. *The Right of the Line: The Royal Air Force in the European War, 1939-1945.* London: Hodder and Stoughton, 1985.

Wilmot, Chester. *The Struggle for Europe.* London: Collins, 1952.

INDEX